# Ports *to* Posts

Latter-day Saint Gathering in the Nineteenth Century

FRED E. WOODS

University of Nebraska Press | Lincoln

© 2025 by Fred E. Woods

Acknowledgments for the use of previously published material appear on pages xi–xii, which constitute an extension of the copyright page.

All rights reserved
Manufactured in the United States of America

The University of Nebraska Press is part of a land-grant institution with campuses and programs on the past, present, and future homelands of the Pawnee, Ponca, Otoe-Missouria, Omaha, Dakota, Lakota, Kaw, Cheyenne, and Arapaho Peoples, as well as those of the relocated Ho-Chunk, Sac and Fox, and Iowa Peoples.

Library of Congress Cataloging-in-Publication Data
Names: Woods, Fred E., author.
Title: Ports to posts: Latter-day Saint gathering in the nineteenth century / Fred E. Woods.
Description: Lincoln: University of Nebraska Press, [2025] | Includes bibliographical references and index.
Identifiers: LCCN 2024024179
ISBN 9781496230706 (paperback)
ISBN 9781496242365 (epub)
ISBN 9781496242372 (pdf)
Subjects: LCSH: Church of Jesus Christ of Latter-day Saints—History—19th century. | Emigration and immigration—Religious aspects—Church of Jesus Christ of Latter-day Saints. | Salt Lake City (Utah)—Emigration and immigration—Religious aspects. | Liverpool (England)—Emigration and immigration—Religious aspects. | BISAC: HISTORY / United States / State & Local / West (AK, CA, CO, HI, ID, MT, NV, UT, WY) | RELIGION / Christianity / Church of Jesus Christ of Latter-day Saints (Mormon)
Classification: LCC BX8611 .W86 2025 | DDC 289.3/3209034—dc23/eng/20241026
LC record available at https://lccn.loc.gov/2024024179

Set in Arno Pro by A. Shahan.

This work is dedicated to my ever-supportive wife, JoAnna.

# Contents

| | |
|---|---|
| List of Illustrations | ix |
| Acknowledgments | xi |
| Introduction | xiii |
| 1. Early Church Beginnings, Teachings, and Gatherings | 1 |
| 2. By Land and Sea to Nauvoo (1840–46) | 9 |
| 3. In and Out of Liverpool | 33 |
| 4. Shipping the Saints | 43 |
| 5. Crossing the Seas | 57 |
| 6. Men in Motion on the Mississippi | 75 |
| 7. The Knights of Castle Garden | 91 |
| 8. LDS Emigration through Missouri by River and Rail (1838–68) | 109 |
| 9. LDS Frontier Outfitting Posts | 119 |
| 10. LDS Emigration and Military Posts | 153 |
| 11. Arrival at the Final Post | 179 |
| Appendix: LDS Emigration Agents (Nineteenth Century) | 199 |
| Notes | 203 |
| Bibliography | 255 |
| Index | 271 |

# Illustrations

1. Jane Charters Robinson Hindley — xvi
2. Brigham Young, ca. 1847 — xvii
3. Heber C. Kimball, ca. 1850 — 7
4. Mary Ann Weston Maughan — 19
5. Alexander Neibaur — 25
6. Nauvoo Temple, ca. 1845 — 31
7. LDS European Mission Headquarters, 1885 — 34
8. Parley P. Pratt, ca. 1840s — 35
9. Samuel W. Richards — 44
10. George Ramsden — 49
11. Ebenezer Farnes — 59
12. John Jaques/Jacques — 66
13. John W. F. Volker and others on ship to Zion, 1885 — 67
14. Isaiah M. Coombs, ca. 1873 — 71
15. George Spilsbury — 76
16. Nathaniel H. Felt — 81
17. Louis Espenschied — 87
18. Castle Garden Immigration Depot — 92
19. "Mormon Emigrants at Castle Garden," 1882 — 93
20. John Taylor, ca. 1870–87 — 94

| | |
|---|---|
| 21. William C. Staines, ca. 1870 | 105 |
| 22. James H. Hart, ca. 1880 | 107 |
| 23. Lilburn W. Boggs | 110 |
| 24. Albert King Thurber, ca. 1880 | 111 |
| 25. Abraham O. Smoot, ca. 1890 | 114 |
| 26. Orson Hyde, ca. 1860s | 121 |
| 27. Hannah Last Cornaby | 126 |
| 28. William K. Belknap, ca. 1860 | 129 |
| 29. Elijah Milton McGee, 1870 | 133 |
| 30. Milo Andrus, ca. 1890 | 135 |
| 31. Jane Charters Robinson Hindley | 137 |
| 32. Amos Milton Musser, ca. 1890 | 148 |
| 33. Joseph W. Young, ca. 1860s | 150 |
| 34. Jacob Weiler, ca. 1880s | 152 |
| 35. Fort Laramie | 154 |
| 36. Jens C. A. Weibye, 1872 | 162 |
| 37. Thomas McIntyre, ca. 1860s | 165 |
| 38. Jim Bridger | 169 |
| 39. Howard Egan, ca. 1865 | 171 |
| 40. Brigham Young, ca. 1870 | 182 |
| 41. Edward Hunter | 187 |
| 42. Tithing Office and Deseret Store, ca. 1870–75 | 191 |
| 43. *Reunion of the Saints* | 195 |

# Acknowledgments

This book was made possible through the assistance of a number of individuals and several institutions. Much appreciation is expressed to the College of Religious Education at Brigham Young University (BYU) for its support of resources and student employees to help produce this work. I am also thankful for the helpful and competent staff employed at BYU Harold B. Lee Library (L. Tom Perry Special Collections), the BYU Faculty Support Center, and the Church of Jesus Christ of Latter-day Saints Church History Library.

I express gratitude to the BYU Faculty Publishing Service for helping to refine this manuscript via the excellent editorial assistance of Kim Sandoval. I am grateful to the University of Nebraska Press, especially acquisitions editor Clark Whitehorn for his selection of excellent peer reviewers as well as his guidance and support throughout the production process.

Portions of chapter 2 previously appeared in Fred E. Woods, *Gathering to Nauvoo* (American Fork UT: Covenant Communications, 2002).

Portions of chapter 4 previously appeared in Fred E. Woods, "George Ramsden, the Guion Line, and the Mormon Immigration Connection," *International Journal of Mormon Studies* 2, no. 1 (Spring 2009): 83–97.

Portions of chapter 6 previously appeared in Fred E. Woods and Thomas L. Farmer, *When the Saints Came Marching In: A History of the Latter-day Saints in St. Louis* (Salt Lake City: Millennial Press, 2009).

Portions of chapter 7 previously appeared in Fred E. Woods, "A Gifted Gentleman in Perpetual Motion: John Taylor as an Emigration Agent," in *Champion of Liberty: John Taylor*, ed. Mary Jane Woodger (Provo UT: BYU Religious Studies Center, 2009), 171–91.

Portions of chapter 10 previously appeared in Fred E. Woods, "Fort Laramie... Half Way to Our Mountain Home (1847–68)," *Annals of Wyoming* 80, no. 3 (Summer 2008): 17–32; and Fred E. Woods, "Mormon Migration and the Fort Bridger Connection (1847–1868)," *Annals of Wyoming* 80, no. 1 (Winter 2008): 2–14.

Portions of chapter 11 previously appeared in Fred E. Woods, "The Arrival of Nineteenth-Century Mormon Emigrants in Salt Lake City," in *Salt Lake City: The Place Which God Prepared*, ed. Scott C. Esplin and Kenneth L. Alford (Provo UT: BYU Religious Studies Center, 2011), 203–29.

# Introduction

This book is the result of over a quarter century of research in Latter-day Saint immigration/emigration narratives from the nineteenth century.[1] It represents a convergence and distillation of scores of academic articles I have written, revised, and built upon. The story takes the reader from the early beginnings of the Church of Jesus Christ of Latter-day Saints in upstate New York (1830) to ecclesiastical gathering places in Kirtland, Ohio, and Jackson County, Missouri (1831–38). It then depicts the journey from international European ports to Latter-day Saint gathering locations in Nauvoo, Illinois (1840–46), and later in the Salt Lake Valley (1847–90) during the peak of this emigrant era known by Latter-day Saints as "the gathering."

*Ports to Posts* reveals the purpose and process by which Latter-day Saints gathered to designated areas in America to build what they called "Zion," which LDS scripture defines as the "pure in heart" (D&C 97:21) and also a place where a righteous people unite for a divine purpose. It introduces readers to the doctrine of gathering, of converts immigrating to Zion to assemble with fellow Saints in America. The ocean crossing is an interpretive narrative based in part on over 1,300 first-person nineteenth-century immigrant/emigrant accounts now compiled on the website Saints by Sea (https://saintsbysea.lib.byu.edu/), of which I am the chief compiler and editor.[2]

These stories are laced with the push-and-pull factors that led emigrants from Europe to the United States and also detail the inspiring experiences of the emigration agents and ecclesiastical leaders who assisted them as they gathered fellow members via ports and posts to Zion. The reader will understand the missionary proselyting process and how European missionaries led converts from Liverpool, the primary place of embarkation, across the Atlantic and into harbors at New Orleans, Philadelphia, Boston, and New York. Authentic voices will attempt to depict the challenges the Saints faced as they left their homelands, navigated sharks on both land and sea, and confronted ferocious winds, wicked storms, and enemies who tried to divert them from their destination. *Ports to Posts* also captures Americans' perceptions of these often unwanted, peculiar pilgrims, who were maligned by both the populace and the press. Also detailed is how unforgettable scenes in the United States such as slave auctions and the American Civil War affected these European converts.

This comprehensive work is an insightful, explanatory treatment based on hundreds of first-person narratives that help complete the Latter-day Saint emigrant story that authors such as Wallace Stegner (*The Gathering of Zion*), LeRoy and Ann Hafen (*Handcarts to Zion*), and William Mulder (*Homeward to Zion*) left unfinished on the plains. *Ports to Posts* is unique in two ways: first, it features more first-person accounts than any other work about the LDS emigration experience, and second, it provides the big picture of LDS emigration by both land and sea, an emigration that was unlike any other in American history. It gives the reader a more complete understanding of how converts were assisted at ports and posts before, during, and after the plains and shares the panoramic portrait of converts, a righteous people of one heart and one mind, fleeing what they considered to be the wicked world (Babylon) in hopes of reaching Zion. This is the story of a covenant people who believed they were led across the Atlantic and through unfamiliar lands by an American Moses, Brigham Young, and other inspired church leaders, just as the ancient children of Israel crossed the Red Sea and traveled in the wilderness to a land of promise.

Latter-day Saints consider themselves literal descendants of the ancient house of Israel and believe in "the literal gathering of Israel."[3] Biblical accounts record God's attempts to gather his people from earliest times. But why? We must go beyond the plains in search of the trailhead to determine why this doctrine has been continually emphasized throughout the ages.

The founding prophet of the Church of Jesus Christ of Latter-day Saints, Joseph Smith, once asked rhetorically, "What was the object of gathering the Jews together, or the people of God in any age of the world?" He answered, "The main object was to build unto the Lord a house whereby

He could reveal unto his people the ordinances of his house and the glories of his kingdom & teach the peopl[e] the ways of salvation."[4]

Yet adherence to the call to gather resulted in dramatic life changes for many, and for some it required an arduous journey to a new homeland. The cost of leaving homelands and loved ones is laid bare in this account. The many miles traversed by tens of thousands of converts raises the question: Where does the trail for Latter-day Saints really begin? One observer queried, "How many branches does [the trail] have, and how shall we compute its duration?"[5]

Though the cost of gathering was often demanding, the Latter-day Saints were willing to embark on this quest because they believed they would receive spiritual rewards in Zion. One British convert, Jane C. Robinson Hindley, penned, "I believed in the principle of the gather[ing] and felt it my duty to go although it was a severe trial to me ... to leave my native land and the pleasing associations that I had formed there. But my heart was fixed, I knew in whom I had trusted and with the fire of Israel's God burning in my bosom I forsook my home."[6] Hindley's compelling witness is a composite testimony explaining why most converts gathered,[7] but what made the Latter-day Saint immigration so successful? The Saints attributed their success to the exceptional principles upon which the gathering was based, principles inspired by and grounded in sacred covenants by which they would consecrate their all to building the kingdom of God. This consecration, as noted in the New Testament (Acts 4:32), entailed giving all to God and having "all things" in common. The Saints promised to bear one another's burdens (Mosiah 18:8) on the journey; to take care of the poor, widows, and orphans (D&C 136:8); and to give their all to help migrate God's children to Zion, leaving none behind (D&C 136:10). They understood that they must give all to receive all God had in store for them (Matthew 10:39; D&C 84:38).

The Saints' commitment to assist their fellow church members is based on a scriptural pattern that one might call the "emigration revelation," which Brigham Young reported he received in 1847 (see D&C 136, especially verse 1). Herein we find what the Saints embraced as divine direction, "the Word and Will of the Lord." They followed what they believed was the inspired direction of the Lord's apostolic leaders, which resulted from much study,

1. Jane Charters Robinson Hindley. Daughters of the Utah Pioneers, Salt Lake City.

counseling together, and prayer. Examples of this direction are evident in records of apostolic leadership councils and the Council of Fifty (established in 1844), in which church leaders worked together with others not of their faith to help move the Saints and other God-fearing people closer to Zion, a people dwelling together in unity and peace.[8]

The gathering to Zion is also laced with examples of wise organizational and economic principles such as the appointment of consecrated emigration agents; the institution of the Perpetual Emigrating Fund (PEF), a revolving financial resource to assist the poor and needy; and the careful selection of routes and conveyances by sail, rail, and trail.

The gathering to Zion is the story of a team, not an individual; of a traveling orchestra, not a stagnant one-man band. And even after gathering to their American Zion in the West, the Saints were willing to extend

2. Brigham Young, ca. 1847. Church History Library, PH 598.

its borders, humbly committing to move yet again to launch hundreds of colonies, starting from scratch, regardless of the sacrifices required. To achieve harmony and beauty, the Saints would apply the same principles used to gather to Zion to further build and expand it.

This pattern was recognized not only by the Saints but also by those who witnessed the immigration by land and sea, including such notables as Charles Dickens and the British House of Commons, as well as scholars such as Katherine Coman, who called the migration of the Saints the best example of immigration in American history.[9] The LDS immigration transported a people not only west but upward toward their God.

# Ports *to* Posts

# 1

## Early Church Beginnings, Teachings, and Gatherings

The Latter-day Saint faith had its genesis in upstate New York in the spring of 1820. An obscure fourteen-year-old farm boy named Joseph Smith Jr., who had been searching for the true church of Jesus Christ, reported that after sincere prayer he had seen God the Father and his Son Jesus Christ, who Smith said told him to join none of the existing churches. Smith recounted that three years later he was visited by an angel who told him about a book that testified of Jesus Christ and his visit to the ancient Americas shortly after his resurrection.

By 1830 Smith had translated the ancient record from gold plates, and in that same year he established what he announced was the restoration of the primitive Church of Christ, in Fayette, New York. Although its beginnings were small, the Church of Jesus Christ of Latter-day Saints, now headquartered in Salt Lake City, has nearly seventeen million members in over thirty-one thousand congregations, with more than half residing outside the United States.[1] The church's missionary force comprises over fifty-five thousand adherents and provides humanitarian services in 188 countries.[2]

### *Latter-day Saint Teachings*

As the name "The Church of Jesus Christ of Latter-day Saints" attests, the message of the church is focused on Jesus Christ, though some Christian denominations do not officially endorse the faith as Christian because of its basic beliefs. For example, whereas mainstream Christianity believes in the literal oneness of the Trinity, Latter-day Saint scripture teaches that God the Father and his Son Jesus Christ are separate and distinct individuals and that the Holy Ghost is a personage of spirit (D&C 130:22).[3] Church doctrine maintains that despite this bodily separation, the Godhead (God the Father, Jesus Christ, and the Holy Ghost) is one in purpose.

Latter-day Saints also maintain that the early Christian church experienced a general apostasy after the death of the apostles in the first century AD. They believe in the Apostle Paul's biblical prophecy that before Christ would return to the earth, His people would experience an ἀποστασία (a Greek word meaning "apostasy"), or as the King James Version translates it "a falling away first" (2 Thess. 2:3). Latter-day Saints also believe that because of this apostasy there was no priesthood authority on earth to perform saving "ordinances"—sacred, formal acts performed by the authority of the priesthood—such as baptism. However, they also believe that Christ sent the apostles Peter, James, and John to restore the priesthood authority back to the earth, which LDS scripture records as having occurred about a year before the restoration of the primitive Church of Jesus Christ in the spring of 1830.

Another point of departure from other Christian denominations is that in addition to including the Bible in its scriptural canon, the Church of Jesus Christ of Latter-day Saints also includes the Book of Mormon,[4] which it maintains is another testament of Jesus Christ that chronicles his visit to his other sheep in the ancient Americas, as previously noted. The Latter-day Saints believe that the Book of Mormon has been instrumental in gathering hundreds of thousands of converts into the fold.

Indeed, Latter-day Saints believe in church president Russell M. Nelson's teaching that "the coming forth of the Book of Mormon is a sign to the entire world that the Lord has commenced to gather Israel. . . . The Book of Mormon is central to this work. It declares the doctrine of the gathering. . . . In fact, if there were no Book of Mormon, the promised gathering of Israel would not occur."[5] According to Nelson, "For centuries, prophets have foretold this gathering, and it is happening right now! As an essential prelude to the Second Coming of the Lord, it is *the most important work in the world!*"[6] However, with the expanded growth of the church, Nelson has also clarified that Latter-day Saints should now gather in their own countries, not in one general location in America as they did in the nineteenth century. He noted, "In the early days of the

Church, conversion often meant emigration as well. But now the gathering takes place in each nation."[7]

### Gathering in the Early Years of the Church

During the second conference of the Church of Christ, less than six months after the church's organization in 1830, Joseph Smith declared that he had received the divine call to gather: "And ye are called to bring to pass the gathering of mine elect; for mine elect hear my voice and harden not their hearts. Wherefore the decree hath gone forth from the Father that they shall be gathered in unto one place upon the face of this land, to prepare their hearts and be prepared in all things against the day when tribulation and desolation are sent forth upon the wicked" (D&C 29:7–8).[8]

Yet missionary work and the gathering was limited to North America during the first decade of the church's existence. Throughout this period the Saints gathered first in upstate New York, with branches in Fayette, Manchester, and Colesville (D&C 24:3). However, following local persecution in these areas, early church members were instructed to gather to the Kirtland, Ohio, region as the year 1831 dawned, to "escape the power of the enemy, and be gathered unto [the Lord] a righteous people, without spot and blameless." They also believed that the Lord had commanded them to move to the Ohio region to receive his law, with the promise that they would be "endowed with power from on high" (D&C 38:31–32), which refers to receiving sacred blessings in the temple.[9]

Church leaders selected this area in northwestern Ohio, known as the Western Reserve, because early Latter-day Saint missionaries had experienced great success there in the late fall of 1830, particularly after the conversion of a former Campbellite minister in Mentor, Ohio, named Sidney Rigdon. Rigdon led many of his Disciples of Christ congregation into the LDS faith. Within three weeks of the missionaries' visit to the Western Reserve, about 130 new converts joined the church, with the number reaching about a thousand by the summer of 1831.[10]

Early convert Newel Knight recalled that during the third conference of the church, held in Fayette, the Saints were "instructed as a people to begin the gathering of Israel." Knight noted, "In obedience to the commandment which had been given, I, together with the Colesville Branch, began to make preparations to go to the Ohio. As might be expected, we were obligated to make great sacrifices of our properties."[11] A revelation received by Joseph Smith during this conference underscored this obligation: "And they that have farms that cannot be sold, let them be left or rented as seemeth them good" (D&C 38:37).

Despite the cost, the New York Saints made the sacrifice and went to Ohio as organized parties under the direction of several designated leaders. Fifty members of the Manchester Branch were led by Martin Harris, "sixty-seven Colesville Saints were led by Newell Knight, [and] the eighty members of the Fayette Branch were under the leadership of Lucy Mack Smith and Thomas B. Marsh."[12]

Some members of these groups recorded that they experienced divine assistance in spite of obstacles as they gathered to the Ohio. For example, Colesville Branch member Jared Carter, who had broken off from the main branch with some men to see if they could catch a vessel going out of Dunkirk via Lake Erie, recalled, "We had not gone far before we met with [a] stiff headwind which made us in considerable dangerous sailing." Yet Carter related that at the time of the ferocious storm, a divine voice spoke to him, saying, "Go and command the winds in the name of Christ to cease." Carter wrote, "I immediately arose[;] . . . I command[ed] the winds to cease, and the wind from that moment began to cease and in about fifteen minutes it was stopped and . . . in a few hours [we] landed in Ohio, at Fairport."[13]

The New York Saints also maintained that they experienced divine intervention when they reached Buffalo and found the harbor frozen over. Observing that the main Colesville group was unable to proceed, the leader of the Fayette group, Lucy Mack Smith, mother of Joseph Smith Jr., boldly declared to members of the Fayette Branch:

> "Now brethren and sister[s], if you will raise your desires to heaven, that the ice may be broken up, and we be set at liberty, as sure as the Lord lives, it will be done." At that instant a noise was heard, like bursting thunder. The captain cried, "Every man to his post." The ice parted, leaving barely a passage for the boat, and so narrow that as the boat passed through[,] the buckets of the waterwheel were

torn off with a crash, which joined to the word of command from the captain, the hoarse answering of the sailors, the noise of the ice, and the cries of the confusion of the spectators, [and] presented a scene truly terrible. We had barely passed through the avenue when the ice closed together again, and the Colesville brethren were left in Buffalo, unable to follow us.[14]

LDS eyewitnesses viewed this captivating scene as an immediate answer to prayer, though nonmembers sarcastically cast doubt on this episode: "Their great prophet Jo, has selected a part of Geauga county, Ohio and pronounced it to be the 'promised land,' and thither the deluded people are flocking, chiefly from New York. . . . They say that a miracle was worked in their behalf, by clearing a passage through the ice at Buffalo." The *Niles Weekly Register XL* added, "Some of them affect a power even to raise the dead, and perchance . . . really believe they can do it!"[15]

Such opposition continued when the local press learned that these unwanted "Mormon" converts had recently landed on the western shores of Lake Erie at Fairport Harbor and settled in the Kirtland region, just twelve miles south. In the spring of 1831, Eber D. Howe, author of the first anti-Mormon book, *Mormonism Unveiled*, and founder and editor of the first anti-Mormon newspaper, the *Painesville Telegraph*, published a derogatory article titled "Mormon Emigration":

> About two hundred men, women and children, of the deluded followers of Jo Smith's Bible speculation, have arrived on our coast during the last week, from the state of New York, & are about seating themselves down upon the "promised land" in this county. It is surely a melancholy comment upon human nature to see so many people at this enlightened age of the world, truckling along at the ear of a miserable impostor, submitting themselves both soul and body, to his spiritual and temperal [sic] mandates, without a murmur, or presuming to question that it is all a command direct from Heaven.[16]

Despite this opposition, LDS missionary work, which began in the 1830s, launched from Kirtland to various places in the United States and Canada, and many Saints migrated in and out of Kirtland via Fairport Harbor, which served as the main local hub for maritime travel.[17]

During this same decade (1831–38), many church members also gathered to western Missouri, hoping to establish the church in that state as well. In fact, church leaders identified Independence, Jackson County, Missouri, as the center place of Zion (D&C 57:3). Yet on October 27, 1838, Missouri governor Lilburn W. Boggs issued an extermination order, forcing the Latter-day Saints to flee the state of Missouri.

Church leaders named a new gathering place for these displaced Ohio and Missouri Saints the following year: Nauvoo, Illinois. In Nauvoo, Saints from Canada and the eastern United States as well as converts from abroad combined their faith and works to build a beautiful city atop a mosquito-infested swampland on the eastern banks of the Mississippi River. The gathering of Saints from outside North America did not begin until the necessary priesthood keys to direct the gathering were restored to the earth, which Latter-day Saints believe occurred on April 3, 1836, just one week after the dedication of the Kirtland Temple. Latter-day Saint scripture notes that in this sacred edifice the ancient prophet Moses appeared and restored to Joseph Smith Jr. and Oliver Cowdery "the keys of the gathering of Israel from the four parts of the earth" (D&C 110:11).[18]

The following year, difficult circumstances disrupted this season of rejoicing. An economic crisis, later known as the Panic of 1837, struck America, resulting in the closure of hundreds of banks. This financial depression did not spare the Saints. Because the Saints had not been able to incorporate a bank in Kirtland, they established their own banking system, the Kirtland Safety Society Anti-Banking Company, which opened for business on January 2, 1837. Other banks would not accept the company's notes, and "anti-Mormons" claimed that the notes were not legal tender. Problems soon arose, and the new company collapsed. A number of Latter-day Saints apostatized during this tumultuous period, though nearly half later returned to the fold.[19]

During this era of crisis, Joseph Smith realized that "something new must be done for the salvation" of the church.[20] In the Kirtland Temple, on June 4, 1837, Smith approached one of his trusted associates, Elder Heber C. Kimball, and whispered to him, "Brother Heber, the Spirit of the Lord

3. Heber C. Kimball, ca. 1850. Photograph likely by Marsena Cannon or Lewis W. Chaffin, copy by George Edward Anderson. L. Tom Perry Special Collections, Harold B. Lee Library, Brigham Young University, Provo, Utah.

has whispered to me: 'Let my servant Heber go to England and proclaim my Gospel, and open the door of salvation to that nation.'"[21] Just one week later (two days before the apostles' departure to England), Smith warned Elders Heber C. Kimball and Orson Hyde, along with five other elders, "to remain silent concerning the gathering... until such time as the work was firmly established, and it should be clearly made manifest by the Spirit to do otherwise."[22] The needed foothold was established after Kimball, Hyde, and their associates had gathered many into the fold.

Early Church Beginnings | 7

During the space of just nine months (July 1837–April 1838), these first LDS missionaries converted over fifteen hundred people in the British Isles.[23] The church grew even more dramatically less than two years later when other apostles led by Elders Kimball and Pratt embarked on another mission to Great Britain (January 1840–April 1841). They traveled to Great Britain not only to expand the work but also to revive the lethargic spirit that had crept in among some of the British converts.[24] These apostles reaped great success in the British Isles, and by the spring of 1840, the church was steadfastly rooted in the land. It was during this season that church leaders determined that British converts should begin gathering to America.[25]

In a council meeting in England on April 14, 1840, the Quorum of the Twelve Apostles declared that the Saints would gather in America: "Moved by Elder Brigham Young, seconded by Elder Heber C. Kimball, that the Saints receive a recommend to the Church in America to move in small or large bodies, inasmuch as they desire to emigrate to that new country."[26] Less than two months later, they began to leave Liverpool for Nauvoo, Illinois, the new gathering place of the Saints.

# 2

## By Land and Sea to Nauvoo
## (1840–46)

The call to build a sacred temple in Nauvoo and partake of the blessings therein encouraged Latter-day Saint converts to gather to the Nauvoo region. While they were eager to meet the Prophet Joseph Smith and gather with their fellow Saints, they also had temporal motives for immigrating to the promised land of America. At the time, the British Isles were experiencing economic problems, and Nauvoo, and America in general, offered a more promising economy.

Missionaries occasionally shepherded their new proselytes across the Atlantic and from various pockets of North America to Nauvoo. One historian observed that at the beginning of the Nauvoo period, "there was a definite shift in area of concentration. Now it was into Illinois, and the cities of Boston, Philadelphia and New York, with thin lines of penetration into the Southern States; whereas formerly, centers had been in Ohio, New York, Canada and New England."[1] Thus, a variety of missionary labors were underway in other areas.

Elijah Funk Sheets, a convert from Chester County, Pennsylvania, who emigrated to Nauvoo in the fall of 1841, was one such missionary who guided his converts from the eastern United States to Nauvoo. After volunteering at age twenty-one to work on the Nauvoo Temple for six months without pay, Sheets left on a mission with Joseph A. Stratton to his home state of Pennsylvania, leaving Nauvoo on September 4, 1842. Sheets and Stratton converted sixty people in Pennsylvania within twenty months and then returned to Nauvoo with a company of thirty converts, arriving on May 4, 1844.[2]

Although missionaries shepherding their converts to Nauvoo served as an ideal pattern, many converts could not afford to travel with the missionaries immediately following their conversion, and in some cases they decided to stay and continue proselytizing to local inhabitants before gathering to Nauvoo.[3] For example, following his baptism in Tazewell County, Virginia, on November 20, 1843, Henry Boyle was determined to earn money to travel to Nauvoo. However, in April 1844 at a local area conference, he was called to labor in his home state of Virginia, where he found success. After completing an honorable mission, he and all the missionaries in this region were released and told to gather to Nauvoo, where Boyle finally arrived on June 25, 1845.[4]

Missionaries also found success in other parts of eastern North America, but their converts often gathered to Nauvoo without them. Some proselytes migrated in groups from various branches of the church. Benjamin Brown, a member of the Pomfret Branch (Chautauqua County, New York), wrote of his family's journey after he was finally able to sell his farm:

> The doctrine of gathering had been taught the Saints at Pamphlet [Pomfret], and, in common with the others, I felt a great desire to gather up and live with the body of the Church. . . . When the time arrived, with my wife and children, and part of the branch . . . I started to find the Church, thinking it was still in Missouri, though we had heard that it had been mobbed and broken up. We journeyed until we came to Springfield, about a hundred miles from Nauvoo, where we met with some brethren, who had been driven out of Missouri, and who told us that the Church was collecting in Nauvoo, then called Commerce. We turned our course in that direction, and arrived there in June the weather being very warm at the time.[5]

One member of this group, Jesse Crosby, noted that fifteen members of this branch departed for Missouri in the spring of 1839. He supported Brown's claim that on the way they met eastbound missionaries who redirected them to Commerce, where this small company arrived on June 6, 1839.[6]

In 1843 Crosby and Brown journeyed east as missionary companions, where their proselyting labors took them through eastern Canada to Nova Scotia. As the first missionaries in what was then predominantly Roman

Catholic Lower Canada and as early laborers in Nova Scotia, they met fierce resistance. After much persistence, they baptized fifty members and organized two branches. Upon receiving word of the martyrdom of Joseph and Hyrum Smith and concerned for their families, Crosby and Brown returned to Nauvoo but did not convoy their converts.[7]

While proselytes who gathered from diverse places usually strengthened the trunk of the church in Nauvoo, the influx often weakened its branches of origin. For example, in May 1842 half of the members of the Charity Branch in Benton County, Tennessee, emigrated to Nauvoo, leaving the few remaining members in a crippled condition.[8] The following year other converts emigrated from the state of Tennessee, further shrinking church membership there. Thus migration came at a cost to local church growth and development. In addition, families were often split apart when one or more of their members left for Zion.

### Emigration Routes by Land to Nauvoo

The Saints who gathered from the southern and central states often traveled by wagon, cart, or foot to reach the bustling city of Nauvoo. Due to severe persecution, one group of eighty to ninety Mississippi Saints journeyed in a company of forty wagons, arriving in Nauvoo in April 1842.[9] Many converts from eastern states made their way down the Ohio River to St. Louis before steaming up the Mississippi River to Nauvoo. Some traveled along the Erie Canal to Lake Erie and then steamed down the Illinois and Mississippi Rivers to their destination.

Benjamin Ashby and his family were converts from the Salem Massachusetts Branch. Ashby described his company's route: they journeyed through Boston to Albany by rail and then via the Erie Canal to Buffalo. They then traveled by steamboat to Cleveland and by canal to the Ohio River down to Cincinnati and up the Mississippi, arriving at Nauvoo in the late fall of 1843.[10]

In America, church leaders had experienced a shift in the perception of the gathering just two months prior to the murder of Joseph Smith and his brother Hyrum. At the April 1844 conference, Smith broadened the concept of authorized gathering places in Zion, which affected priesthood assignments and ecclesiastical units in the United States:

You know there has been great discussion in relation to Zion—where it is, and where the gathering of the dispensation is, and which I am now going to tell you. The prophets have spoken and written upon it; but I will make a proclamation that will cover a broader ground. The whole of America is Zion itself from north to south, and is described by the Prophets, who declare that it is the Zion where the mountain of the Lord should be.... I have received instructions from the Lord that from henceforth wherever the Elders of Israel shall build up churches and branches unto the Lord throughout the States, there shall be a stake of Zion. In the great cities, as Boston, New York, &c., there shall be stakes.[11]

This same month, the LDS periodicals the *Nauvoo Neighbor* and the *Times and Seasons* published a list of 337 missionaries who would be sent to various locales throughout America to preach and electioneer for Joseph Smith, who was running for president of the United States. This was the most intense missionary effort initiated during Smith's lifetime.[12] However, due to Smith's martyrdom just two months later, all missionaries throughout the United States were called home.[13]

As early as mid-August 1844, the *Times and Seasons* published "An Epistle of the Twelve," clearly demonstrating that church leaders intended to implement ecclesiastical programs that would echo the policies of their beloved martyred prophet. Among other things, the epistle specified, "The United States and adjoining provinces will be immediately organized by the Twelve into proper districts in a similar manner as they have already done in England and Scotland, and high priests will be appointed over each district, to preside over the same."[14]

Less than two months later, at the October conference in Nauvoo, Brigham Young appointed eighty-five high priests "to go abroad in all the congressional districts of the United States, to preside over the branches of the church." He also clarified their mission and instructed them "that it was not the design to go and tarry six months and then return, but to go and settle down, where they can take their families and tarry until the Temple is built, and then come and get their endowments, and return to their families and build up a stake as large as this."[15]

James Linforth explained that church leaders still wanted to build up Nauvoo during this postmartyrdom period, but they introduced a policy for Saints emigrating from Britain: those "who were wholly dependent upon their labour for support, were advised to emigrate to New York, Philadelphia, Pittsburgh, Salem, Boston, and other large towns in the eastern states, . . . where employment could be procured, which would give the emigrants the means to go west, when the way should open."[16] Although some may have clustered to these economic centers, the vast majority of British Saints who immigrated to America during the Nauvoo period (1840–46) gathered directly to Nauvoo, which the Saints considered to be the core of Zion during this era.

### British Gathering to Nauvoo across the Atlantic and up the Mississippi River

While most Saints were gathering to Nauvoo from the eastern and southern regions of the United States by wagons and river/canal travel, the British Saints began their overseas immigration to Nauvoo in Liverpool, England. Before setting sail, most British converts made their way to Liverpool by rail. One LDS convert, a silk manufacturer bound for Nauvoo, wrote of his rail journey from Staffordshire, England, to Liverpool: "We were booked for rail for Liverpool which cost us 10/-each second class, they charged us 1/6 per cwt for luggage above a hundred weight for each passenger. . . . Were kindly treated by Mr. Woods at the station house at Liverpool."[17]

The first group of British converts began their Atlantic crossing on the *Britannia* on June 6, 1840, led by Englishman John Moon.[18] Hugh Moon recalled that members of the Quorum of the Twelve were present to lend their support to Saints boarding the *Britannia*: "We found Elders Brigham Young and Heber C. Kimball aboard. They had stretched a curtain across our cabin and commenced blessing the company. They bid us walk in."[19]

After the company arrived safely in Nauvoo, John Moon's brother Francis wrote home to England describing the favorable temporal and spiritual conditions they found there. He referred to Nauvoo as a refuge in the troubled last days and noted that a purpose of gathering the people of God in any age was to "build a sanctuary to the name of the Most High."[20] Francis expressed both a spiritual and a temporal hope that his words would encourage his fellow British Saints to gather:

> Now I would . . . say if you can get to this land, you will be better off than in England, for in this place there is a prospect of receiving every good thing both of this world and that which is to come: . . . Then those who have the means delay no longer but come and unite with us in building the house of the Lord, and in bringing to pass the great things belonging to the kingdom of our God. My fellow-Englishmen and brethren, you may rely upon what I say, for it would be nothing to my profit for to deceive you, then believe me when I say this land is good—the things that have been taught you are true, and Joseph Smith is a prophet of the Most High.[21]

This opening voyage charted the course for thousands of other British Saints who soon followed them to Nauvoo. Francis's glad tidings to his homeland and letters from other early immigrants encouraged the Saints of England to gather. An article titled "Emigration," published in February 1841 in the new British LDS periodical the *Latter-day Saints' Millennial Star*, reported, "News from the emigrants who sailed from this country last season is so very encouraging that it will give a new impulse to the spirit of the gathering."[22]

These letters also reinforced the call issued a few months earlier (in August 1840) by the First Presidency to build a temple in Nauvoo:

> Believing the time has now come, when it is necessary to erect a house of prayer, a house of order, a house for the worship of our God, where the ordinances can be attended to agreeably to His divine will, in this region of country—to accomplish which, considerable exertion must be made, and means will be required—and as the work must be hastened in righteousness, it behooves the Saints to weigh the importance of these things, in their minds, in all their bearings and then take such steps as are necessary to carry them into operation.[23]

This call to build a temple certainly influenced immigration to Nauvoo in the subsequent years. One historian noted thirty-two LDS companies left England for Nauvoo between June 1840 and January 1846, with the possibility of another undocumented voyage in 1846. Further research suggests that there were thirty-four LDS voyages and thirteen additional voyages not chartered by the church, consisting of small groups composed of families or individuals.[24] Jenson estimated that about five thousand British Saints gathered to Nauvoo during these years.[25] These statistics suggest that about one-fourth of the Saints who gathered to Nauvoo before the 1846 exile were British converts.[26]

### *The Challenge of Leaving Home*

The Saints' enthusiasm to gather to Zion was balanced by the difficulty of leaving loved ones behind. Seventeen-year-old Mary Haskin Parker Richards remembered the pain she felt leaving her family and friends before climbing aboard the *Alliance* in December of 1840: "Nevver shall I forget the feeling that shriled through my bosom this day. while parting with all my dear Brothers & Sisters. and all my kindred who were near & dear to me by the ties of nature."[27]

Twenty-one-year-old convert Thomas Callister left his homeland, the Isle of Man, on January 9, 1842, for Nauvoo. He wrote, "I left all my relatives and friends for the gospel sake."[28] Although his parents were not alive to bid him farewell, one sibling saw him off: "His brother John went with him to the ship and there offered him half of all he owned if he would only give up going to America. When he refused, his brother said he would be happier if he could lay him away on the hill with his parents."[29]

Two years later, in 1844, Priscilla Staines left England two days after Christmas aboard the *Fanny*. She also recalled the difficulty of leaving her homeland:

> I left the home of my birth to gather to Nauvoo. I was alone. It was a dreary winter day on which I went to Liverpool. The company with which I was to sail were all strangers to me. When I arrived at Liverpool and saw the ocean that would soon roll between me and all I loved, my heart almost failed me. But I had laid my idols all upon the altar. There was no turning back. I remembered the words of the Saviour: "He that leaveth not father and mother, brother and sister, for my sake, is not worthy of me," and I believed his promise to those

who forsook all for his sake; so I thus alone set out for the reward of everlasting life, trusting in God.[30]

As previously mentioned, the impetus to gather tore some families apart. Family members who stayed behind experienced homesickness and grief, and some felt a sense of betrayal, distrust, and division. Nevertheless, the Saints believed in the words of Matthew 10:37: "He that loveth father or mother more than me is not worthy of me: and he that loveth son or daughter more than me is not worthy of me."

*Economic Obstacles*

The cost of crossing the Atlantic varied from year to year.[31] The *Millennial Star* posted rates to keep the Saints apprised of the changing rates. For many Saints, economic factors determined if and when they would be able to gather to Zion. Sometimes families were temporarily separated. In the fall of 1841, Robert Pixton decided that he would lead the way to Zion, even though it meant leaving his wife behind. He wrote, "I spoke to my wife about it and she was willing that I should go and leave her behind until I could send for her as we had not sufficient means for both to go. . . . This was a sad parting but I was reconciled to go."[32]

George Cannon, who voyaged on the *Sidney* in 1842, wrote, "Nothing caused me so much regret as leaving so many of the Saints behind, anxious to go but without the means to do so."[33] Some, such as Robert Crookston, a passenger with Cannon, exercised great faith and made significant sacrifices. He recalled, "We had to sell everything at a great sacrifice. But we wanted to come to Zion and be taught by the prophet of God. We had the spirit of gathering so strongly that Babylon had no claim on us."[34]

Liverpool served as the primary port of departure for these voyages. By 1840 Liverpool was the most active international port of emigration in the world due to its prime location for rail connections in the British Isles and its excellent navigable channels in the Mersey River.[35]

By the spring of 1841, the Quorum of the Twelve had appointed an agent in Liverpool to help steer the Saints through the immigration process and to arrange for group travel, which had economic advantages. The following

"Epistle of the Twelve" was published in April 1841 to counsel those who desired to emigrate:

> We have found that there are so many "pick pockets," and so many that will take every possible advantage of strangers, in Liverpool, that we have appointed Elder Amos Fielding, as the agent of the church, to superintend the fitting out of the Saints from Liverpool to America. Whatever information the Saints may want about the preparations for a voyage, they are advised to call on Elder Fielding, at Liverpool, as their first movement, when they arrive there as emigrants. There are some brethren who have felt themselves competent to do their own business in these matters, and rather despising the counsel of their friends, have been robbed and cheated out of nearly all they had.
>
> A word of caution to the wise is sufficient. It is also a great saving to go in companies, instead of going individually. First, a company can charter a vessel, so as to make the passage much cheaper than otherwise. Secondly, provisions can be purchased at wholesale for a company much cheaper than otherwise. Thirdly, this will avoid bad company on the passage. Fourthly, when a company arrives in New Orleans they can charter a steam-boat so as to reduce the passage near one-half. This measure will save some hundreds of pounds on each ship load. Fifthly, a man of experience can go as leader of each company, who will know how to avoid rogues and knaves.[36]

Most of the immigrating Saints followed this sound counsel.

Probably for logistical reasons, in 1841 three separate groups of Saints chose to depart from the port of Bristol and entered North America at Quebec before making their way to Nauvoo via the St. Lawrence River and the Great Lakes.[37] All other LDS voyages destined for Nauvoo embarked from Liverpool except for three early voyages that entered the United States through the port of New York, continuing their journey through canals and on the Ohio River before steaming up to Nauvoo.[38] All other LDS voyages disembarked at the port of New Orleans.[39] Apparently the decision to arrive in New Orleans (beginning in December 1840) instead of the port of New York was influenced by a letter Joseph Smith had sent to the apostles in England two months earlier. Smith wrote, "I think those that came here last fall, did not take the best possible route, or least expensive."[40]

Six months later the *Millennial Star* ran an "Epistle of the Twelve" offering counsel about when and how British converts should immigrate to Nauvoo: "It is much cheaper going by New Orleans than by New York. But it will never do for emigrants to go by New Orleans in the Summer on account of the heat and sickness of the climate. It is, therefore, advisable for the Saints to emigrate in Autumn, Winter, or Spring."[41]

### Hygiene and Order

Church company voyages were known for their hygiene and order, even during this early sailing era.[42] Robert Reid, one of 212 LDS passengers on the 1843 voyage of the *Swanton*, over which Lorenzo Snow presided,[43] wrote, "The order of the ship was, that the bell went round at six o'clock in the morning for all to arise, which has been attended to: prayer meetings every night at seven o'clock; preaching Tuesday and Thursday nights, and twice on Sunday, with church meeting in the afternoon."[44]

### Divine Intervention in Times of Storm and Human Tempests

Regardless of outstanding order or the route of choice, the immigrants faced the same obstacles encountered by others who sailed across the treacherous Atlantic. Mary Ann Weston Maughan, who crossed the Atlantic in 1841, recalled one memorable storm: "Soon after our Mast broak a young Man in our Company took off his shoes and went on deck[;] going to the forepart of the Ship he raised his right hand to Heaven and in the name of Jesus Christ rebuked the Wind and the Waves and Prophysed that the storme should abate and the good ship *Harmony* [italics added] would carry her load of Saints in safety to their destination."[45]

In addition to the raging winds and angry sea, potential human tempests often threatened each vessel as well. During a storm on the 1841 voyage of the *Rochester*, an observer noted that a cook had his hands full fighting with Irish passengers.[46] Enclosing several nationalities in tight quarters under adverse conditions for an extended period of time was like lighting a powder keg with a very short fuse.

The human element often exacerbated conditions and put other passen-

4. Mary Ann Weston Maughan. Utah State University, Merrill Cazier Library, Special Collections and Archives.

gers in peril. Alexander Neibaur wrote that the captain of the 1841 voyage of the *Sheffield* declared to his LDS passengers that the ship was in a state of mutiny after one of his crew members threatened him.[47] William Clayton observed that human nature often overrode professed beliefs when, on board the 1840 voyage of the *North America*, he said that "some are not saints who profess to be."[48] He further related the challenge the brethren faced of keeping the sailors away from female church members. Surely some of those indiscretions were two-sided. The crew greatly resented such interference from the LDS men.[49]

One captain, Captain Peers (Pierce), displayed extreme behavior on the 1842 voyage of the *Henry*. The *Henry* carried 157 Saints on this passage, of whom one, Alfred Cordon, recalled the following: "The Captain swore he would keep us on the ship untill we were starved to death. On the 14th of November 1842 we came to the mouth of the Mississippi river [and] remained there six days on account of the evil disposition of the Captain, who was determined to provoke us as much as possible. When Captain Taylor came on board to examine the Log Book he found a charge against Elder [John] Snider [company leader] and James Morgan for Mutiny."[50]

Despite these incidents, most voyages ran fairly smoothly, and the captains and crew generally looked upon transporting Latter-day Saints favorably. For example, upon reaching the port of New Orleans in 1844, William Kay, LDS company leader on the *Fanny*, reported, "I believe no people that ever crossed the Atlantic ever had a more prosperous voyage ... such a captain and crew for kindness I believe could scarcely be met with; his liberality exceeds all that ever came under our notice; indeed I am at a loss for words to express the respect he has manifested to all."[51]

### *Relationship between Saints and Mariners*

While most captains and crew liked to transport Latter-day Saint cargo, some even took time to play with the children. Mary Haskin Parker Richards, a young passenger on the 1840 voyage of the *Alliance*, recalled, "Our captain was an American and was very kind to us. He would often bring a couple of chairs out of the cabin for Ann and me to [sit] on, in the porch of the cabin door, and would then give each of us a rope from the mast which stood in front of us to balance ourselves by and would then ask if we ever enjoyed a nicer rocking then we was then taking."[52]

While on the 1842 voyage of the *Sidney*, George Cannon remembered:

> Perhaps a more agreeable ship's company, both of Saints and seamen, never crossed the Atlantic. The Captain and officers are kind and humane men and so far from disputes or hard feelings that the sailors say they never saw a family who agreed better: and they wonder how a company of people who were many of them strangers to each other can bear and forbear in the manner they do. One of the sailors, an intelligent man, told me that he had been in the passenger line of shipping for years and never saw anything like it: in general the Captain kept his distance and did not allow of freedoms from the passengers: but here he allowed them every indulgence, took

pleasure in having the children round him on the quarter-deck and would play with them as if they were his own. May the Lord bless him for his kindness![53]

## Ocean Leisure

The adults also allowed time for recreation. For example, Wilford Woodruff, an avid fisherman, took time to observe marine life on several occasions. On May 5, 1841, he wrote, "We saw a large school of porpoises." Two weeks later he recorded, "Saw a school of Macerel." A few days later he penned, "We saw 50 fishing smack waiting for bait."[54]

Yet no form of recreation could equal the joy of the seagoing Saints when they finally arrived at a North American port after a long voyage. For most, that port was New Orleans, established as the principal port of arrival during the Nauvoo period and remaining so until the spring of 1855.[55] All but ten LDS-chartered Atlantic voyages during this fifteen-year period docked at New Orleans, carrying about eighteen thousand Saints.[56]

During the sailing era of the 1840s, the voyages to New York averaged about five weeks. The trip to New Orleans took an average of nineteen days longer.[57] Despite the extra distance, church leaders chose New Orleans as the port for the Saints to disembark, primarily for economic reasons and the accessibility of the Mississippi River, which provided a direct route to Nauvoo.[58] With the exile of Nauvoo church members in 1846, and problems with yellow fever and cholera on the Mississippi, the Saints were rerouted to ports on the East Coast nearly a decade later.[59]

## Challenges Landing at New Orleans

Although the Nauvoo-bound Saints were thrilled to arrive at the port of New Orleans, they faced potential hazards heading up the Mississippi. As the Saints entered the Gulf Coast region, they had to cross a dangerous sandbar at the mouth of "Old Man River." They did so with steam-powered tugboats, which pulled the ships across the bar and towed them about one hundred miles into port.

The tugboats were accompanied by pilots who resided in "the Balize." One historian described this uninviting habitation that the Latter-day Saints would have gazed upon as they entered America in the early 1840s:

The Balize, as it was known, where the pilot stations were established was little more than a mud bank situated a short distance above the North East Pass. One such station contained sixteen or eighteen houses built upon piles in the midst of the morass. The houses were connected one with the other by raised walks or bridges, laid on the mud, constructed of timber, logs and wrecks of vessels. The pilots at each station were mostly ex-merchantmen, chiefly English with some Americans, French and Spaniards. The monotonous existence at these stations resulted in the deterioration of the conduct of their inhabitants and they became notorious for the frequent occurrences of riots and brawls.[60]

Conway explained further that "once a sufficient number of ships had gathered at the mouth of the river and this rarely involved a long wait, the tow boat would take six ships upstream, one on either side and four towing behind. This allowed easy communication from one ship to another."[61] James Palmer, who voyaged on the *Hanover* in 1842, noted a variation of this process:

> The first mate was on the look out for land and soon discovered from the main gallant topsail that we [were] sailing direct towards the mouth of the mississippi river[;] shortly we saw a vessel approaching from our left, that came from Germany and a steam tug came booming over the bar to meet us[.] Thay threw their large cables and made fast to our ship and soon we ware anchored safely in the mouth of that king of all rivers, and soon our German friends ware made fast along side and we ware booming up towards New Orleans.[62]

The Saints were no doubt eager to quickly travel the hundred-mile distance from the mouth of the Mississippi to New Orleans. LDS convert George Whitaker, who took the steamer *Palmyra* in 1845, noted that it took his party three days to cross this stretch of the river and described its beautiful banks: "I thought I never saw anything so beautiful as the sights going up the river. This was in the beginning of March. Everything looked fresh and green—the oranges were hanging on trees. I thought I would very much like to live there."[63]

Upon arriving at New Orleans, Whitaker recorded, "This was the first time I had set my foot on land for about seven or eight weeks. We stayed there one day. I sold some of my shawls and got a good price for them. We met some of our brethren from Nauvoo, who had come to work there through the winter. They did not give a very pleasing account of things at Nauvoo, which discouraged some few of the Saints, and they remained there."[64]

During the Nauvoo era, some Saints who were not as economically fortunate as Whitaker were forced to stay for a time in New Orleans or elsewhere along the river. Economic issues were not unique to Latter-day Saints emigrating through New Orleans—or any other port, for that matter.

## *Land Sharks*

In addition to the financial concern of securing enough money for their passage, LDS immigrants also faced the continual threat of land sharks (thieves), who waited to rob them as they passed into the Crescent City. Although this problem would later be ameliorated, as it had been in Liverpool, by engaging LDS emigration agents, no church agents were on hand to help protect the arriving immigrants during the Nauvoo years. Church immigration agent Lucius Scovil provided a colorful account of these river thieves' tactics at New Orleans:

> Yesterday, I fell in with one of those sharks, his name is Cook, and the head of one of a company of ten in number, who are engaged in taking out permits and re-shipping passengers. They speak five or six languages, and are determined to monopolize the business.... They would send some person ... on board to make confusion, ... bringing bills from some boat, and saying that they were captain or clerk of said boat, and would carry them for one dollar to St. Louis.... On this account the last company had to stay here six days, just because they were bamboozled by these runners. I consider that there is but one way to do business for the best good of the Saints, and that it is for one person to do all of the business.... Those sharpers are threatening me all the time, but I do not fear them. I am satisfied that the church has not known the extent of their speculations from them, and yet were soaping them all the while.[65]

## A Sad Look at Slavery

The issue of slavery also caught the attention of the Saints in New Orleans. Alfred Cordon, arriving in the Delta City in November 1842, remembered, "There were many slaves working in the streets chained together both men and women." Yet the Saints did not always share the same view as they passed on their way, differing in their opinions about the institution of slavery. The reaction of William Staines, who immigrated to Nauvoo at age twenty-four in the spring of 1843, is especially noteworthy:

> When about nine years of age [Staines] had been informed that these [American] slaves all worked in chains upon rice and sugar plantations in the Southern States. His sympathies were so aroused by the woeful tale that he refrained from eating sugar in order that the money saved might go to a fund that was being raised in England for the emancipation of the slaves in America. Concerning his observations at New Orleans and along the Mississippi, he [said]: "Here to my surprise I found them driving fine mule teams, being trusted with cartloads of valuable merchandise, taking the same to all parts of the city and country, apparently equal with the free white man, except in being slaves and owned by someone. I found them working as porters, warehousemen, firemen on steamboats, etc., and their food was as good as that of white men performing like labor. I must confess that this surprised me, and for the first time I regretted that I had quit eating sugar to help to free the negro. I found him in slavery having all the sugar he needed and with a better breakfast than any farm laborer in England could afford to eat."[66]

Yet slavery was not as sweet as Staines here implies. Another Saint who passed through the New Orleans region summarized her detestable experience of watching hundreds of sunbaked Negroes laboring on plantations by exclaiming, "Oh! Slavery, how I hate thee!"[67] This statement may have reflected the opinion of most passing church emigrants, and even though Staines may have succumbed to sugar, he was not relieved of his repugnant feelings toward the institution of slavery in general.[68]

5. Alexander Neibaur. In *Utah Genealogical and Historical Magazine*, April 1914.

### River Towns

Alexander Neibaur noted that the cook on the voyage of the *Sheffield* had been sold in New Orleans, "[it] being one of the chief slave states."

On April 1, 1841, he also described the Saints boarding the steamboat *Moravian* headed to Quincy, Illinois, and provided a vivid portrait of life along the river. At the town of Plaquemine (which he maintained was "about 150 miles N.W. of the Gulf of Mexico"), he reported, "Several Negroes coming on board some with vegetables, eggs, apples[,] pies, etc." Neibaur described Natchez as "a neat town" where they stopped to get wood for fuel. He portrayed Vicksburg as "an imposing town built upon rising ground; courthouse built upon a hill. Numerous turtles upon the shore." Memphis was "a neat little place on a hill." But this "little place" was soon struck by a terrifying scene:

At midnight it thundered and the lightning illuminat[ed] the objects around us for many a mile. At the same time a terrific storm shook the boat, the Captain and his men being frightened out of their wits, sparks of fire flying about in the sterrage. Many of the passengers were awakened by the fear of fire. The Captain gave orders to stop the engine and make for the land until daylight appeart, the cooks window being blown out of the kitchen. It was terrifying. Broke all the windows in the tophouse (wheel house).[69]

Also to be reckoned with was nonmembers' abhorrence of the Saints as they steamed up the Mississippi on the church-owned steamboat *Maid of Iowa*.[70] William Adams described the following vivid experience he had in March 1844:

We were very much anoyed also persecuted in towns along the river. News went ahead that a Boat filled with Mormons were on their way to Nauvoo[;] necessity caused the Boat to land to get supplys. Men would rush on to the Boat calling us foul names. Joes rats was a common salutation we received[.] Natchez a town on the east side of the river set the Boat on fire. . . . The fire was extenguished in a short time with the loss of several feather beds and bedding[;] it was a narrow escape for the crew and passengers also the Boat.[71]

Priscilla Staines remembered that the town was Memphis, not Natchez, adding that the fire was started by "some villain [who] placed a half consumed cigar under a straw mattress."[72] She also recalled the following incident wherein a mob gathered and threw stones through the cabin windows. This disturbed Captain Dan Jones, so he commanded the brethren to parade with loaded muskets and told the mob that if they would not cease their behavior, he would shoot them down like dogs. The mob, so warned, slithered away.[73]

William Adams, a second witness to this episode, added the following:

Another town that we landed late in the evening Captain Jones ordered that no Person be allowed aboard the Boat, but men came rushing aboard and would not be held back. Br. James Haslem [Haslam] went on the herricon [hurricane] Deck and fired a gun in hopes it would be a warning to the mob that we would not be run over by them, but in quelling them they run for firearms and fired off several shots. Things looked serious, Steam was got up as speedily as possible the Boat was shoved off and they landed three miles up the River and lay over to the next morning ... but we were not molested. ... I will state one incident where the company was in eminent danger of looseing their lives and sinking the Boat, [which] also shows their hatred against the Later-Day Saints. The Lower Mississippi had quite a number of First class Steamboats running between St. Lewis and New Orleans that made the round Trip every week[;] each time they passed the *Maid of Iowa* we would have a grand salute by cheering and laughing and calling us bad names. One of those Boats I forget her name tried to run us down and would if Captain Jones had not been on the Herricon [hurricane] deck as he was always on duty, made them shear off by hollowing and threatening to shoot the Pilot[.] This took place at night when the Company were in there beds.[74]

In addition to these challenges, the Saints faced the normal obstacles of river travel, including sandbars, snags, currents, and ice. The *Sidney* and the *Medford* were each stuck on the sandbar at the mouth of the Mississippi for nearly a day and a half.[75] Alexander Wright made the best of the situation: while the *Sidney* was caught on the bar, he managed to catch enough catfish to feed his fellow passengers.[76] Saints from the two companies then joined together in New Orleans, took the steamboat *Alex Scott* upriver, and were stuck for three weeks ninety miles below St. Louis because the river water was so low. By the time they got to St. Louis, the river had frozen over, forcing them to spend the winter there.[77]

A month later another LDS company crossed the Atlantic on the *Emerald* and was detained in the river cities of Alton, Chester, and St. Louis for three cold months due to ice on the Mississippi.[78] Parley P. Pratt, the company leader of the *Emerald*, decided against staying in St. Louis: "I landed with my family in Chester, Illinois—eighty miles below St. Louis. The company continued on to St. Louis. My reason for landing there was, that I would not venture into Missouri after the abuses I had experienced there in former times."[79]

The following year a number of converts from the 1844 *Norfolk* voyage found themselves stuck in St. Louis for a different reason: they didn't have sufficient funds to continue the journey to Nauvoo.[80] Generally speaking, most Nauvoo-bound Saints wanted to pass through St. Louis in a hurry, where they faced not only the threat of cholera and yellow fever but also a hardness in the hearts of the St. Louis apostates, which seemed as cold as the winter ice on the Mississippi.[81] Such hardness sometimes affected church members on their way to Nauvoo. For example, Hiram Clark, who gathered to Zion with a group of 181 Saints in 1841, noted that about 30 members of his group had been "disaffected through false reports" and therefore chose to tarry at St. Louis.[82]

Thomas Wrigley, who gathered to Nauvoo in 1843 to prepare the way for his British family, met opposition on two fronts. When he visited his sister's nonmember family, he related that "they tried their best by every means to persuade [him] to give up [his] faith."[83] When he returned to St. Louis the following year to bring his family up the Mississippi, he was delayed there for a season. He described the dark conditions in the city: "We for some time felt afraid of the exterminating orders of Governor Boggs, which were still in force, but our numbers began to increase in that city and we took courage and a few met in a private house and organized a branch of the Church and the Lord blest the faithful but it was hard work having to contend with the prejudice of the people of the world and every apostate that left Nauvoo came there and did their best to bring persecution on us."[84]

Joseph Fielding, company leader for more than two hundred Saints on the 1841 voyage of the *Tyrian*, summarized his view of the apostate spirit in St. Louis in a letter: "At St. Louis we found a number of Saints, at least who have a name among the Saints, some of these prove a trial to those who call there. They tell you many evil tales; I wish they would stop all who are like themselves. The faithful need not be troubled by them; let them talk and have all they can get, they seem afraid to suffer affliction with the people of God, and so go to Missouri, where there are none, thinking also to get a little more money."[85] In his journal Fielding added, "Here we saw some poor, faithless Saints something like spiders webs set to catch flies. They came to us with fair words as our best friends, but their counsel was that of enemies, but did not prevail to stay any of our company except two."[86]

This determined spirit helped push most Saints to their desired haven. After crossing the Atlantic on the *Metoka* in 1843 and finally reaching Nauvoo that fall, William Rowley wrote of the stark contrast between the negative reports he had heard about Nauvoo while traveling up the Mississippi and what he actually found there:

> You may suppose we were most pleasingly surprised, after having had our ears continually assailed with the doleful accounts of "the wretchedness of the place," its "log and mud" built "cabins," its "knee deep" muddy streets, the "poverty and starvation" that awaited us, the "villainy and roguery" of its inhabitants, the "awful delusion of Mormonism," "beware of old Joe Smith," and a thousand other such salutations; you may judge then, how much we were gratified at beholding the striking contrast, while gazing with rapturous delight, first upon the "temple," which already assumes a lofty bearing from the commanding eminence on which it is being erected; then the Nauvoo House; the Mansion House (the residence of him of whom the world is not worthy); the masonic, music, and public halls; some completed, and others are being so, besides numerous well-built and substantial brick stores, and private dwellings.
>
> The whole site and aspect of the city, presenting a most cheering picture of the enterprise and industry of its inhabitants, exhibiting a remarkable difference to many of the western towns which we passed in coming up the Mississippi, of far longer standing and origin.[87]

### *Nauvoo Reception*

Once the British converts reached Nauvoo, they encountered not only a beautiful city but also a warm welcome by fellow Saints, which seems to have caused the inbound converts to forget for a time some of the rough challenges of their journey. Hiram Clark, who arrived in Nauvoo in 1841, was grateful for the reception he received, which no doubt brought light to his night voyage: "We landed in Nauvoo on the 18th of April, about eleven o'clock in the evening, yet many of the brethren stood on the shore to welcome us on our arrival."[88] Alexander Neibaur, who immigrated with Clark, wrote, "A number of the brother[s] was ready to receive us; they kindly offered their houses, many slept in a large stone building belonging to one of the brethren, myself & William Gross, [while] some others kept up a large fire all night and stayed with our luggage. Some of the brethren that had come here before us kept us company. Early in the morning a number of the brethren came to Inquire whether all of us had obtained habitations. We got in very comfortable with a brother."[89]

In a letter to the *Millennial Star*, Heber C. Kimball related the warm welcome members of the Quorum of the Twelve and over a hundred immigrating Saints received in the summer of 1841: "We landed in Nauvoo on the 1st of July, and when we struck the dock I think there was about three hundred Saints there to meet us, and a greater manifestation of love and gladness I never saw before. President Smith was the first one that caught us by the hand."[90]

James Burgess, who left Liverpool in the fall of 1842 for Nauvoo, remembered, "When our boat arrived at the city there were hundreds to welcome us."[91] Robert Crookston also left England in 1842 for Nauvoo with a company of Saints. He testified, "As we approached the landing place to our great joy we saw the Prophet Joseph Smith there to welcome his people who had come so far. We were all so glad to see him and set our feet upon the promised land so to speak. It was the most thrilling experience of my life for I know he was a Prophet of the Lord."[92]

The Saints who crossed the Atlantic on the *Emerald* and came upriver on the *Maid of Iowa* were also warmly greeted, first by the prophet Joseph Smith, who described the following: "I was present at the landing and the first on board the steamer, when I met Sister Mary Ann Pratt (who had been in England with Brother Parley) and her little daughter only three or four days old. I could not refrain from shedding tears; so many of my friends and acquaintances arriving in one day kept me very busy receiving their congratulations and answering their questions. I was rejoiced to meet them in such good health and fine spirits; for they were equal to any that had ever come to Nauvoo."[93]

The *Maid of Iowa* also carried the Saints who had crossed the Atlantic on the *Fanny* in 1844. When this group of British converts reached the shores of Nauvoo, William Adams noted the joy of being greeted by Joseph and Hyrum Smith and two hundred others.[94] Priscilla Staines felt that she

6. Nauvoo Temple, ca. 1845. Daughters of the Utah Pioneers, Salt Lake City.

would be able to recognize the prophet Joseph Smith among the masses who had assembled to greet the Saints. Staines said, "I felt impressed by the spirit that I should know him. As we neared the pier the prophet was standing among the crowd. At the moment, however, I recognized him according to the impression and pointed him out."[95]

William Clayton penned the following words to a fellow church member in England, explaining that the British Saints would have trials on their way to Zion but adding that the journey would be worth it:

> It is impossible for pen to describe to you the difficulties you will have to endure.... You must either come or suffer the vengeance of heaven and for my part I will say that if I was in England now and had

*By Land and Sea* | 31

experienced all the journey it would not in the least deter me from coming for I have often found that in the greatest seasons of suffering we have the greatest cause of rejoicing and so it has been with us for when we have been enduring things which we should once have thought impossible even then was our happiest moments.[96]

This letter is an illuminating summation of the spirit of the gathering to Nauvoo. It is imbued with a sense of the unity the Saints felt as they gathered. Perhaps it also describes how the gathering did more than bring a people from one location to another; it also served as a rallying point for these covenant people to meet and overcome obstacles together and to reach their desired haven, prepared with one mind and one faith. After the Nauvoo Temple was erected, over 5,600 adult Saints (including many British converts) made sacred covenants there to assist others who desired to gather.[97] These exiles from Nauvoo, beginning in the winter of 1846, made their way again on the Mississippi, only this time they crossed east to west, eventually establishing a new Zion in the Salt Lake Valley.[98]

# 3

## In and Out of Liverpool

Following the gathering to Nauvoo, Saints from the British Isles and other European converts continued to assemble at Liverpool before crossing the Atlantic. The *Latter-day Saints' Millennial Star* remained as a guide for the emigration operation throughout the nineteenth century.

### *The* Millennial Star

The *Millennial Star* was established in Manchester in April 1840, just two months before the first LDS emigrants launched from Liverpool. However, just two years later, in April 1842, its operations moved to Liverpool.[1]

Elder Parley P. Pratt was the first editor of the *Millennial Star*. Among other things, Pratt indicated in his prospectus issued May 27, 1840, that the purpose of the periodical was to spread the truth, gather Israel, and shine as a star of light for the faithful to prepare for the second coming of Jesus Christ and the ushering in of the millennium. Within its pages, the *Star* created the feeling that the second coming (of Christ) was nigh at hand, which no doubt influenced converts and the doctrine of the gathering. The first article of the opening issue indeed dealt with the doctrinal topic of the millennium and reviewed the teachings of ancient prophets regarding the restoration and gathering of Israel in the last days.[2]

This Latter-day Saint periodical proved to be an essential instrument for church leaders and LDS agents, providing continual information and direction to the passing emigrants. These emigration agents chartered vessels each year, and the *Star* regularly published departure times in various editions throughout the nineteenth century.

The *Star* offered guidance in minute detail for each and every aspect of the emigrants' journey to Zion. For example, in August 1841 the periodical

7. LDS European Mission Headquarters, Liverpool, 42 Islington Street, 1885. Church History Library, PH 2368.

published an article titled "Information to Emigrants" providing several pages of general information regarding immigration to North America, as well as practical counsel about what emigrants should take on their voyage. Such advice included taking no furniture but only "necessary articles of beds, bedding, wearing apparel, pots, cooking utensils, &c., which will come in useful both on the ship and on the steamboat, and after they arrive." Emigrants received this additional instruction: "Everything which is not designed for use on the passage should be carefully packed in strong boxes or trunks. Emigrants will not have to pay anything for freight of their usual household goods and furniture on the ocean; but it will cost something for freight up the Mississippi River for every article except a certain quantity which is allowed each passenger free as travelling luggage."

The *Star* also offered meticulous advice on the best route to take, including specific guidelines for purchasing tickets, paying for travel, and avoiding extra lodging costs:

> New Orleans is by far the cheapest route for emigrants to Illinois; and emigrating in large companies may save much more money.

8. Parley P. Pratt, ca. 1840s. Photo of engraving. Church History Library, General Authority Portrait Collection, PH 700.

Those who wish to avail themselves of these advantages, and who are intending to emigrate this autumn, are informed that the name and age of each passenger, together with money to pay their passage to New Orleans and to purchase provisions, must be forwarded . . . at least 10 days previous to the time of sailing, so that a ship may be chartered and provisions purchased according to the number of passengers, and thus avoid all hurry and confusion.

The money and names being forwarded ten days previous to the time of sailing, the passengers and goods need not arrive till two or three days before the time of sailing. Thus when all things are prepared, they can go immediately on board, and begin to arrange the berths, beds, provisions, &c., and avoid the expense of living a while in the town of Liverpool. Perhaps the passage money and provisions for each passenger from Liverpool to New Orleans will be not far from four pounds. Children under fourteen years of age, half-price; under one year nothing. . . . When the ship arrives in New Orleans the company will need to send their foreman, or leader, or committee, to charter a steam boat for Nauvoo or St. Louis, which will probably be from 15 s. [shillings] to 25 s. per head, and provisions to be purchased for about two weeks; so the whole passage money from Liverpool to Nauvoo will probably be from £ 5 to £ 7.[3]

The *Star* also encouraged immigration with reports by those who had reached America. For example, an article titled "Emigration" commented, "The news from the emigrants who sailed from this country last season is so very encouraging that it will give a new impulse to the spirit of the gathering."[4] Church leaders also provided written instructions that encouraged immigration to Nauvoo so the Saints could build the temple and partake of its blessings.[5] British converts were influenced by these leaders' excellent organization and dependability, both in Liverpool and Nauvoo and later in Salt Lake City.

In addition to providing useful instructions to departing LDS emigrants, the *Millennial Star* also published the dates when various transatlantic voyages would depart. In addition, church leaders selected an emigration agent to carry out arrangements in Liverpool. As previously noted, in as early as April 1841 the *Millennial Star* had published an "Epistle of the Twelve" detailing the appointment and advantages of having an LDS agent who could arrange for better pricing for travel and provisions and also help navigate around those who would take advantage of the Saints.[6]

However, such an assignment certainly had its challenges. One agent said this concerning his service: "There is much to do when a vessel is preparing to sail for some days; from ten to twenty emigrants coming to the office; one wants this and one wants that, and the third wants to know where he shall sleep all night, with a dozen or more women and children in the office to run over; one wants tin ware, another is short of cash and their children are hungry."[7]

### Post-Nauvoo Advice for Departing Emigrants and Descriptions of Liverpool

Following the Nauvoo exodus, the Saints began to stream into the Salt Lake Valley in 1847. During this emigration period, the agents continued to provide valiant service, and the *Millennial Star* continued to offer instruction to emigrants leaving from Liverpool: "We beg to inform the Saints intending to emigrate that we are now prepared to receive their applications for berths. Every application should be accompanied by the names, age, occupation, country where born, and £1 deposit for each one named, except for children under one year old. Passengers must furnish their own beds and bedding, their cooking utensils, provision boxes, &c. Every person applying for a berth or berths should be careful to give their address very distinct, in order to insure the delivery of our answer to them by letter carriers." The article also noted:

> By reference to STAR no. 32, it will be seen that £10 each was named as the lowest sum upon which single persons or families could be encouraged by us to emigrate from Liverpool to Great Salt Lake City....
>
> Our first vessel will sail in the fore part of January 1853; and as soon as our arrangements are complete, the passengers for that ship will be notified when to be in Liverpool, and receive all further necessary information; the same routine will be observed in reference to the succeeding ship. Deposits may be forwarded until the close of the year, or later, as may hereafter be noticed.[8]

Liverpool was better positioned than London as a hub of emigration. Not only was Liverpool located between the British Isles and Ireland, but it also had rail connections to the eastern ports of Hull and Grimsby. In addition, the Mersey River was easier to navigate than the Thames, and it was a day closer than London. Conway Sonne further noted, "Most important in Liverpool's growth was a 200-acre dock system, forming a belt along the waterfront that extended three and eventually seven miles."[9]

During the latter half of the nineteenth century, Liverpool served as headquarters for both the European and British Missions and therefore created an additional reason to focus migration efforts from this important communication center. By 1851 the British census noted that Liverpool had a population of 367,000, making it the second-largest city in England. LDS historian Bruce A. Van Orden observed that in 1851 "more than 32,000 members of the Church resided in Britain; this figure, an all-time high for the nineteenth century, exceeded the total membership of all the Church in all of North America including Utah."[10]

Upon arriving at Liverpool, LDS converts were greeted by their shipping companies' agents as well as by LDS-appointed emigration agents and church leaders. As the primary port of LDS embarkation, Liverpool provided a variety of scenes to many who had never been to a metropolis. By the mid-nineteenth century, Liverpool was the most active international port of emigration in the world, and with more than two thousand pubs, it was considered a sailors' paradise:[11] "Liverpool was a sailors' town. Dockside pubs were everywhere.... The sound of... sea shanties was heard from the tavern doorways as the sailors spent their few days' leave and their hard-earned money on beer, women and song. Prostitutes roamed the streets and solicited the mariners."[12]

Yet to Latter-day Saints and other respectable emigrants, such scenes were repugnant. Historian Terry Coleman explained, "Away from the handsome classical buildings and houses of the merchants, the rich city of Liverpool was narrow, dirty, and infested, and itself a great inducement to emigration."[13]

Author Nathaniel Hawthorne, Liverpool's American consul in the mid-nineteenth century (1853–57), knew something of Liverpool's filthy environment. Coleman succinctly described Hawthorne's dismal view of Liverpool's socioeconomic condition in the mid-nineteenth century:

> Almost every day Hawthorne walked about the city, preferring the darker and dingier streets inhabited by the poorer classes. Women nursed their babies at dirty breasts. The men were haggard, drunken, care-worn, and hopeless, but patient as if that were the rule of their lives. He never walked through these streets without feeling he might catch some disease, but he took the walks all the same because there was a sense of bustle, and of being in the midst of life and of having got hold of something real, which he did not find in the better streets of Liverpool. Tithebarn Street was thronged with dreadful faces—women with young figures but with old and wrinkled countenances, young girls without any maiden neatness, barefooted, with dirty legs. Dirty, dirty children, and the grown people were the flower of these buds, physically and morally. At every ten steps there were spirit vaults.

Placards advertised beds for the night. Often he saw little children taking care of little children.... At the provision shops, little bits of meat were ready for poor customers, little heaps and selvages and corners stripped off from joints and steaks.[14]

Hawthorne carefully described in a single picturesque sentence the deplorable conditions that existed in Liverpool: "The people are as numerous as maggots in cheese; you behold them, disgusting, and all moving about, as when you raise a plank or log that has long lain on the ground, and find many vivacious bugs and insects beneath it."[15]

Hawthorne's descriptions of Liverpool are remarkably similar to those of LDS converts who passed through during the mid-nineteenth century. For example, Latter-day Saint German migrant Hans Hoth wrote in December 1854, "Saw adults and children go around barefoot, and frequently almost quite naked."[16] Two years later an LDS British couple noted, "Liverpool is the dirtiest place we ever saw."[17] Hans Peter Lund wrote, "We saw poverty."[18] Another convert remembered, "Liverpool was a smoky, dirty looking place."[19] In 1876 Thomas Griggs wrote, "Liverpool is dirty and disorderly, large numbers of barefooted women & girls, many bruised faces."[20] Others described the port of Liverpool as a "noisy, smoky, city of ships."[21] Robert Schmid remembered its "cobble rock streets."[22]

Some emigrants walked those stony streets and found more than just dirt as they did a bit of sightseeing. Thomas Atkin wrote, "We got our luggage on board [but were delayed,] which afforded us a splendid opportunity to visit some of the many places of interest in the town of Liverpool."[23] Andrew Gowan recalled, "Went to the Botanical Gardens which was a treat to behold to see everything is so fine, arranged in order."[24] Amos Milton Musser took advantage of a chance to visit "the circus with several of the brethren."[25]

Others found time to buy books and to take "a good look at the city."[26] David H. Morris noted, "Went to the Alexandria theater where the 'Harbor lights' was presented in fine style."[27] William Davidson remembered that the harbor was "six miles long, constantly filled with ships from every country of the world."[28] Andrew Gowan observed, "As for the shipping of

Liverpool, it is like a dense forest for miles and the steamers running up and down the river and every moment which is pretty to behold. Some very splendid vessels here."[29]

### Lodging and Provisions in Liverpool

Gowan had plenty of time to see this maritime metropolis as a letter notes he "stayed in Liverpool seven days then stayed in the ship two days." During this time of transition before embarkation, LDS emigration agents tried to ease the transition process as much as possible, including directing converts to temporary lodgings while they awaited their departure. When possible, the agents preferred to make arrangements for the emigrants to sleep on the vessel to minimize the time spent in this unsanitary, crime-ridden city and to avoid extra lodging costs. Frederic Gardiner remembered, "We arrived in Liverpool the same night it being Aug. 30th [1849], and stopped at the Music Hall, which had been rented for the reception of the ship's passengers, until it would be ready to receive us on board. Sept. 1st we all shipped on board the ship James Pennell."[30]

Thomas Evans Jeremy, emigration agent for the Welsh Saints, further noted, "I settled my accounts with President Cameron with regard to emigration from Wales. I am his agent in emigration matters in Wales. . . . The Saints came to Liverpool and I took them all to comfortable lodgings in Hunter Street." The following day the Welsh Saints boarded the ship *General McClellan*, "as also did the English, Danish and Scots."[31]

Depending on the circumstances, some emigrants even stayed temporarily at mission headquarters. George Dunford recalled, "I took leave of our good brothers and sisters of the Birmingham Conference and we stayed the latter part of the above day in the Church office in Liverpool and on the following morning . . . we went on board the steamship."[32] Other Saints simply found lodging for themselves. For example, James Farmer wrote in 1853, "Procured good lodgings at Robinson's Temperance Hotel. . . . They treated us kindly and we were well situated."[33]

Other European converts also used Liverpool as their main port of embarkation before crossing the Atlantic. Most were British proselytes, but many Scandinavians also responded to the call to come to Zion, which thus led them to Liverpool to join with other Saints before departure.[34] For these Scandinavian Saints, their journey generally began after traveling to Copenhagen before they transmigrated through the port of Hull, on the eastern coast of England, and then took the rail to Liverpool.[35] Between 1852 and 1894, over twenty-four thousand Scandinavian Latter-day Saints traveled to Utah through England. Nearly two hundred vessels carrying the Saints left Scandinavia bound for Hull. From Hull they traveled by rail to Liverpool.[36]

Church leaders and LDS emigration agents were keenly aware of the groups of Saints who would be passing through Liverpool and therefore were in a position to assist them with lodging as well as food. For example, the first large group of Scandinavians to transmigrate through Hull to Liverpool arrived on December 29, 1853, and "lodging and meals, previously ordered, were prepared for them." Three days later they boarded the packet ship *Forest Monarch*.[37]

A fifteen-year-old LDS youth who traveled in 1888 described how the train he rode was an improvement compared to the trains he had previously ridden: "The passenger trains were different than any I had seen before. The coaches were divided into compartments that would accommodate from 6 to eight passengers; they would be locked in. A running board on the outside of the train that the conductor used to go from compartment through the whole train. I thought it a practical way to check all passengers without disturbing those already checked."[38]

Rail services from Hull to Liverpool began in 1840 when the rail line between Liverpool and Selby was extended to Hull.[39] The North Eastern Railway (NER), which took control of this route in 1851, chartered emigrant trains from Hull to Liverpool for trade purposes. The journey lasted up to seven hours. In 1854 one Scandinavian convert described his nighttime rail journey: "In Hull we were but three hours. We went the same evening by train to Liverpool. . . . It was bad, we went through England in the night, as we passed many trains and cities and through tunnels and over rivers and lakes. We rode 44 miles in 7 hours and arrived in Liverpool 3 o'clock a.m."[40]

The rail route out of Hull varied according to arrangements made in advance between the railway and steamship companies and the LDS agents; and as the scale of transmigration grew, the local rail line facilities improved. Most emigrants headed on the NER's trains via Leeds, Manchester, and

Bolton before arriving at Liverpool's Lime Street Station. The Saints saw little of the port of Hull. One passing Saint recorded:

> I did not see anything of Hull beyond the streets through which we went to reach the railway station. The railway station itself was beautiful and imposing. We left for Liverpool on a special train at 3 o'clock in the afternoon, and came through the towns of Howden, Selby, Normington [Normanton], Brandford [Bradford], Leeds Hudbersfild [Huddersfield], Manchester and Bolton to Liverpool. But as it became dark at an early hour, I saw little or nothing at all of the cities and the country we passed through. The country around Hull was pretty, flat and fertile. Farther away it was more mountainous. The railway was frequently on a higher level than the towns and villages, and sometimes it also went along below the surface at considerably long stretches.[41]

Regardless of the route they took, all migrants traveled the 140 miles to Liverpool by steam train. The scenery they passed through varied as greatly as the backgrounds of the passengers on board. From the flat hinterlands of the Humber to the rugged terrain of the Pennines, the journey was an experience they would never forget—especially for those like Joseph Hansen, who wrote, "This was the first and only time that my father rode in a railway train."[42]

# 4

## Shipping the Saints

Men in the maritime emigration business observed the passing Latter-day Saints and their impressive mode of operation throughout the nineteenth century.[1] Two Liverpool shipping agents interviewed in 1852 noted, "With regard to 'Mormon' Emigration, and the class of persons of which it is composed, they are principally farmers and mechanics, with some few clerks, surgeons, &c. They are generally intelligent and well-behaved, and many of them are highly respectable."[2]

Two years later Samuel W. Richards, president of the British Mission, received a remarkable invitation. Richards recalled, "In early May, 1854, I received a very notable document, sealed with wax, in which was the impress of her majesty's official seal. . . . I found it to be an order, not a mere invitation for Mr. Richards, the shipping agent of the 'Mormon emigration' to appear in London before a committee of her parliament, to answer such questions as might be required by them."[3] This created no small stir among the Saints, Richards added, and no doubt caught the immediate attention of Richards himself.

The committee, under the direction of the queen and led by John O'Connell, comprised sixteen parliamentary members who were charged with finding a solution to the high mortality rate on sea vessels in the mid-nineteenth century. Richards, whose lodging and travel costs were paid in full by the British government, took the train to London for the meeting but upon arriving learned that the requested meeting had been postponed until the following day. Richards explained, "[At the appointed hour] I was . . . invited to a seat inside of a large, half-circular table around the outside of which this committee was seated, facing inwardly, so that all could look me in the face while I could not look directly at each of them.

9. Samuel W. Richards. In Andrew Jenson, *Latter-day Saint Biographical Encyclopedia: A Compilation of Biographical Sketches of Prominent Men and Women in the Church of Jesus Christ of Latter-day Saints*, vol. 1 (Salt Lake City: Andrew Jenson Company, 1901), 718.

Close by my side sat a reporter to take every word of my answers to the questions propounded."[4]

Richards then related that O'Connell explained why he had been summoned to the meeting, "having been represented as conducting the best shipping agency of emigrants in the kingdom. He wished [Richards] to explain how it was done, and wherein it differed from other agencies conducted under the law." O'Connell added, "If you can tell us anything that we can do to better the condition of our emigrants who go to sea, we want you to do it."

President Richards then described the effective LDS emigration operation, which, he noted, "[he] did very minutely." Richards explained, "By this system, I could call the emigrants into Liverpool mostly in one day, issue to them their tickets the following day, and let them go immediately on board where they were made comfortable till the sailing, on the day or two following, instead of lying for weeks in the docks without shelter and sometimes without food, as many did under the ordinary way of treating emigrants."[5]

Because of Richards's willingness to answer the committee's queries, committee members asked additional questions, some of which were not even relevant to the subject at hand. Richards noted, "Every one seemed anxious to have his own peculiar views satisfied by drawing out the desired information[,] and questions were plied with a zest and zeal that I had never before encountered in my experience, but all with an evident desire to become acquainted with the facts." Richards further observed, "When any question was asked irrelevant to the legitimate subject under investigation, I was frankly reminded that I was under no obligation to answer, if not my pleasure to do so. In this respect the utmost courtesy prevailed such as only gentlemen delight to indulge in."[6]

After a compelling four to five hours of free-flowing conversation, the interview concluded with each committee member shaking Richards's hand. A number of the committee members extended an invitation for Richards to stay at their home whenever he made a trip to London. O'Connell, who was Catholic, even ordered the clerk to pay double the fees to compensate for Richards's time away from his duties in Liverpool. O'Connell also insisted that Richards meet him the next morning so that he could introduce him to some of his parliamentary friends. Richards noted, "After a warm greeting and introduction, to quite a number of the members, he assured me that if the house had known of the interest attached to my examination every member would have been there to hear it. I was taken to the House of Lords for a like introduction."

Richards summed up his experience as follows: "No man on earth could have asked for higher considerations than what were bestowed so freely upon the European president of the 'Mormon' people, while representing the purpose of the King of Kings in the gathering of his people from the nations of the earth, and in answering the summons of the queen of England. . . . Among all of my experience in missionary life, as varied, perhaps, as those of any other man living at the present time, I place this as among the most interesting and satisfactory of them all."[7]

Richards's encounter with the House of Commons also caught the attention of a London newspaper correspondent, who wrote:

> I heard a rather remarkable examination before a committee of the House of Commons. The witness was no other than the supreme authority in England of the Mormonites, and the subject upon which he was giving information was the mode in which the emigration to Utah, Great Salt Lake, is conducted. . . .

*Shipping the Saints* | 45

At the close of the examination, he received the thanks of the committee in rather a marked manner. According to his statements, about twenty-six hundred Mormonite emigrants leave Liverpool during the first three months of every year, and are under the care of a president. On arriving at New Orleans they are received by another president, who returns to Mr. Richards an account of the state in which he found the ship, etc. At any rate there is one thing which, in the emigration committee of the House of Commons, they can do—viz., teach Christian ship owners how to send poor people decently, cheaply, and healthfully across the Atlantic.[8]

### Guion Shipping Line and Agent George Ramsden

Building upon the impressive LDS model for maritime immigration, the Saints joined hands with a shipping company the following decade that enhanced their profile and ensured their comfort and safety. In the late nineteenth century, over forty thousand Latter-day Saints crossed the Atlantic Ocean on a dozen steam vessels owned and operated by the Guion Line, a British shipping company.[9] Spearheaded by Stephen Barker Guion and his business partners John S. Williams and William H. Guion, Stephen's older brother, the enterprise was registered in 1866 as the Liverpool and Great Western Steamship Company, though it was commonly known as the Guion Line.[10]

Stephen Guion, an American born in 1819, had moved to Liverpool in 1851 to work for the Black Star Line, where he had previously partnered with Williams and Guion, who specialized in immigrant transportation from Liverpool to New York. Fifteen years later, though his colleagues had relocated to New York, Guion was stationed in Liverpool, where he served as the company's primary representative. Not only was the name Guion Line strongly influenced by Stephen's mere presence in England, but it is also asserted that the title sprung from his request that all maritime employees wear shirts with his name on them.[11] While familiarity and respect for Stephen's character grew among the community, so did his business; both the Latter-day Saints and the shipping industry held the Guion Line in high regard.[12]

This esteemed shipping line was easily identifiable because most of its vessels were named after American states, although the ships were British by law.[13] The Guion steam vessel *Wyoming* alone made thirty-eight church-chartered voyages, transporting over ten thousand LDS passengers. This represents a considerable number of the over eighty-five thousand LDS immigrants who traveled to America in the nineteenth century, and about 98 percent of those who went by steam.[14]

While the vessels themselves were impressive, perhaps most impressive was their main shipping agent, Mr. George Ramsden. Ramsden was born in Huddersfield, Yorkshire, England, in 1831.[15] He and his wife, Ellen (Hellen), also from Yorkshire, had eight children.[16] In 1853 Ramsden moved to Liverpool to supervise the passenger shipping business of the Black Ball Line, where he worked for a number of years and gained the experience he would need to take on a more active role in managing the Guion Line.[17]

Ramsden's warm relationship with the Saints began on May 13, 1869, when he met with LDS British Mission president Albert Carrington in Liverpool to arrange for the passage of a company of LDS converts aboard the *Minnesota*.[18] According to Ramsden and Carrington's plan, the Saints boarded the *Minnesota* in Liverpool on June 1, 1869. The British Mission Manuscript History recorded, "On their arrival on board they were provided with tea, and everything was done by the manager, Mr. G. Ramsden, for the comfort of the Saints. They had the best part of the steamer entirely for themselves and could use the aft part of the ship in common with the cabin passengers."[19]

Five years later European Mission president Joseph F. Smith discovered that he could secure a better financial deal with a different shipping firm. Ramsden, whom Smith defined as "a very shrewd, keen man, with both eyes open to business,"[20] quickly made a counteroffer to keep the Latter-day Saints' business. This proposal affected the entire shipping conference cartel, which allowed the Guion Line to offer lower rates to LDS passengers only.[21]

The extraordinary relationship between George Ramsden and the Latter-day Saints lasted for a quarter of a century. In praise of the Saints' trust in Ramsden, British Mission president Anthon H. Lund noted that Ramsden had worked with the church for decades without a written contract.[22] Furthermore, by 1880 the entire maritime industry held the Guion

Line in great esteem because it had "never lost a life" during its shipping years.[23] Not only did the seagoing Saints receive exceptional service, but they traveled in peace, confident in Guion's impeccable safety record. In addition, the successful conversion from sail to steam on the journey westward significantly reduced travel time to America.[24] Ramsden's trusted leadership, paired with the timely and safe voyage the Guion Line offered to Saints, created a truly thriving partnership and business.

Within this relationship, the Saints also found support and protection against those who wished to do them harm. In 1879 U.S. secretary of state William M. Evarts campaigned against the LDS practice of polygamy by sending a circular to a number of European countries, ultimately hoping to halt the Saints' immigration to America.[25] In response, "several of Mr. Ramsden's friends engaged in the shipping business warned him of the risk he ran of having [their] people sent back should he attempt to land them in America; but this did not deter him from booking them. He saw how unjust this measure was, and knew that it had its origin in prejudice and religious intolerance."[26]

Anthon H. Lund related that when a consul put up posters announcing that Latter-day Saints couldn't land in American ports, Ramsden came aboard a Guion ship and took charge: "In a towering rage [Ramsden] commanded the Consul to pull down the notice. The latter said he was acting [on] order from the government. Ramsden replied that the government had nothing to do with his ships, and that he did not ask a passenger what his religion was. His strong stand saved our emigration from being stopped."[27]

In addition to having dedicated employees who helped the Saints, the Guion Line also published annual guidebooks providing a variety of information about transatlantic travel, suggesting they had established a well-organized system. For example, in 1875 the Guion Line advertised that it was running to New York, Philadelphia, and Boston "TWICE A WEEK, Forwarding Passengers to all parts of the UNITED STATES and CANADA, at Low Rates. New York is the best, safest, and quickest route for all Passengers going to the United States of America." In addition, the line provided rates and booking instructions: "Children under 12 years of age £2. Infants under 12 months 10s [shillings]. Passengers can be engaged

10. George Ramsden. Church History Library, PH 2016.

by a deposit of Two Pounds on each berth. . . . Passengers booked to all parts to the States, Canada . . . and San Francisco at low rates."[28]

Steerage passengers were informed that upon arriving in New York, they would "[land] at the Government Depot, Castle Garden, where they [would] receive every information respecting the departure of trains, steamboats." Furthermore, all passengers were told that they would receive three quarts of water every day, "with as much provisions as they [could] eat,

*Shipping the Saints* | 49

which [were] all of the best quality, and which [were] examined and put on board under the inspection of Her Majesty's Emigration Officers, and cooked and served out by the company's servants." Breakfast was served at 8:00 a.m., dinner at 1:00 p.m., and supper at 6:00 p.m. As far as sleeping arrangements were concerned, the Guion Guide stipulated that "married couples [would be] berthed together. Single females [would be] placed in the room by themselves, under charge of the stewardess."[29]

The Guion partners were also skilled in initiating and maintaining business relationships with other shipping lines. For example, they wisely joined hands with the Wilson Line based in Hull, England, which brought thousands of transmigrant Scandinavians (including thousands of Latter-day Saints) through Hull to Liverpool before engaging a Guion steamship across the Atlantic.[30] Both the Wilson and Guion Lines profited from their role as carriers of LDS converts.

The Guion and Wilson Lines provided a standard of steamer that surpassed most of its North Sea rivals. An example of this excellent service is evidenced by the Guion Line's hiring of Charles Maples, a Hull-based emigration agent who met migrants upon their arrival in port and escorted them safely to the railway station.[31] Maples, like many of his counterparts, was noted by LDS transmigrants for assisting the foreign converts en route to Liverpool.[32] Organized groups, such as the Saints, gained a reduction in price by purchasing their tickets in bulk. Booking with experienced agents and trusted shipping operators ensured that they received a high standard of service at minimal cost.[33]

The Guion Line treated the Saints very well. LDS convert Alma Ash explained:

> At the Guion Office we were told that it was too late to go aboard and they would find us lodgings for the night for a reasonable sum. It was evident to us that the agents were looking more after the money they could get out of the emigrant than his comfort and well-being. We informed them that we wanted to find the docks and go aboard that night if possible and asked them to direct us to 42 Islington, the office of the church in Liverpool, and which the Guion company were very familiar with. Just as soon as we mentioned 42 Islington

they changed their tune and treated us very politely and directed us where to go.[34]

At times, however, the Saints ran into obstacles that not even the Guion Line could avoid. A letter from LDS New York emigration agent James H. Hart revealed that in late August 1886, forty-five Saints were detained and threatened with expulsion back to Liverpool.[35] There was no valid reason for such an action, as the Saints were not paupers or suffering from poor health conditions. Soon thereafter the *Millennial Star* noted, "We learn from Mr. Ramsden that all the Saints who were detained in New York have been permitted to continue their journey Zion ward, with the exception of a woman and three children."[36]

A few days later, Daniel H. Wells of the church's First Presidency wrote of this unfortunate incident and described to other church leaders (John Taylor and George Q. Cannon) the value of dealing with Mr. Ramsden and the Guion Line:

> I trust that our emigrants will have no difficulty or interruptions in New York by the Government officials. The American Consul here has visited with Mr. Ramsden of the Guion line to make enquiries.... Mr. Ramsden has written a favorable letter on the subject... giving a statement of the number, age, sex of our Emigrants sent through them for the last few days and adding that the Mormon Emigrants are the most orderly, cleanly, intelligent and best to do for any class of Emigrants that they carry across the sea, and if they do not as a rule have much money, they have their fares paid through to their destination.... It would be very unfortunate for us to be obliged to break our connection with Guion & coy as we cannot only get better terms with them than others, but their influence in our favor and assistance in many ways... is of great value to us and I am quite sure will continue to be exercised in our favor when we may need it more than at the present.[37]

A number of accounts and letters published in the *Star* further attested to Ramsden's excellent service to the traveling Saints. For instance, an emigration report of 1874 noted, "It is very gratifying to us to state that the kind and agreeable arrangements as made by Mr. Ramsden, General Passenger Agent and Manager[,] ... have been in every respect satisfactory." The report also mentioned the "courtesy and gentlemanly good feelings extended by [the] Captains."[38]

The following year C. C. Larsen and others wrote, "In Hull we were met by Mr. G. Ramsden, of Liverpool, ... a gentleman of first class business tact, whom we found ready and on hand to make all arrangements necessary for the comfort and convenience of forwarding our company."[39] Additionally, in a letter to European Mission president Albert Carrington, Junius F. Wells wrote, "Please remember me to all of the brethren, and to Mr. Ramsden."[40]

An 1877 telegram published in the *Millennial Star* further substantiated the attention Ramsden continued to show to his LDS clients even after their voyage had ended: "By courtesy of G. Ramsden, Esq., of Guion & Co., we are informed that the *S. S. Wisconsin* arrived in New York at 4 a.m. on the 7th inst. All well."[41] In another notice titled "Departure," the writer noted, "Mr. Ramsden, of Guion & Co., met the company at Hull, and by his irrepressible force and indefatigable labor, aided materially in bringing them safely to Liverpool."[42]

Furthermore, in preparation for an 1879 voyage on the *Wyoming*, Ramsden unrelentingly labored to make "all necessary arrangements for the comfort of the Saints, and in this he was highly successful. The portion of the vessel assigned to the company was fitted up in a manner highly commendable to his ability to render the situation as pleasant as possible."[43]

Later that year two other articles reported Ramsden's painstaking labor and commitment to provide excellent service to the Saints: "As usual, Mr. Ramsden and his aids were indefatigable in their efforts to provide for the well-being of the passengers, and the company were in fine spirits."[44] Further, "As usual, Mr. Ramsden, assisted by his aids, was on the alert to make matters [as] agreeable and comfortable as possible on shipboard. His part in connection with seeing to the well-being of the people is always well and willingly performed."[45]

Nearly a decade later the *Millennial Star* provided a composite testimony of the excellent treatment the Saints had received on their many transatlantic voyages with Mr. Ramsden and the Guion Line: "The Guion

Company, whose steamships have carried our people across the ocean, have secured many eulogies from the companies of Saints emigrating for the uniform kindness, care and consideration they have received at the hands of George Ramsden, Esq., their agent, and the officers of their excellent line of steamships. It would be impossible for emigrants to be treated with greater consideration, and they have freely expressed verbally and in writing to the captains and officers their appreciation of the treatment received."[46]

On Christmas Day 1892 the *New York Times* reported that the Guion Line had "leased its pier to the White Star Line [which] was taken as an indication that the former company was going out of business. This was confirmed later in the afternoon by the Guion agents." Although the agents did not want to discuss the details of this business transaction, it was clear that the line was closing down. The *Times* also noted that the "Guion Line [had] been much affected by the attitude of the Government, as it [had] derived its principal revenue from its steerage business. Its entire fleet [was] now lying idle in Liverpool."[47]

With its outdated fleet, the Guion Line simply could not compete with other shipping companies, although it managed to hold on for another year, after which the Guion Line Corporation was finally liquidated in 1894. Yet the outdated fleet was not the only problem that spelled financial disaster for the business. In this same year, LDS church leaders counseled that foreign converts "'should not be encouraged to emigrate until they [were] firmly grounded in the religion by labor and experience,' and that those who were earning good wages and were in relatively favourable circumstances should not be encouraged to emigrate to this place, where labor is so scarce."[48] This statement led to an even steeper decline in the LDS immigration business, which had already significantly decreased in the early 1890s, factors that certainly affected the Guion Line's revenue.[49]

Nonetheless, when the Guion shipping business closed its doors, it went out with a global reputation for "quickness, regularity and safety of [its] passengers," having brought more than a million people across the Atlantic without losing a single life by accident.[50] At this time of transition, Ramsden helped Latter-day Saint British Mission president Anthon H. Lund arrange for a transfer of business to the Allan Line, which changed its LDS base of operations that year from Liverpool to Glasgow, Scotland.[51]

Two years later, on May 26, 1896, George Ramsden died at the age of sixty-five.[52] The following day the *Liverpool Mercury* eulogized his life: "No man was more respected and admired than Mr. Ramsden. His attitude to all was consistently kind and courteous, which in business he proved himself a man of strong determination and commendable foresight. Doubtless his long illness was due to a great extent to the misfortunes which overtook the once flourishing Guion line."[53] The *Liverpool Daily Post* added that he was "a man of great integrity, ability and determination [and] . . . successful in securing and retaining for many years for his shipping company a contract with the Mormon elders for the conveyance of their emigrant proselytes, large numbers of whom were sent across the Atlantic. Brigham Young's converts were then a flourishing source of revenue for this port."[54]

Lund also praised Ramsden at the time of Ramsden's death in an article titled "A Good Friend Gone." Publicly, he wrote to his readers that with the death of Ramsden, "Latter-day Saints [lost] one of their best friends, . . . a man of integrity and honor." Lund noted that although Ramsden "did not share the religious views of the Latter-day Saints, . . . his business connections with them for so many years had convinced [Ramsden] of their honesty and integrity, qualities which he highly treasured, possessing them as he did in so high a degree."[55]

Shortly after attending Ramsden's funeral on Friday, May 29, 1896, Lund privately recorded his feelings about Ramsden, his dear and trusted friend:

> In the afternoon Bro. Burrows and I went over to the Wallesey Church to attend the funeral of Mr. Geo. Ramsden. We sent a wreath to him which cost ten dollars[.] I felt that in him we lose one of our best friends in this country. He has ever been on hand to help us. . . . There was a large turn out. The hearse was full of wreaths but only one was nicer than the one we had sent. The parson read the service of the English Church. It was a cold formal burial not a word was spoken originally[.] I would have liked to [have] had the same chance of speaking and would have liked to read the text . . . (1 Cor. 15). His sons came up and shook hands with us. I do not think his family there was any who mourned his loss more than we.[56]

George Ramsden's name certainly deserves to be held in high regard for his assistance in transporting nearly half of the Latter-day Saint converts across the Atlantic during the late nineteenth century. His example of integrity and trust certainly merit a chapter in LDS history as one of the most loyal and admired friends of the Saints. This relationship no doubt strengthened outsiders' view of the Latter-day Saints' immigration system. In fact, in the early twentieth century, historian Katherine Coman stated that the Latter-day Saint system of transporting converts "was[,] taken all in all, the most successful example of regulated immigration in United States history."[57]

# 5

## Crossing the Seas

As with those who crossed the Atlantic to America in the 1840s, later Saints continued to struggle as they left loved ones to gather and cross the seas to America before heading overland to Utah. Regardless of when or from where converts left their homelands, the emotional wounds incurred from leaving family, friends, and home were poignant.[1] Mary E. Fretwell Davis recalled, "[In June 1863] I bid farewell to my father, brothers and sisters and sailed on the 'Amazon.' . . . I felt very sad as we sailed away, to see old England fading away out of sight, and those I loved and did not know that I should ever see them again."[2] Caroline Martine Anderson, who voyaged across the Atlantic a year later, had similar feelings. She anguished, "My heart is filled with pain when I think of those that are left in Babylon, and also that there are my relatives."[3]

This same year James T. Sutton vividly recalled the poignant scene when his family departed on the *Hudson* from the port of Liverpool:

> That was a sight to be remembered! Some were crying, . . . and others fainting at the thoughts of leaving their loved ones never to see them again. My father fainted on the deck as the ship began pulling away from the wharf. We thought for a few minutes that my brother Henry would not be with us. My cousin, James Thomas, was holding him on the dock trying to keep him from leaving but at the last moment he broke away and with a run and a big jump, caught hold of one of the ropes on the side of the boat and climbed aboard.[4]

### The Solace of Poetry and Song

These brave converts were in dire need of solace and comfort as they began their voyages. Poetry and song served as the ointment for their pain and the balm for their souls. In a poem published in the *Millennial Star*, LDS convert J. Riley poetically proclaimed the invitation to gather as noted in the first few stanzas of his lengthy poem:

> Come ye Saints of ev'ry nation,
> Flee to Zion's safe abode;
> Hail with joy the great salvation,
> Offer'd you by Christ the Lord.
>
> Glide across the mighty ocean,
> Bid the winds your canvass swell;
> Put the gallant ship in motion,
> Anchors weigh, and hoist your sail.
>
> Go behold the restoration,
> Of all things declar'd of old;
> Build the wastes of generations
> By Isaiah long foretold
>
> Though it may appear but simple,
> Sure an angel God hath chose,
> Who shall measure out the Temple,
> Whence for you a foundation flows.[5]

The Saints often put such inspirational words to music and sang them as they left Europe for America, or as they would say, "Babylon for Zion." The *Millennial Star* noted that while on the voyage of the *Metoka*, "Saints on board gave expression to their feelings in various hymns, which they sang as the vessel was towed into the river."[6] The following year, Ann Pitchforth described her feelings when the *Fanny* left the docks of Liverpool: "When the farewell hymn was sung on ship-board, I felt what it was like to leave all for the truth."[7]

John William South recalled that on the day hundreds of Saints departed on the *Horizon* in 1856, Silas H. Wheelock quickly composed a song for them: "Our gallant ship is underway to bear me out to sea. And yonder floats the steamer gay that says she waits for me. The seamen dip their

11. Ebenezer Farnes. Church History Library, PH 1700 5063.

ready oars as ebbing waves oft tell, To bear me swiftly from the shore, my native land, farewell."[8] Other passengers on board also wrote of melodic memories at sea. Mary Goble Pay remembered that the Saints would "sing [the] songs of Zion."[9] Of this same voyage, Joseph Beecroft recorded, "The Saints are singing in groups[;] . . . one has just turned out with his fiddle which I am very glad to see for having heard about him."[10]

The Saints also sang as they worked. Ebenezer Farnes, who crossed the Atlantic in 1862 on the *William Tapscott*, recalled that a man who emptied water from the vessel would "sing all the time[,] making up the song as he pumped." Farnes noted, "Some of the words of the song were good and some ridiculous, but it helped break the monotony."[11] Singing work songs and the hymns of Zion had a unifying magic for the Saints. Long, idle hours voyaging across the Atlantic became moments of rejoicing when heart and voice found expression through song.

## Entertainment at Sea

The Saints mingled their songs with dance and were encouraged to maintain a balance between spiritual and temporal matters. An 1847 revelation by Brigham Young admonished, "If thou art merry, praise the Lord with singing, with music, with dancing, and with a prayer of praise and thanksgiving" (D&C 136:28). Fanny Fry Simons, a passenger aboard the *William Tapscott* who immigrated in 1859, recalled, "We had dancing and music every evening, with few exceptions."[12] John McAllister, an LDS passenger aboard the 1862 voyage of the *Manchester*, remembered seeing "Saints on deck dancing, singing, knitting, sewing &c. Violin and concertina in full blast."[13]

Elizabeth White Steward observed that the Saints weren't the only ones singing. She remembered being entertained while "listening to the sailors singing while they were pumping the water out from the bottom of the ship. They never worked without singing, so they could all pull together." Steward also noted, "When the sea was calm we could occupy our time in reading, sewing, and taking our walk on deck."[14]

Along with these activities, a teenaged B. H. Roberts also recalled "games for the children; among others, marbles for the boys when the ship was steady enough for the marbles to stay in the rings until shot out by the players."[15] John Eden remembered, "The boys my age had a good time playing games & running from top to bottom of the deck."[16] The adults also made time for exercise, but sometimes the children could not resist participating. George Dunford delightfully recalled memories of children on deck joining him in his daily exercise routine as he walked briskly from stem to stern. He noted, "The children would crowd around me and would put their little hands in mine and walk back and forth and play with and so amuse me."[17]

Sometimes captains and crew joined in on the Saints' recreation and even encouraged it. John S. Fullmer noted, "The captain had a place cleared on deck and had some of the invalids brought out to sun themselves, which others that were more able he had to jump the rope. In fact, he loves to sport with children, and he actually took one end of a rope and helped to swing it for an hour while the children and even the lasses jumped it like good ones."[18]

## Seasickness

Despite the joyful recreation and song, these Latter-day Saint converts faced a long voyage across the treacherous Atlantic and the ever-present probability of seasickness. James Palmer, who voyaged in 1842 on the *Hanover*, recalled how the sea suddenly changed its motion: "This company left the dock singing and rejoicing . . . and shortly the passengers became sick and all their mirth was turned into sadness."[19] Two decades later another Saint recalled that the entire company suffered several days of intense seasickness. Some finally came out on deck, while "others lay in their berths afraid they would die, and others afraid they wouldn't die."[20]

Some passengers became ill as soon as they began their maritime journey to reach the main designated gathering place in Europe. One such passenger was teenaged Jensine Marie Jensen Moulton, who became gravely sick soon after stepping aboard a vessel in Odense, Denmark, bound for Copenhagen. From there she would again voyage by sail and rail to reach the main body of the Saints in Liverpool in 1874 before crossing the Atlantic on the steamship *Wyoming*. Jensen wrote of her sudden seasickness traveling among animals as a third-class passenger in steerage:

> The boat or sailing vessel had not gone very far from land when I got seasick. There were three fat steers on board and just a wooden picket fence between their heels and where I fell and lay there until nearly six o'clock the next morning. I was so deathly sick, laying there on the bare floor vomiting, and almost straining my life out. I couldn't raise my head, not a pillow or a mat under me and everybody saying "just as well throw that child out in the sea first as last, for she will never live to see Utah" and just imagine my poor little sister pulling and tugging at me trying to drag me away from the heels of the cattle, scared to death that they would kick and kill me. But I was too sick to care or even to think, so I lay there at the heels of the cattle on the rough dirty floor from about 5 p.m. until the next morning when we got close to land.[21]

Some passengers were spared such sickness. One young woman remembered, "After we got out in the sea, the people began to be seasick. I do not think . . . ten escaped and I was one of the favored ones. I was not sick a half hour all the voyage through."[22] While most travelers experienced some degree of seasickness and eventually recovered, others never did return to health and were ultimately lowered into the angry deep.[23]

### Death and Burial at Sea

Some families felt the sting of death at sea more than others. Such was the case for H. N. Hansen, who sailed in 1864 on the *Monarch of the Sea*, a vessel carrying 973 Latter-day Saints, the largest number of Saints known to have crossed the Atlantic together on a voyage up to this time:[24]

> Our family did not escape. In a few days from the day of sailing my oldest brother took sick and he died in about a week and my youngest brother again in about a week after him. It soon became a common thing to have several deaths a day. I think about 60 children died which included nearly all the little ones found among us. . . . The disease among the children was said to be the measles, but why it should prove to be so universally fatal I cannot now understand, and . . . [I'm] rather inclined to think that it was the scarlet fever, and perhaps both. It was truly a trying time for parents and relatives of the little ones. No sooner was life extinct, but they would put their body in a coarse sack together with a piece of iron and dump them overboard without ceremony. The iron being in the sack to cause the body to sink. Having two brothers thus buried in the great deep the word of God which says, that: "The sea shall give up the dead which are in it," is not without significance and comfort to me.[25]

John Johnson, aboard this same voyage, noted, "There were much sickness among the people. 67 died and dumped into the sea. The way it was done was to sew them up tight in burlap or canvas, then fasten some iron to their feet, then lay them on a plank over the edge of the ship, lift up the end of the plank on deck until it got so deep they would slide into the ocean."[26]

Ebenezer Farnes, who had witnessed two deaths aboard the 1862 *William Tapscott* voyage, explained:

> Burial at sea is a sad thing. The body is sewn in a canvas and a ball of iron placed at their feet so as to make the body sink feet first so the

sharks cannot get it. A long plank is placed on the rail of the ship, part on the ship and part over the water, and the body is placed on the plank, feet to the water. After the burial ceremony the plank is lifted at one end and the body slides into the sea. You can see the body go slanting down for a long distance.[27]

While the Saints often held burial services for their loved ones, at times the captains discouraged the passengers from having them. Ellen Burton Beazer recalled memories of her voyage aboard the *Arkwright* in 1866, during which seven passengers died: "The captain did not want any burial services held, but the people insisted. The funeral services were held at the front of the ship, then the officers would rush to the other end & slide the bodies over the side. The bodies were first wrapped in a material similar to canvas & had weights tied to them. The sharks followed the ship all the time & the officers were afraid that if they came too near the boat there would be trouble."[28]

### Regulations for Passengers at Sea

Although seasickness and disease could not be avoided, the general conditions of ocean travel improved slightly with the 1842 Passenger Act, a result of parliamentary recommendations based on suggestions made the previous year by the Colonial Land and Emigration Commission. The commission's objective was fourfold: "1st. To regulate the number of emigrants conveyed in the different vessels, and to provide for their proper accommodations on board; 2ndly. To ensure a proper supply of provisions and water; 3rdly. To provide for the seaworthiness of the vessels; and 4thly, to afford the poorer class of emigrants protection from the numerous frauds practiced upon them before they leave this country; to provide for their being carried to their stipulated destination; and to secure them a reasonable time for making arrangements before they are landed from the ship."[29]

This new and improved British law stipulated the follow requirements:

Each passenger to be given weekly seven pounds of bread, biscuit, flour, oatmeal, or rice, or the equivalent in potatoes. This was to be supplied uncooked, and was intended as no more than an insurance against starvation. Passengers were expected to bring their own sea-store [and the Mormons certainly did!].

Emigrants to be paid 1s. [shilling] a day subsistence money if the vessel did not sail on the date stipulated on the contract ticket. Passenger brokers and agents to be licensed. Only three steerage passengers to be carried for each five tons of the vessel's tonnage. Each passenger to have at least ten square feet of space between decks. Two children under fourteen to count as one statute passenger. Children under one year not to be counted at all. Drinking water to be carried in sweet containers [three quarts of fresh water per passenger for each day].

Spirits to be neither sold nor drunk on board, on pain of a fine of up to £100. At those ports where emigration officers were stationed, they and not the customs officers were responsible for carrying the Act into effect—for inspecting water and provisions, assessing the seaworthiness of the vessel, and prosecuting for breaches of the Act.[30]

In addition, Ray Jay Davis noted that each passenger was allowed a berth that could not be less than six feet long and eighteen inches wide. Vessels were inspected for seaworthiness, and two to four lifeboats were required on each ship. Passage brokers also had to be licensed, and passengers were to be issued money receipts.

Davis observed, however, that the commissioners' goals fell short of the legislative expectations: "The statutory space requirements were not very commodious. Required provisioning was monotonous and inadequate. Steerage passengers needed lifeboats in the event of trouble as much as did cabin passengers. Doctors could have helped in cases of injuries or disease. Nothing was said about personal security, light, or ventilation."[31]

Therefore, most emigrants, including the Latter-day Saints, still had some personal concerns over lodging conditions, provisions, and serious disease. Yet the *Millennial Star* provided advice to help the sailing Saints, as did church leaders. The book *Route from Liverpool to the Great Salt Lake Valley*, published in England in 1855, also offered meticulous instructions.

The helpful directives of the updated and improved Passengers Act of 1852 and the wise advice in *Route from Liverpool* encouraged the Saints to leave "all unnecessary things . . . behind [as] the expense of transporting such goods ... [was] frequently more than they [were] worth, or the owner [had] money to pay." Emigrants were also reminded that "many articles [were] now being made in Utah ... with an endless variety of goods." Emigrants were also encouraged "to take good fire-arms, especially rifles, for use upon the plains and afterwards." Further, they were advised, "A general assortment of choice seeds ... should be taken." Limited space for luggage was also spelled out, as was the price for passage and suggestions for provisions, cooking utensils, and medicine.[32]

## *The Orderly Conduct of the Saints versus Other Immigrants at Sea*

As noted previously, ships' captains noticed the Saints' orderly conduct at sea. LDS immigrant John Jacques, aboard the 1856 voyage of the *Horizon*, recalled the captain's remarks:

> More than once did I hear him remark on the superior morality, order, and cleanliness which our people exhibited, when compared with ordinary emigrants. I knew this before, but still it is pleasing to me to hear Captains, as well as others, frankly acknowledge the truth about us. He was rather surprised that he had 850 people on board, and did not hear an oath from them. It was warm and trying work at the cooking galley very often, but he favourably contrasted our conduct there with that of other emigrants, especially Irish, instancing their numerous bloody quarrels, and stating that his favorite and most effectual arbitrator and peacemaker was the hose, whose services he frequently found himself under the necessity of applying for.[33]

James Thompson, who immigrated aboard the *Lucy Thompson* that same year, wrote, "Before we were long on board we were found to be the most clean in our habits. We kept our berths clean, washing them frequently. The Gentiles were annoyed, as the officers only gave them half allowance of water till they went and did likewise. Towards the end of the voyage the officers seldom visited us, as they considered it unnecessary."[34]

In addition to providing wise counsel regarding hygiene and order, church leaders (mostly returning missionaries) were appointed at Liverpool to preside over the seagoing Saints. Church units were organized,

12. John Jaques/Jacques. Portrait by C. R. Savage. Church History Library, PH 4477.

and ecclesiastical leaders made certain that members adhered to daily and weekly schedules that included church meetings. They also ensured that the Saints maintained general good order and proper hygiene and offered daily prayers.

### Challenges at Sea from Confederate Warships during the American Civil War

Prayers were certainly on the rise during the years of the American Civil War (1861–65), as was the desire to gather quickly to Utah. Many Saints seem to have taken to heart the promise of safety in Zion and trusted that the Lord would protect them as they traveled. During the Civil War, Confederate warships posed an additional threat to LDS immigrants. In 1864

13. John W. F. Volker (*back row, third from right*) and other elders on a ship shepherding Saints to Zion, 1885. Church History Library, 1968, fd. 1, item 3.

David Coombs wrote that the captain of the *General McClellan* had sailed off course, far north among icebergs, for fear of meeting a Confederate ship at sea.[35] Some plying the oceans were not as fortunate. The Confederate warship *Alabama* posed a continual threat during the war years and eventually sank a total of sixty-five Yankee ships—more than any other Confederate vessel.[36] The crew of the *Alabama* may have taken particular notice of a ship bearing the name of a Union general—George B. McClellan.

Less than two weeks after the *General McClellan* left England on its 1864 voyage, the *Hudson*, with 863 Saints aboard, faced a threatening encounter on the Atlantic. A Confederate warship pulled alongside the *Hudson* to determine what kind of freight it was transporting. The sailors aboard the warship yelled out, "Say your prayers, you Mormons, you are all going down!" Fortunately, nothing came of the boastful threat. At least two LDS passengers aboard the *Hudson* reasoned that they were spared because the passengers were from foreign countries. Charles William Symons recalled, "The Confederate gunboat *Georgia* [italics added] hailed us and brought us to a standstill, for be it remembered the War of the Rebellion was now in full sway. After inquiries from our captain we were permitted to move on for they ascertained that 1100 British subjects were on board. Consequently they had no means of handling that many persons and the would-be prize was given up, the gunboat's band playing a farewell."[37]

In spite of the dangers at sea, over eleven thousand foreign converts sailed on thirty-two known voyages to eastern American ports during the war years, departing between February 1861 and June 1864. Not one immigrant ship carrying Latter-day Saints was sunk by enemy fire during this time.

### Deliverance from Tumultuous Storms at Sea

The weather was unpredictable during nineteenth-century sea crossings, and at times so was the behavior of travelers. One noteworthy incident occurred among some Irish immigrants who had joined a body of seagoing Saints. Charles W. Nibley, then just a boy, recalled a storm that made the sea so turbulent "most of the people thought [they] were going to the bottom and the cries and prayers and curses of those wild Irish people [were] still well remembered."[38]

Ann Pitchforth also told of a sudden storm that occurred while she crossed the Atlantic:

> The winds arose and our fears with them; wave dashed on wave, and storm on storm, every hour increasing; all unsecured boxes, tins, bottles, pans, &c., danced in wild confusion, cracking, clashing, jumbling, rolling, while the vessel pitched and tossed and bounced till people flew out of their berths on the floor, while others held on with difficulty; thus we continued for eight days—no fires made—nothing cooked—biscuits and cold water; the waves dashed down the hold into the interior of the vessel, hatchway then closed, all in utter darkness and terror, not knowing whether the vessel was sinking or not; none could tell—all prayed—an awful silence prevailed—sharks and sins presenting themselves, and doubts and fears; one awful hour after another passing, we found we were not yet drowned; some took courage and lit the lamps; we met in prayer, we pleaded the promises

of our God—faith prevailed; the winds abated, the sky cleared, the fires were again lit, then the luxury of a cup of tea and a little gruel.

Oh! how ungrateful are we for our mercies, because they are so common. We soon sailed joyfully and pleasantly along, rescued a sinking vessel with nine human beings from a watery grave; they had been seventeen days up to their waists in water, sleeping by turns, held up by the others. Oh! we wept for joy to be the means of saving them, remembering our own perilous condition. We arrived at New Orleans. The sight of land caused every face to smile, though on a foreign shore.[39]

Christopher Alston described another harrowing voyage when the ship he was on struck an enormous iceberg in a thick fog:

It was a fearful experience. Everything that was not lashed down tight was thrown from side to side—people, utensils and luggage in one great pile. The rattle of pans, dishes and baggage, and the cries of women and children, the shouts of men, the commands of officers, the banging and bumping of the ship against the iceberg made it seem as if two monsters were trying to beat each other to pieces and the great floating mountain of ice would overwhelm the sturdy ship and sink her in the deep sea with all on board. But it was not to be so, we were in the hands of the "master of ocean and earth and skies."[40]

Several first-person accounts such as these attest to the Saints' belief in God's power to harness the angry deep. Such episodes bolstered Latter-day Saints' faith that their vessels would not go down into the depths of the sea while journeying to Zion. Mary Ann Rawlings Aveson, a passenger aboard the *Hudson*'s tumultuous 1864 voyage, recalled, "We had not fear. We were Mormons and we said no ship would go down with such precious cargo."[41]

The Saints reported that they witnessed miracles during both the sail and steam era at sea. Church member Isaiah M. Coombs wrote the following journal entry on January 23, 1876, relating his belief that divine power had calmed the elements on the steam vessel *Montana*:

I heard one of the stewards exclaim, "My God if that wave strikes us we can never recover from it." I got up, dressed myself, and staggered to the saloon just as the ship was shaking this huge wave from its decks. The sight and sounds outside were truly fearful. I went back to my room and kneeling down asked the Lord to give me power to rebuke the winds and waves that the ship might go safe into port for my sake and for the sake of the few saints on board. . . . Found our good captain drenched to the skin, but not otherwise injured. This room was covered a foot deep with saltwater and the carpenter was replacing the windows while some boys and men were dipping up the water by the bucketful and throwing it on deck. I went to the door that leads out into the main deck and which had been tied partly open for the purpose of ventilation and looked out on the wildest and most fearful sight that my eyes have ever beheld. The wind was blowing fearfully and the waves were absolutely mountains high and sweeping the deck from stem to stern with relentless fury. It seemed as if we were about to be swallowed up in the depths of the ocean. I stood there at the door looking at the fearful sight, and raising my heart to God for strength, I, in the name of Jesus Christ, and by the authority of the holy priesthood, rebuked the winds and waves, and commanded them to subside that our ship with its precious freight of souls might go safe into port and called on God to seal the rebuke in heaven as I had on earth. My prayer was answered almost immediately. In less than half an hour the wind died away, the waves lessened, and the blessed sun was shining upon us. The infidel would say it would have been so anyway, I say give God the glory. Oh praise God! I went to the breakfast table for the first time and ate a small piece of steak and then going to my room wept for joy.[42]

Such experiences were part of the miraculous story the Saints told of God preserving them on the sea. It is notable that all LDS voyages crossing the Atlantic, and all but one voyaging on the Pacific, arrived safely in America in the nineteenth century.[43] In contrast, at least fifty-nine non-LDS-immigrant-carrying vessels sank just between the years 1847 and 1853.[44]

Such a record in spite of storms left a memorable impression on non-LDS passengers, captains, and crews who voyaged with the Saints. In a severe

14. Isaiah M. Coombs, ca. 1873. Church History Library, PH 1700 2710.

Atlantic storm in March of 1851, the captain of the Yankee ship *Olympus* gave the following orders to one of his crew members:

> Go tell the Mormon captain—Elder William Howells—that if his Mormon god can do anything to save his people and this ship, he'd better be doing it and that pretty d—d quick, for I have done all I can, and our chances are good for landing at the bottom of the ocean before daylight. Elder Howells' reply to the Captain was, "Give my regards to Captain Wilson, and tell him to fear not, we embarked for New Orleans and by the help of our God we will land safely there." A council of twelve of the brethren was called, young Nowers was one of them, and they kneeled in a circle on the lower deck and prayed to

their God to still the tempest and to hush the storm. Each prayed in turn as he was called upon, the President offering the closing prayer. Immediately the ship had a different motion, instead of tossing and pitching and rolling which had been going on for hours, there was a trembling or quivering motion felt. . . .

The next day, Sunday services of praise and thanksgiving were held, and so impressive were those services that a number of people from a company of Welsh and Irish emigrants occupying the fore hold of the ship came forward desiring membership in the church. A large barrel was brought up and filled with water, and twenty-seven souls were added to the church through the ordinance of baptism that day. On the same day, twenty-one men were baptized in the ocean. This was accomplished by lashing a hatch to the side of the vessel and placing a heavy belt around the person to be baptized. Elder Thomas Smith sat upon this improvised platform, held the candidate by the belt and clothing at the back of the neck, and immersed him in the sea. Under the arms of each person a rope was tied and held by the people on deck, so that in case of slipping or other accident the two could be drawn up. Altogether there had been two deaths, one birth, and fifty baptisms during this journey of fifty-five days from Liverpool to New Orleans.[45]

Two years later the ship *International* also encountered a terrible storm two weeks after leaving Liverpool. The fierce winds finally abated after the Saints prayed earnestly for two days. Captain David Brown then had a remarkable dream "that himself, mates and crew were all baptized in the Mormon faith, and when he awoke he found himself at prayer."[46] Following the storm a celebration marking the twenty-third anniversary of the church was held, on April 6, 1853. Henry Maiben wrote a ten-verse song for the occasion, to be sung to the tune of "Yankee Doodle" by the 425 Saints onboard. Its lyrics illuminate the company's makeup and its organizational structure, as well as the Saints' determination. Two sample verses will suffice, coupled with the chorus:

> On board the International all joyful and lighthearted,
> Bound Zionward, from Liverpool we started.

We'er English, Irish Scotch, and Welsh, Assembled here together;
Resolved to do the will of God, What'er the wind and weather. . . .

And Elders are appointed to Take charge of wards and sections,
And do all things according to the President's directions.
Thus ev'ry regulations made Which is found to be needed;
So that there's not a soul on board Whose welfare is unheeded.

CHORUS
Then, sing aloud, ye Saints of God In one united chorus;
Old Babylon, we'll leave behind, For, Zion is before us.[47]

Upon reaching America's shores, the *International* LDS company leader, Christopher Arthur, reported, "I am now glad to inform you that we have baptized all on board, except three persons. We can number the captain, first and second mates, with eighteen crew, most of whom intend going right through to the Valley."[48]

Some mariners, however, had not been baptized for the right reasons, and church leaders put necessary precautions in place the following year. Thomas F. Fisher, who voyaged on the *Marshfield* in 1854, wrote, "Two of the crew—the carpenter and a sailor, are going with us to Zion. They have been engaged as teamsters by some of the passengers, and will be baptized after leaving the ship. It is not prudent to baptize seamen on board—it has proved that they sometimes get baptized on board merely to assist in their designs upon the honor of our sisters. We might have baptized all our crew, mates and all, but President was too old for them."[49]

Nevertheless, most mariners appreciated their Latter-day Saint cargo due to their order and hygiene, and especially for security's sake. On the 1874 voyage of the *Idaho*, Emma Palmer Manfull wrote that after a terrible storm, Captain William Forsyth said, "If it hadn't been for the Saints on board nothing could have saved us."[50] Captain J. Morgan, who transported a company of Saints in 1872 aboard the steamship *Minnesota*, seems to have felt the same as Captain Forsyth did. Mary Ellison Vincent recalled the following memory of a violent storm aboard this voyage: "The ship was badly broken up and the hatchway was nailed down and we were without food or drink for forty-eight hours. One of the portholes being broken we were drenched and had to be carried from place to place. I was only eleven years old and was very frightened. During the worst of the storm the dear old captain told us to be of good cheer for he always felt assured he would be safe if he had Mormon emigrants on board."[51]

These captivating accounts demonstrate the collective faith of these foreign converts, who believed in the psalmist's words:

> They that go down to the sea in ships, that do business in great waters; These see the works of the LORD, and his wonders in the deep. For he commandeth, and raiseth the stormy wind, which lifteth up the waves thereof. They mount up to the heaven, they go down again to the depths: their soul is melted because of trouble. They reel to and fro, and stagger like a drunken man, and are at their wits' end. Then they cry unto the LORD in their trouble, and he bringeth them out of their distresses. He maketh the storm a calm, so that the waves thereof are still. Then are they glad because they be quiet; so he bringeth them unto their desired haven. Oh that *men* would praise the LORD *for* his goodness, and *for* his wonderful works to the children of men! (Ps. 107:23–31)

# 6

## Men in Motion on the Mississippi

The Saints disembarked at two primary ports when they arrived in America in the nineteenth century. The first was New Orleans (1840–54), and the second was the Castle Garden Immigration Depot in New York (1855–89), which, until it burned down, was the predecessor of Ellis Island. After vulnerable immigrant passengers touched the shores of the United States, they often worried about securing enough money for the passage west to Utah. During the early Nauvoo years (1840–46), some Saints who had arrived in New Orleans were delayed in their travels to Nauvoo due to economic challenges. Yet the *Millennial Star* informed the seagoing Saints that it was better to reach the American shores (Zion) than to stay in Europe (Babylon) and that they should be content "to make their way by degrees."[1]

One British convert wasn't satisfied to remain temporarily at New Orleans. Arriving penniless with his family in the spring of 1843, George Spilsbury described his determined efforts to find immediate resources to bring his stranded family up the Mississippi to Nauvoo, despite the adverse conditions they faced:

> We were in a strange land and in a hot place with no money to buy our provisions nor to pay our fare on the steamboat. My wife wept like a child at our humiliating circumstances. Nevertheless I did not feel discouraged. Another ship load of Saints arrived on the morrow after us, and I went on board and found a man going to Nauvoo. I borrowed the money from him to pay our fare by giving him my clothes for security. Thomas Bullock loaned us money to bring our provisions to Nauvoo. So by hard struggling and the blessing of the

15. George Spilsbury. Church History Library, PH 327.

Lord I accomplished the desire of my heart in getting to Nauvoo and seeing the Prophet of the Lord and shaking hands with the man who had seen God face to face.[2]

Having insufficient funds was not unique to Latter-day Saints emigrating through New Orleans, or any other port, for that matter. A. A. Conway explained the three options available to immigrants disembarking at New Orleans in the nineteenth century: "If he possessed sufficient money to pay his passage upstream, he could immediately transship himself with his luggage to a river steamboat and continue his journey inland. If he had insufficient funds to pay his passage, he could take a position at New

Orleans until such time as he had accumulated sufficient money to defray the cost of transportation upstream. If he landed destitute, there was no alternative, but to look for employment and to trust to charity to support him in the meantime."[3]

In addition to financial concerns, there was also a continual threat of thieves who waited to rob vulnerable immigrants as they passed into New Orleans, also known as the Crescent City, the fourth largest city in America in the mid-nineteenth century.

## New Orleans's First LDS Emigration Agent

Lucius Scovil was the first known LDS emigration agent assigned at New Orleans. He not only assisted incoming immigrants at New Orleans, but in early 1848, he also accompanied William Clayton to St. Louis to arrange for five thousand copies of Clayton's *Latter-day Saints' Emigrants' Guide* to be published by the Missouri Republican Steam Power Press, Chambers and Knapp. Fellow emigration agent Nathaniel H. Felt, who was stationed in St. Louis, reported to President Young, "Br Scovil & Clayton arrived here on the 29th Feby well and in good spirits. . . . Arrangements have been made to secure the publishing of Bro [Wm] Claytons book entirely satisfactory to Br C. he will have 5000 copys printed."[4] This book proved to be of significant worth not only to LDS emigrants but also to other westbound travelers before the advent of the transcontinental railroad.[5]

Just one year later, in 1849, the California gold rush brought argonauts from all over the world to the American West. Scovil continued to help LDS transmigrants through New Orleans and up the Mississippi to St. Louis during this period. These converts, also heading west, were searching for a spiritual treasure they valued far more than California gold.

As the winter of 1849 lingered, Scovil grew a bit despondent, given his own financial circumstances as well as the poverty of the incoming Saints. Most needed more funding to advance to St. Louis and eventually reach their destination in the Salt Lake Valley.

This adverse condition was exacerbated by the fact that some of the Saints had been struck by gold fever and others by another malady— cholera. In this trying state, on March 2, 1849, Scovil meditated over the difficult conditions. While pondering, he felt impressed to go to an area in the French Quarter known as Calaboose Square and walk to a nearby bookstore. Upon arriving at the bookstore, he bought a lottery ticket from the French clerk. Although conceding "the thought was foreign to [his] natural feelings as anything could be," Scovil explained:

> When I entered the store I felt that I had been very familiar with the Frenchman at some previous time. I inquired if he had lottery tickets for sale. He asked me who told me he had lottery tickets for sale, as there was no lottery tickets for sale in Louisiana, it being contrary to law, but, said he, "I have lottery tickets for sale and the drawing is tomorrow." He then spread out the tickets before me on the counter and I soon discovered a half ticket of the number I wanted, 9998. I asked him the price of it and he said $2.50. I took the ticket and paid for it.

Ten days later, Scovil, on learning he had won one hundred times the money he paid for the lottery ticket, felt gratitude that God had opened the way for him to perform his appointed task in New Orleans and advance the incoming British converts to St. Louis.[6]

## Gathering to St. Louis

Because of the high volume of British converts passing through St. Louis, church leaders decided to establish temporary lodging for the Saints during this post-Nauvoo era. Minutes from a May 3, 1849, meeting indicate that many of the brethren "urged the propriety of procuring some place, as a rendezvous for the saints emigrating from Europe so that the Poor might have some place to put up at until they would be enabled to get Houses. [It] was recommended that the Mound House if Possible be procured for the purpose."[7]

The following month Nathaniel H. Felt, church president of the St. Louis Conference, suggested the rental of another building, and eventually church leaders leased the Concert Hall in St. Louis for the price of twenty-five dollars per year.[8] Many of the Saints clearly strove to help the church in any way they could; however, not all wore halos, and apostasy among the St. Louis church members again reared its ugly head. In 1849 LDS immigrant Charles Dutton Miller wrote upon his arrival in the city,

"I found St. Louis abounding with Saints & apostates."[9] In this same year David D. Bowen remarked, "I found the Saints in the sixth ward meeting in Bywardrobe. They locked the door for fear of the apostates."[10]

Yet another malady swept St. Louis in 1849, this time in the form of Asiatic cholera. In late spring the disease began to advance rapidly throughout the region and continued through the sweltering heat of summer. Noted St. Louis historian James Neal Primm wrote, "The disease idled along until May, when it began to strike with triphammer blows reaching a peak in July, when 145 persons died in one grisly day and 722 in one week. By July 30th 4,547 cholera victims had been buried in the city since the first of the year."[11] John Martin, a passing convert, was an eyewitness to the devastating epidemic. Offered a job at the city hospital, he was responsible for transporting cholera victims in need of medical treatment as well as burying those who died. In 1849 he wrote:

> As I had got so far towards the gathering place of the Saints I was very desirous to get the remainder of the way. Yet I accepted the offer to run one of the city hospital vans and stayed until the cholera had died out. The death rate was very great for three months. Three of us were kept busy running light wagons and we took two loads a day each and four dead bodies on each wagon at a time. As we took only such people known as paupers, this compared with the others filling more respected graves would make the numbers somewhat alarming.[12]

In a June 14, 1849, church meeting, President Felt prayed for the end of the cholera epidemic among the Saints in St. Louis.[13] The following month he asked the six branch presidents in the area to provide a report about branch members. Such reports expressed the true magnitude of the sickness's destructive path as it swept through the city, and indicated that the "assistants were faithfully discharging their duty, administering to the sick and comforting the hearts of the saints." President Felt counseled those in the leadership meeting "to exercise faith in administering to the sick, and to comfort the afflicted &c."[14]

LDS historian Andrew Jenson recorded that during this period Felt "was constantly called for by the afflicted people, and responded by visiting, administering to and comforting them, scarcely taking time to eat or sleep."[15] Furthermore, a Felt family historian provided this vivid picture of his selfless, Christlike service:

> Every morning the "dead wagon" made its round, accompanied by the awful cry "bring out your dead." Accompanying these wagons were immunes who would enter, take the corpses, sometimes without any preparation, to the vehicles, and then on to the cemetery where, due to the heavy death toll, the corpses were buried in trenches, hundreds at a time. Occasions like that required all the devotion, strength and love the Conference President possessed. He was called on constantly by the afflicted people. Hour after hour, without stopping sometimes to eat or sleep, President Felt visited the sick, administering to them, comforting them in their pain.[16]

Despite his continual contact with this dreaded disease, Felt's life was spared from the epidemic. By the end of the year, the cholera outbreak had finally ceased, though it had taken 8,423 lives in St. Louis alone.[17] With the passing of this plague, Felt turned his attention to the gathering. In mid-December 1849 he spoke on this theme, urging the Saints to emigrate to Salt Lake City as soon as possible. He further desired that "this idea go forth, that all gather up, if it be only to the Bluffs" (meaning Council Bluffs, Iowa). Just two months later he advised the Saints who had temporarily congregated in St. Louis to "go to the Valley go to the Bluff. . . . Go; Go; as far as you can."[18]

LDS European converts were not the only ones to pass through St. Louis during the mid-nineteenth century; LDS missionaries traversed the region as well while journeying to their various fields of labor. Such visits created many opportunities for Felt and other church members to provide aid. Elder Eli B. Kelsey, on his way to England with Elder George P. Dykes, traveled through St. Louis in 1849. In an article to the editor of the *Millennial Star*, Kelsey reported warmly, "We spent one week in St. Louis. Brother Felt . . . treated us with great kindness, and [has] given us means sufficient to bear our expenses to New York. . . . I can confidently say to all the emigrating Saints, who are *compelled* to stop in St. Louis for want of means to proceed further, that if they will hearken to the counsel of Brother Felt and his counselors, it will be well with them."[19]

16. Nathaniel H. Felt. In Frank B. Esshom, *Pioneers and Prominent Men of Utah* (Salt Lake City: Western Epics, 1996), 249.

John Forsgren passed through St. Louis on his way from Utah to initiate missionary work in Sweden. He rejoiced in the local branch and observed a good spirit among the St. Louis Saints.[20] The following week Joseph Toronto passed through the city on his way to Italy. The minutes of the council meeting for January 19, 1850, noted, "Bro Toronto . . . said the news of the Valley was good[;] he had nothing to say but what was good. they had plenty to eat. and they felt well. he said he was going to a catholic country to preach. This seemed hard to do. Yet he relied upon the Lord."[21]

In late January Elder Erastus Snow of the Quorum of the Twelve Apostles also passed through St. Louis on his way to preside over the Scandinavian Mission in Copenhagen. He praised the local Saints for their good spirit and indicated that thanks to the establishment of a peaceful gathering place in the Salt Lake Valley, the Twelve needed "to call upon the Saints to come up and help Build up mighty 'Cities Temples' &c."

In addition, Elder Snow said the Twelve "were now about to go to call and bear the message of the Gospel to the Nations who leys [sic] in darkness. He advised, all there; and every where to gather to the Valley. He counseled the Brethren to act in unison; to hearken to the Council of Bro Felt." Elder Snow also prophesied that those who did would be blessed. He then fervently prayed that "God would bless and open up the way before [them]. He wished that the next time [they] met it would be in the Vallies of the Mountains; or among the Nations of the Earth; bearing the Torch of Truth. for said he we want to turn the World upside down; and you are the men to do it. the Leaver [lever] had been applied." Finally Elder Snow noted that St. Louis was a "half way House where all nations might pass through to here [sic] the Gospel. Their light was not hid under a bushel."[22]

Elder John Taylor spoke the following week to St. Louis church leaders, with Elders Erastus Snow and Lorenzo Snow in attendance, stressing the importance of the gathering. As one amanuensis from the branch meeting recorded, Elder Taylor "said he admired [their] organization of wards. [Their] care for the poor. the destitute, and the stranger. said it was good." Elder Lorenzo Snow informed the congregation that he agreed with Elder Taylor's words regarding the emigration doctrine and felt that "the Brethren would be much better off there [in the Salt Lake Valley] both temporally and spiritually. He said the Valley was the place where the Lord would pour out temporal blessings.... He said if the saints could but realize their situation; as the sons and Daughters of God [they] would consider it a small matter to move to the Valley."[23]

Some emigrants, however, did not have the means to make it all the way to the Salt Lake Valley. Bingham Bement was forced to return to St. Louis for employment, leaving his new wife in Kanesville, Iowa. Writing in this same year (1850) to his wife, he told of the lingering effects of cholera in the city and of the loneliness he felt after many of his church associates had emigrated west to Utah: "O Sarah you cannot tell how lonely I feel[;] all of the Saints with whome I was acquainted have left and no one to associate with."[24]

Bement's struggles to obtain financial resources are described in several letters he sent to his wife over the next few months from St. Louis: "Gone to a regular boarding house, provisions are very high[.] I have to pay 2,50 a week for bord 50 ct more then I ever payed before."[25] "A pity to earn $2,00 [a] day (or three when I work nights)."[26] In a subsequent letter, he wrote, "I earned 18,00 this week which payes the Company all that I owe them."[27]

After years of diligently helping Saints in need, such as Bement, Nathaniel Felt completed his service in St. Louis and left in the spring for Utah. The St. Louis Saints rallied to help support Felt and his family on their journey. Hezekiah Mitchell, a passing emigrant, wrote in his journal on April 14, 1859, "Gave half a dollar to President Felt's subscription to help him to the valley."[28]

In late April 1850, Felt offered his formal resignation as president of the St. Louis Conference. According to minutes kept on April 20, 1850, in his farewell address, President Felt remarked that "he much regretted leaving so many with whom he had been associated for the last three years. Yet he hoped it would not be long before he met them all in the Valley[;] he did not feel that [they] parted to meet no more[.] He felt glad that it was his privilege to go to the Valley." Felt then recommended that his counselor, Alexander Robbins, be sustained as successor and president.[29]

Despite Felt's move west to the Valley of the Great Salt Lake, the LDS community in St. Louis continued to prosper. In the spring of 1851, a prominent St. Louis newspaper, the *Missouri Republican*, praised the Saints' positive influence on the city:

> Although we have no Mormon Church in St. Louis, and though these people have no other class or permanent possession or permanent interest in our city, yet their numerical strength here is greater than may be imagined. Our city is the greatest recruiting point for Mormon emigrants from England and the Eastern States, and the former especially, whose funds generally become exhausted by the time they reach it, generally stop here several months, and not infrequently remain among us for a year or two pending a resumption of their journey to Salt Lake....
>
> There are at this time in St. Louis about three thousand English Mormons, nearly all of whom are masters of some trade, or have acquired experience in some profession, which they follow now. As was said, they have no church, but they attend divine services twice each Sunday at Concert Hall, and they ... perform their devotional duties with the same regularity, if not in the same style as their brethren in the valley.

> We heard frequently of Mormon balls and parties, and Concert Hall was on several occasions filled with persons gathered to witness Mormon theatrical performances. We have witnessed the congregation as it issued from the hall at the religious meetings on Sunday, and certainly we think it does not compare unfavorably with congregations.[30]

Unfortunately, by the year's end, negative reports from Utah territorial officials, largely about the practice of polygamy among Utah Saints, had soured St. Louis citizens' opinion of Church members.[31] In early December 1851, Bingham Bement wrote to his wife, "The Utah officers have come back with sutch a report, the Public opinion is very mutch agitated against the Mormons. I do not know what the result will be nether do I care mutch, I expect we will have to fight until we are an independent People."[32] Two weeks later he wrote: "There is a great difference manifested towards our people sinse our U.S. Officers have returned[;] it is visible in all most every man which does not belong to the church and a grate many that does the devision line is about to be drawn [end of p. 1]. I am well satisfied that it is time that all good saints had aught to be out of St. Louis and all other palses in the states."[33]

According to the journals of William Gibson, between the time of Felt's departure in 1850 and Gibson's arrival in St. Louis in the spring of 1851, Thomas Wrigley served as the president of the St. Louis Conference. Yet Gibson wrote that with Wrigley's departure in the spring of 1852, "[Gibson] was appointed & took the Presidency of St. Louis Conference."[34] At this time Gibson further noted, "There was six wards in the St. Louis Branch & two Presidents to every ward[;] money matters were allowed to go pretty loose."[35] During a weekly council meeting held on June 1, 1852, at Gibson's "206 Market St." home, the president announced his plan to establish a local Perpetual Emigrating Fund that would cater specifically to members in St. Louis; and just weeks later a generous $29.20 was collected from the area's seven branches.[36]

In the fall of 1852, Gibson elaborated on some of his duties in preparing for the emigration season. His journal provides a transition to the Horace S. Eldredge era; Eldredge replaced him the following spring when Gibson left with his family to Salt Lake City:

Fall [1852] I received a letter from SW Richards in Liverpool saying that there would be a large Emigration next spring & he would need from 300 to 500 waggons & he desired me [to] look around & find out where they could be got best & cheapest the waggons before this [they] had mostly come from Cincinati so I wrote there to find out their prices now & having got that I went around to all the wagon makers in St. Louis & round about it. I found that the Cheapest best & most reliable waggons were made by Mr. Espenschied of St. Louis they cost about ten dollars less each waggon than those from Cincinatti & to judge from those we had received from there were much superior waggons accordingly I wrote back to Br Richards but some how he delayed sending me on the final order for them which in the end was the cause of the loss of several thousand dollars to the Emigration Fund. . . . As I was to go to Utah in the spring [of 1853,] Horace S. Eldredge was sent to take my place as President of St. Louis Conference he stopped at our house & I continued to act as his assistant while I staid . . . [until in] 1853 May I started with the Saints from St. Louis [for Utah].[37]

In a unique attempt to play an even more active role in emigration matters during his stewardship, President Gibson frequently visited coffeehouses "in search of men with whom he [could make] contracts" for a "large number of wagons." Because many of these men could not speak English "sufficiently to make the necessary agreements for the work," President Gibson graciously accepted their invitations to meet at locations of their choice where a friend could interpret.[38]

Although Gibson was innocent of any ill behavior, various individuals misunderstood his efforts, and according to the *St. Louis Record* of 1852–56, "Many stories were in circulation reproaching him with frequenting coffee houses & being drunk &c all of which was false & calculated to injure him and lessen him in the confidence of the church."[39] Further, "All his actions had been watched, & he had been dogged about from morning till night & even the Police had their eye upon him. . . . Every trifling circumstance was timed to his disadvantage."[40] While these slanderous reports and rumors aimed to discourage the Saints and slow the church's missionary progress, they proved unsuccessful. President Gibson maintained the full support, faith, and confidence of the members.[41]

The following year church leaders called Eldredge to preside over the St. Louis Conference. He recorded his new assignment in his journal on November 21, 1852: "Sunday. I attended meeting at concert Hall a very convinent [sic] and pretty place. I was presented to the meeting by Br. O [Orson] Pratt as being appointed to preside over the conference and was unanimously accepted by the meeting."[42]

Eldredge did quite a bit of traveling in his new calling as both St. Louis district president and general emigration agent for the westbound Saints. In early spring church clerk James Cantwell recorded, "President H. S. Eldredge spoke on emigration and recommended the Saints to put their means together, forming companies, and by so doing many might go that otherwise could not." James Armstead from LaSalle (a suburb of St. Louis) echoed President Eldredge's words and the impression of the St. Louis members: "The saints there, are in good standing, a spirit of love and unity prevail, they also have the spirit of gathering, and some are on the eve of moving away, prejudice is giving way, and the people are enquiring into the nature of the work, A number of school houses are now opening for preaching."[43]

Two weeks later hundreds of St. Louis Saints gathered to listen to their church leaders at a conference held on April 3, 1853, in the Concert Hall on Market Street. At this time over 1,200 members from a dozen LDS Church branches were reported to be living in the area, yet many of them were busy making plans for their move to the Salt Lake Valley.[44] About this same time, President Eldredge recorded his efforts to obtain wagons for the Saints' westward journey from a German emigrant in St. Louis named Mr. Louis Espenschied. On February 23, 1853, Eldredge noted, "We engaged 14 wagons of Mr. Espenshead [Espenschied] at $58. per wagon."[45]

Several entries from Eldredge's journal in late March of 1853 confirm that he was very busy with his assignment as General Emigration Agent in purchasing wagons and cattle and arranging steamboat travel up the Mississippi River to Keokuk, Iowa, for LDS emigrants:

> 21st I attended to some business with Br. [Isaac C.] Haight. dealt out provisions to the Saints.–in the evening we attended a party at the

17. Louis Espenschied. Missouri Historical Society, St. Louis.

Jefferson Hall; during which time Bro Vincent Shurtliff [Shurtleff] arrived on the steamer Hindoo which brot [brought] 50 ox wagons from Cincinnatti

22 We spent the day preparing for emigration

23 B. Elijah Thomas arrived from the east on his way to the Valey. In the evening Br.s Haight & Shurtliff [Shurtleff] left on board the Hindoo for Keokuck. . . . I attended meeting in the office with the saints that are a going to emigrate, and again I gave them counsel and instruction

25th H. I. Hudson from Alton called at the Office in the morning.–I made some purchases for the brethren and engaged some wagons. . . .

26th I attended to some more business pertaining to the emigration; received a letter from Maj J. Brown and answered it.[46]

*Men in Motion* | 87

> 30th Last night the latter part of the night the steamer landed with about 300 Saints from Wales and Eng[;] a part of them were shipped aboard the Hindoo for Keokuck. about 50 of them . . . stopped in St. Louis[.] We obtained a house for the Danes and them for $80.00 per month and got them moved into it. . . .
>
> 31st We made a contract with the Keokuck Packet Co to take up our emigration and freight to that point at the following rates, for cabin passengers $3.50 adult cabin passengers $1.00 Children 2 year old to 14 50¢ &c In the afternoon Bros Pratt Haight [Cyrus H.] Wheelock and myself went out in the country about 6 p.m. to see some cows.[47]

Additional journal entries by Eldredge in June 1853 reveal that he made a trip up the Missouri River to St. Joseph to purchase flour and twenty head of oxen.[48] Records also attest that he took care of the spiritual needs of the local Saints and enjoyed doing so. That summer he noted, "I made several calls[.] I take great pleasure in calling on the Saints & incouraging and cheering them up." Finally, on the celebration of the Saints' entrance into the Salt Lake Valley (now known as Pioneer Day), he wrote, "July 24th Sunday. I attended meeting at Jefferson Hall read the ninth General epistle of the Presidency to the saints."[49]

While addressing matters of emigration, President Eldredge hoped to create a spirit of camaraderie among the Saints by establishing a variety of social activities, including a Social Club responsible for obtaining "funds to provide fuel for the widows of the church in this city and to clear the debt on the church."[50] Eldredge also created a choir and called an organization of sisters to decorate the meeting hall.[51] At a "complimentary benefit" arranged by the Social Club on January 30, 1854, to express gratitude for Eldredge's work, the Saints' presented him with a ring and the following letter:

> We the "Mormon Social club" having viewed with entire satisfaction, your labours in the Responsible situation which you occupy; And having seen with what anxious care, you have discharged that arduous duty, And with what impartiality you've administered to the Saints; We approbate the same with please and therefore we voluntarily give

unto you this complimentary benefit, And also herewith present to you this Gold Ring, as an abiding testimony of the same, That we, The "Mormon Social club["] have not, alone, been interested observers of your conduct; [for it] is manifest by this crowded Hall of saints and friends, who have assembled with us, to contribute their need of praise, and by their presence to express their approbation of this testimony of our esteem, Our wishes are for you in the future, That Your course, may continue prosperous, and always found in the path of goodness.[52]

Eldredge succeeded in taking care of the multifaceted needs of the St. Louis Saints. Although he was diligent in his dual role as district president and general emigration agent, his journal entries indicate that he spent most of his time providing supplies and arranging for the launching of transmigrant Saints from the Mississippi River to the Salt Lake Valley.

By April 1854 Brigham Young and other church leaders had designated St. Louis as a location where the "Saints might gather with approbation who were unable to go directly through to Utah."[53] Elder Erastus Snow was chosen to journey to St. Louis, organize a stake, preside over the region, and oversee general emigration matters in Iowa and Missouri. Elder Snow organized the St. Louis Stake that fall, on November 4, 1854,[54] and appointed Milo Andrus as stake president (with Charles Edwards as first counselor and George Gardner as second counselor).[55] Yet the stake lasted less than three years as attitudes toward the Saints changed due to widespread negative press and apostasy.[56]

In addition to contending with apostates, the St. Louis Saints also faced other enemies as U.S. soldiers, during the so-called Utah War, marched on Utah Territory to suppress rumored sedition among Latter-day Saints. As a consequence, all Latter-day Saint elders who were serving abroad, including those in St. Louis, were called home.[57] This event effectively marked the end of the St. Louis Stake,[58] and although the spirit of the St. Louis Saints continued to burn for a time, its bright flame eventually dwindled to a mere flicker. By early June 1857, St. Louis stake president James H. Hart and his family quietly left the Mound City due to the threat of war against the Saints in the Salt Lake Valley.[59]

Another significant factor had curtailed the Saints' emigration into St. Louis three years earlier. Just months prior to the organization of the stake, Brigham Young penned an influential letter dated August 2, 1854, directing Elder Franklin D. Richards, stationed in Liverpool, to change the immigration route to avoid entry into New Orleans. Young wrote, "You are aware of the sickness liable to assail our unacclimated brethren on the Mississippi river, hence I wish you to ship no more to New Orleans, but ship to Philadelphia, Boston, and New York, giving preference in the order named."[60] Thus, the following emigration season, the incoming European Saints were rerouted into ports on the eastern U.S. seaboard, a decision that would impact tens of thousands of converts who would follow.

# 7

## The Knights of Castle Garden

Philadelphia was short-lived as a port of preference for immigrants, as was Boston, largely because in 1855 New York City completed the first American immigration depot, known as Castle Garden.[1]

This important government immigrant station offered protection and direction for incoming foreigners and thus became the port of choice for the bulk of European LDS converts and other immigrants throughout much of the nineteenth century.

Castle Garden apparently did not fit its descriptive name. When Charlotte Ann Hilstead, a twelve-year-old Latter-day Saint girl, landed at the depot, she remarked, "We landed on what they called Castle Garden, but I did not see a castle nor a garden. It was just a big wooden shed with a roof across it."[2] A coastal artillery battery originally known as Fort Clinton (named after George Clinton, former governor of New York from 1805 to 1812), Castle Garden was located at the extreme end of Manhattan Island. After the War of 1812, the federal government gave the fortress back to New York City, which utilized it as a resort and occasionally as a place to host foreign visitors.

In 1847 the fortification was renamed Castle Garden and transformed into an amusement hall with a new roof, flooring, and stage. That same year the New York Commissioners of Emigration was formed to protect arriving immigrants from thieves and undesirables who abused and took advantage of the vulnerable foreigners. In 1855 the commission successfully arranged for the amusement center to be converted into an immigration depot, though they retained the name Castle Garden.[3] With the establishment of America's first official immigration reception center, "so severe a blow was struck against the business of the swindlers that it aroused

18. Castle Garden Immigration Depot. In George J. Sveyda, *Castle Garden as an Immigration Depot, 1855–1890* (National Parks Service, U.S. Department of the Interior, 1968), Appendix H.

resentment and opposition from the 'runners,' who saw in it an interference with their private vested interests."[4] The new center provided greater insurance against potential threats by issuing rigid medical inspections and requiring proper registration from all entering immigrants.

One *New York Times* reporter visited the depot on New Year's Day in 1856 and described a Latter-day Saint company that had just disembarked from the *Emerald Isle*. Among other things he noted, "The majority of the men in the Castle were engaged in paring and washing potatoes; the women were generally sitting . . . or nursing and dressing the children. Quite a large group was standing around a stove, and another listening to a violin played by an old German. The children were at play." He further noted, "All seemed happy and contented with their prospects and bore with quietness the inconvenience of travel."[5]

While Castle Garden provided a sense of security for incoming foreigners, the Latter-day Saint agents, the valiant "knights near Castle Garden," provided even greater security for the arriving Saints. These faithful LDS men helped vulnerable foreign converts make the transition to a new country and find their way through the crowded cosmopolitan city of New York, providing general counsel, direction for lodging needs, and

19. "Mormon Emigrants at Castle Garden," 1882. Miriam and Ira D. Wallach Division of Art, Prints and Photographs: Picture Collection, New York Public Library Digital Collections, image #833646.

economic opportunities and assistance in continuing the journey west to Zion.[6] The first agent to do so was John Taylor.

### John Taylor as Eastern Church Leader, Editor, and Emigration Agent

In 1855 President Young appointed Elder John Taylor to oversee the entire LDS Eastern Mission from New York.[7] In addition to supervising church units in the eastern region, this gifted, versatile British convert also launched and edited the Latter-day Saint periodical *The Mormon* and supervised the multiple needs of over eight thousand incoming LDS immigrants who disembarked at New York City, Philadelphia, and Boston.[8]

From Taylor's own writing, it is clear he knew exactly why he had been sent to this large cosmopolitan region during the mid-nineteenth century. In a letter to Brigham Young, Taylor wrote, "When I came on this mission

20. John Taylor, ca. 1870–87. Church History Library, fd. 1, item 1, PH 4468.

I understood that I had two things to perform; one was to publish a paper, the other was to preside here and . . . to counsel & direct the emigration in this country & in their journey west."[9]

Taylor also used his literary skills to defend the unpopular doctrine of polygamy, which had recently come under public scrutiny.[10] Joseph Smith knew of Taylor's gift and had previously informed Taylor that his service in writing would be greater than his preaching.[11] Apparently, Elder Taylor drew strength from Joseph Smith's prophetic pronouncement, for when Taylor arrived in New York City to inaugurate *The Mormon* he deliberately chose to rent rooms for his office on what was known as "newspaper row," between two of the most powerful periodicals in the nation, the *New York Tribune* and the *New York Herald*.[12]

Taylor then took up his pen and in the very first issue of *The Mormon* (February 17, 1855), on the front page and bottom of the masthead, wrote the words "IT IS BETTER TO REPRESENT OURSELVES THAN TO BE REPRESENTED BY OTHERS."[13] Then, with a courageous fervor, he symbolically laid down the gauntlet: "We defy all the editors and writers in the United States to prove that Mormonism is less moral, scriptural, philosophical; or that there is less patriotism in Utah than in any other part of the United States. We call for proof; bring on your reasons, gentlemen, if you have any; we shrink not from the investigation, and dare you the encounter."[14]

Encounters with additional New York newspapers also shed light on Elder Taylor's bold stance toward the press. Soon after Taylor arrived in New York City, the editor of the *New York Mirror*, a Mr. Fuller, wrote a slanderous report about the Saints. Elder Taylor immediately replied and challenged Fuller to a public debate, but the editor declined. Later, in *The Mormon*, Taylor noted Fuller's cowardly act and determined deception.[15]

The *New York Sun* also attacked the Saints with degrading insults. To one such libelous report, Elder Taylor responded, "Your contemptible falsehoods fail to ruffle a feather in our caps. The God of Jacob in whom the Mormons trust—He who brought up Israel out of Egypt—He it is who sustained the Mormons in their tedious journeyings over the barren deserts. . . . He sustains them still and will cause them to shine forth."[16]

### Advising Emigration Matters

As noted previously, in addition to his editorial role and local ecclesiastical leadership, Taylor supervised immigrants' efforts to reach the Salt Lake Valley. The year 1855 was a transient year: it marked the change of the Latter-day Saints' port of disembarkation from New Orleans (which the Saints had used since late 1840) to the eastern coast of the United States. Such a change in course required a multitalented man in motion who could handle distant branches, the New York press, and traveling missionaries, as well as the manifold needs of the newly arrived European converts.

In this demanding setting, Brigham Young counseled Elder Franklin D. Richards, then overseeing the British Mission, to keep Elder Taylor informed of the needs of inbound European converts:

Whenever you ship a company, whether it be small or large, be careful to forward to Elder John Taylor, at New York City, a correct list of the names of the persons in each company, with their occupation, and approximate amount of property or means, and forward it in season for Elder John Taylor to receive it before the company arrive in port, that he may be so advised as to be able to meet them, or appoint some proper person to do so, and counsel them immediately on landing as to the best course for each and all in every company to pursue—viz., whether to tarry for a season to work in the place or immediate neighbourhood of their landing, or proceed to Cincinnati and its region, &c.[17]

To provide needed counsel, Elder Taylor used *The Mormon* to assist European converts upon their arrival. In its first issue, dated February 17, 1855, Taylor explained the primary purpose of this new periodical:

We shall endeavor to be always prepared to impart the latest information relative to the best course to be pursued by Emigrants on their arrival in Boston, New York, and Philadelphia. Our emigration [has] heretofore, almost exclusively, gone by the way of New Orleans, but will hereafter land in the Eastern cities, and one of the principal objects of establishing "THE MORMON," is for their information, as well as all other emigration arriving in this country.

We shall take special interest in seeking out the cheapest, best and most convenient mode of conveyance from this and other points, as well as to observe the course pursued by agents in the accommodation for travelers on the routes, and make of "THE MORMON" a directory, to which all Emigrants and Travelers may refer with some degree of safety.[18]

Besides serving as a directory for routing emigrants west, this Latter-day Saint newspaper included dates of port arrivals as well as employment opportunities for those who needed to raise money to continue their journey to the Salt Lake Valley. Two weeks after the establishment of *The Mormon*, local missionaries received the following instruction from Taylor: "As there will shortly be many of our brethren here from Europe who will be in want of employment, in various trades and occupations, you are requested to send to this office, directions whereby we may know where to send those that are in need of employment, on their arrival in this country."[19]

Though *The Mormon* was short-lived,[20] this LDS periodical proved most effective in helping European immigrants locate much-needed employment. For example, just three weeks after Taylor's request for employment information, one local area reported that they had an abundance of mining jobs.[21] In a letter to church headquarters, Taylor wrote, "We have been doing what we could lately in assisting the emigrating operations, and not withstanding the bad times, with the united efforts of the brethren, we have succeeded in obtaining work for all, with very few exceptions, and they are provided for by the others." He wrote further, "I am in hopes we shall be as successfull with the remainder; You will see by the published lists, in the 'Mormon' the names of those coming."[22] Less than two months later Taylor informed Brigham Young, "Although 30,000 persons have been out of work in New York and the same proportion in Phila, yet our brethren I believe have all got employment."[23]

Taylor also devised a plan to assist individuals who could not find employment. In a letter to President Young dated February 20, 1856, Taylor related, "We have had pretty hard times with many poor saints here; but shall see it through. I am raising a loan fund something after the order of the P.E.F. [Perpetual Emigrating Fund] to be kept for the purpose of assisting those that are poor untill they get employment, & then to be returned."[24]

Taylor continued to provide direction and aid to improve conditions for the arriving Saints. He regularly corresponded with President Young, whose counsel he valued and implemented.[25] An extract from a letter written to Brigham Young in April 1855 provides a glimpse into Taylor's efforts to assist in the immigration process. Having just informed Young that the ship *Siddons* had not yet arrived in Philadelphia, Taylor offered the following plan for the remaining season of emigrant rail travel:

> Concerning emigration I have made all the enquiries I can & am decidedly of the opinion that the best rout at present will be by Burlington Iowa to which place a railroad goes direct. I mean for those

who go through. The expense will be quite as little to say nothing of time & they will go by railroad in about four days Through a healthy country & thus avoid the whole length of the Ohio, the detention in Pittsburg & St Louis, & the river voyage up the Mississippi or Missouri rivers. It is expected that before another season a railroad will go to within two hundred miles from Council Bluffs or St. Joseph. I suggest these things for your consideration a reference to the late maps will show the routes from any of these eastern cities several weeks would I believe be saved by this route which would facilitate greatly the emigration in their progress west however saving them from the uncertainty & unhealthiness of the river transit.[26]

Three months later Taylor again wrote to Young about emigration matters: "When I first came here I found a strong combination among the railroads. I have managed however to break into them, and I think that contracts can be made to take the Saints comfortably from N. York to Iowa City for about $9. & from 7 to 7 50/100 to Saint Louis." He also carefully noted, "I throw out these suggestions and leave it for your superior wisdom to dictate."[27]

This letter reveals not only Taylor's intricate involvement in negotiating emigration business but also his humility and sense of place, as President Young ultimately oversaw all aspects of the emigration operation from beginning to end. Taylor's submissive attitude and involvement in emigration rail/trail matters is also apparent in another letter he wrote to Young as the new year dawned: "According to your instructions, I have sent out Bro. A. Cunningham and McGaw to examine the rout and facilities for emigration at Iowa City and between that place and Council Bluffs. Further, I have also directed them to ascertain the position of things, at or near Wood River, and if practicable to see the Governor of Nebraska Territory, to visit the place and report to me in relation to the feasibility of the location."

In addition to delegating the inspection of the upcoming season's route, Elder Taylor also visited St. Louis and, according to Young's previous instruction, ordered the construction of one hundred handcarts. However, in reference to the handcart plan, Taylor noted in his letter, "I must confess, that at first sight it looked rather like 'Jordan's a hard road to travel.'" He also wrote concerning his involvement with the season's arrangements for rail travel: "I am now negociating with Rail Road companies and making every practical arrangement to facilitate the movements of the brethren."[28]

In his multifaceted assignment and with the demands of sail, rail, and trail travel, Elder Taylor was assisted in New York by his son George and other elders. One elder of particular note was Nathaniel H. Felt, an experienced, wealthy tailor from Salem, Massachusetts. As noted previously, Felt had also been a St. Louis church leader and emigration agent at that inland port several years before. Felt helped to ease the heavy workload at Taylor's New York office.[29] Elder Taylor informed President Young, "Br. Felt & my son George are with me, as I found their assistance absolutely necessary. They are all well & doing well."[30] Elder Taylor no doubt sensed the breadth of Felt's competency and delegated to him some responsibility for correspondence, including writing to Brigham Young to notify him about various emigration situations. For example, it was Felt who wrote Young about the first Latter-day Saint converts who had disembarked in Philadelphia, an integral part of the Eastern States Mission over which President Taylor had stewardship.[31]

Although Elder Taylor visited the Saints in Philadelphia during conference sessions, he also sent Felt on multiple trips to the City of Brotherly Love to assist with emigration tasks.[32] A letter Taylor wrote to Brigham Young in the spring of 1855 provides a sense of the price Felt paid in assisting with emigrant rail travel and hints at his appreciation of Felt's efforts:

> In negotiating with the "Penn. Railroad Co." for the conveyance of passengers, Bro Felt, with much exertion, obtained a drawback of 50 cts per passgr from the general terms; There is a combination of the R.R. companies, and such things are generally discarded, this was obtained out of extra allowance which they had on account of extra trouble in obtaining passengers at this end of the rout[e]; they would not make a reduction in the fare; and this could only be obtained, by the President through the board of directors, upon the anticipation of a heavy emigration. Bro Felts expenses in travelling, to and fro, two or three times to Phila and once to Pittsburgh to make arrangements, were something like $50.[33]

President Taylor also sent Felt to meet incoming LDS immigrants at the New York City docks. One convert who crossed the Atlantic on the *Thornton* wrote, "At sun down we landed at the Castle Gardens, a large building appropriated for emigrants, where we were visited by Elder Felt who kindly welcomed us."[34] Taylor was also involved with such greetings. James G. Willie, captain of the soon-to-be-ill-fated handcart company, was on this same voyage and recorded, "On our arrival at Castle Gardens, New York, we received a hearty welcome from President John Taylor and Elder Felt."[35]

The *New York Daily Times* also kept abreast of the incoming Latter-day Saint voyages. One journalist described the disembarkation of "a rich cargo of humanity" from the ship *Emerald*. Among other things, the paper noted that 345 of the 666 passengers aboard the ship were Latter-day Saints. Following a visit to Castle Garden on New Year's Day to inspect these foreign converts, the writer explained, "Their appearance betokened their origin. In England they might have been the industrious laboring class. Men of strong arms and women of ardent hopes, each seeking a bettered condition." Further, "There were but few aged persons, but one or two sick, and the others with ruddy cheeks . . . showed their ability to labor and live."[36]

Such positive reports of the incoming LDS converts influenced the media representing a variety of New York City newspapers. John Taylor's competency and integrity also impressed the press. The following year, in 1857, the *Times* carried an article titled "Mormonism in New-York," which acknowledged, among other things, the "Valedictory of President John Taylor" prior to his departure and the appointment of Elder [William] Appleby, who replaced him as president of the Eastern States Mission. The article also revealed Taylor's positive impact on the larger New York City community and the respect members of this high-powered metropolitan newspaper had for him:

> President Taylor was a popular gentleman in his dealings with the Saints and Gentiles of suasive manners and imposing presence. His age is about 55, and he has been a Mormon for many years; once edited a Mormon paper in Paris, and established one afterwards in London and has published several works. Since its commencement,

he has conducted the *Mormon* with considerable ability and tact.... He has directed the emigration of foreign Mormons setting it in the right road to Utah,—has made arrangements with railroad companies for the transit parties of Mormons.[37]

Thus, John Taylor's impressive editorial skills and his competency in managing the emigration process did not go unnoticed by the New York press. However, with the Utah War of 1857, Taylor's talent and wisdom were needed back in Utah, and he soon left his East Coast labors.

## Arrival of European Converts at American Eastern Ports during the Civil War

Several years later, the American Civil War broke out. Of the thirty-two vessels that took companies of Saints across the Atlantic during this period (1861–65), none arrived through Philadelphia, three South African voyages came to port in Boston, and the remaining twenty-nine voyages, carrying mainly British and Scandinavian converts, first touched the American shore in New York, where the Castle Garden immigration depot was located. The LDS immigrants were well chaperoned—priesthood leaders saw them off at the Liverpool docks, returning missionaries accompanied them on the transatlantic voyage, and immigration agents awaited them at the ports on the East Coast.

The first group of South African converts to gather to Zion during the war selected Boston as their port of arrival. While the procedures for all immigrants at New York's Castle Garden Immigration Depot are well documented,[38] the immigration experience at the Boston port, which received less LDS immigration activity, is not as familiar. Eli Wiggill, an LDS convert who immigrated to America from South Africa, provided an interesting account of his experience in Boston after he and thirty-two of his companions (including a small Black African boy named Gobo Fango, who was smuggled through customs) arrived in Boston on April 19, 1861.[39]

Wiggill explained that just before the passengers stepped on shore, "the Pilot came on board and brought papers and also the news that the War had broke out in the United States."[40] Wiggill indicated that the local Saints welcomed them upon their arrival. He noted that the Bostonians were surprised by the color of the South Africans' skin, as they did not know there were white people in Africa. Wiggill also explained that as soon as the ship docked, the local Boston branch president telegraphed LDS emigration agent Nathaniel V. Jones in New York for instructions on how to proceed. Jones told them to wait in Boston until a ship of Saints came into New York, then the South Africans were to continue on to New York before heading west.

While the Saints stayed in Boston for nearly a month, "it was all comotion with the Bands of Music Fife and drum and recruting parties and Flags Flying in every direction it being the comencement of the War of 1861 between the North and the South."[41] Wiggill later noted that after they reached New York and journeyed west by train, free Black men spotted the young Black boy traveling with the South African Saints and mistakenly assumed he was being taken into slavery. The child was therefore in danger of being abducted. The Talbot family, who were caring for the boy, hid him by disguising him in a girl's dress and bonnet; they later concealed him under a woman's large petticoat.[42]

Elders Nathaniel V. Jones and Jacob Gates were assigned as immigration agents just as they were returning from missions to England. Gates recorded that he had received word in late 1860 that he was to supervise immigration at Florence (North Omaha), Nebraska Territory, while Jones was to be the first immigration agent assigned to New York City during the Civil War. By February 1861 they had arrived from England at the port of New York.[43]

Jones remained in New York for some time to assist the arriving immigrants.[44] He described the situation there in a letter to his wife, Rebecca, on April 22, 1861, just ten days after the Civil War began: "Things here are in a very alarming condition while I am wrighting this. They are without doubt fighting in Baltimore & Washington. They have been Skermishing in the former place since yesterday but of this you can read from the Papers which I will Send with this."[45]

The *Manchester* was the first ship to bring seagoing Saints to New York during the Civil War. John McAllister, a passenger aboard the *Manchester* in 1862, recorded in his journal that he "read to Capt. T[rask] Joseph Smith's views on the p[o]licy and Govt. of U.S."[46] This conversation seemed to have greatly affected Captain Trask, who three days later assembled his passengers on the quarterdeck and addressed them just prior to their disembarkation in New York City: "Assembled Soldiers of Zion—assembled because you are Mustered, if not Soldiers in reality you are Soldiers in embryo hence you are seed mustard. Seed of Zion, to you I would Say be strong and Steadfast."[47]

In his speech Captain Trask suggested that the Saints had a greater battle to fight than the one being waged between the North and the South. The Saints enjoyed not only his speech but also his overall conduct on their voyage. They drafted a resolution to show their appreciation to Captain Trask, wherein they praised him for his "gentlemanly and courteous bearing, liberal acts, and solicitious [sic] spirit," and then presented it to him just as the pilot stepped aboard prior to their docking in New York.[48]

On the previous voyage of the *Manchester*, in 1861, the passengers had encountered men of a different spirit gathered in New York at the time of their arrival:

> We had our luggage all packed and ready for starting immediately by Steamer for Castle Garden, but Bro. N. V. Jones, who was Emigration Agent, visited us, and on account of the above place being occupied by U.S. Troops, he deemed it wise for all hands to remain on board ship. Counsel was given to the company to that effect. On account of the dreadful, warlike attitude of the North and South, these troops were collected there. They were a very mean set, too, and Bro. Jones had informed the proprietors, that unless the Garden was cleared of them, he should not land his people there.[49]

F. W. Blake, who arrived on the *Underwriter* a week later, reported a less intimidating but more boisterous arrival: "The hour arrived for the crowd of Saints & stock of Luggage to be removed from the ship & it became my unfortunate lot to stay on board while the large vessel was drawn towards shore. Handkerchiefs and hats were waving & loud hurrahs were heard sounding over the waters competing with those engaged in the national cause. (they were frequently making the air echo with the power of their voices)."[50]

Elijah Larkin described the arrival of the *Amazon* in the New York harbor two years later, on July 17, 1863:

A stream [*sic*] troop ship passed us at 8 a.m. . . . Sighted Fire Island at 6 p.m. A pilot came on board at 6.30 the New York Papers were read on board informing us of the Riots that were going on there, which caused great excitement on board. Port Hudson was taken by Federals. . . .

18th. . . . A transport loaded with Troops for the City passed us, & we were informed there was 4500 Troops alreaddy there to quell the Riot.

we anchord in the harbor about P.M. Our Band played the Star Spangled Banner,

& we gave several hearty [cheers].[51]

### New York Emigration Agents after the End of the Civil War until 1889

After the conclusion of the American Civil War, LDS agents such as William C. Staines, who acted faithfully in this position from 1867 until his death in 1881, continued to serve in New York. Despite his faithfulness, Staines faced challenges, as did other agents who offered advice after observing thousands of incoming immigrants.

For example, in a letter to Albert Carrington, president of the European Mission and stationed in Liverpool, Staines advised:

> If any Saints emigrate to New York without means to go to Utah, they should be competent to take care of themselves, and not rely upon us, as I have not means to further them with. Their luggage should not be mixed up on the ship with that of those who are going through to Utah, but should be kept entirely separate. This will prevent a great amount of trouble and unpleasantness and probably some difficulty. Two sisters came to me this morning, with a Frenchman to interpret, as they cannot speak a word of English. They brought a letter from Brother Ursenbach to Brother Miles, wishing them to be sent on to Utah, but they have only sufficient to provision them a few days. I think it is unwise to send people in this way, unless it is known that funds have been deposited here to assist them—not the case in this instance.[52]

During his tenure of service, Brother Staines "made regular annual trips between Salt Lake City and New York, his duties requiring his presence in the East during the spring, summer and fall, after which he would return

21. William C. Staines, ca. 1870. Church History Library, PH 7954.

to spend the winter with his family and friends in Utah."[53] In the spring of 1871, before his annual departure to the East, he was given a special blessing at the hands of Wilford Woodruff, who acted as voice; Lorenzo Snow; and Franklin D. Richards. Among other things, the men commended Brother Staines for his service and gave the following instruction to assure him that he would not be laboring alone:

> Again go forth unto your field of labor, in the United States, to take charge of the emigration and to preside over the same. You have labored for seasons past and gone in this work, you have been faithful to your charge, to God and to your brethren, and for these things you have been blessed. We say unto you, let your heart be comforted before the Lord; you shall have your reward for all the good you have

done. Therefore, go in peace, trust in the living God, as you have done in times that are past and gone; for we say unto you in the name of the Lord Jesus Christ; the Spirit of God shall rest down you; you shall be filled with light and truth and with understanding, and nothing shall come in your way, but success shall attend you, and you shall be greatly blessed in the emigration, in laboring for the benefit of your brethren and sisters.

The angels will be round about you; you shall be preserved while attending to this mission, and the Lord will open your way in many respects. Whenever you come to a position where all may seem dark, you shall see your way open up before you. Whenever danger shall lie in your path, whether upon railroads or else-where, the Spirit of God shall reveal unto you that danger and you shall escape the same. Whenever it shall be right to make contacts for the emigration it shall be clearly made known to your mind. Your labors will be accepted of the Lord God of Israel, and you shall be preserved by His power.[54]

On May 6, 1881, President John Taylor set apart James H. Hart as "emigration agent" at New York City to replace Staines. Agent Hart kept President Taylor informed of his labors throughout his seven-year tenure, as evidenced by the sixty-two letters he wrote to Taylor, who had once held the same position. During the years Hart served as an agent, he commuted back and forth between emigration seasons, returning to Bloomington, Idaho, to serve in his calling as first counselor to William Budge in the Bear Lake stake presidency. He also spent two years working as a prosecuting attorney.[55] Hart had previous experience handling immigration matters in St. Louis, where he had served as president of the St. Louis Stake from 1855 to 1857.[56] His prior experience as a lawyer, coupled with his labor as a farmer and postmaster and his service in the Idaho Territorial Legislature for three terms, provided him with a wealth of experience prior to taking up his assignment on the East Coast.[57]

Upon Hart's arrival in New York City, and continually thereafter, newspaper reporters clamored to interview him. In the words of one of his grandsons, Edward L. Hart, "He was, in that metropolis, the visible Mormon—the genuine specimen that could be seen and interviewed."[58]

22. James H. Hart, ca. 1880. Church History Library, PH 1700 518.

Besides facing the media and assisting thousands of passing converts, Hart also managed correspondence from Church members, which kept him very busy and at times tried his patience. Such correspondence included the following letter sent by Jno. Scofield on July 3, 1883: "Dear Brother I have sent you $37 dollars for you to purchase my ticket from Chicago to Salt Lake City Utah. I would like to leave St. Catherine's on the 6 or 7 that is next Friday or Saturday. It will [be] Saturday the 7 of July. Please and rite back how to go on, yours very truly."[59] Another engaging letter followed about three months later, written by a Brother Schofield on October 24: "Will you be kind enough to hand the enclosed seven dollars to Sister Sarah Woodenden or any of her family who are emigrants (on the next company) from Brighouse Yorkshire and you will confer a great favor. P.S. They are my relatives."[60]

In addition to managing such correspondence, Hart also effectively handled important decisions that affected emigration on a much broader scale. One of the most notable changes was his suggestion to President John Taylor that the Saints no longer use the New York trains to travel West. In light of immigration procedures, costs, and the passage of the Interstate Railway Act of 1887,[61] he suggested that the church transport the incoming Saints from New York to Norfolk, Virginia, by ship and then proceed through the port of Norfolk west on their railroads. President Taylor implemented his suggestion, and over five thousand LDS converts traveled west through the port of Norfolk to Utah between 1887 and 1890.[62]

As the nineteenth century drew to a close, the Latter-day Saint gathering, which had once flowed at a rapid rate, slowed to a trickle. Antipolygamy laws had affected immigration, and in 1887 the Edmunds-Tucker Act had, in effect, halted the Perpetual Emigrating Fund. Yet by this time, tens of thousands of European converts had been successfully transported to Zion under the wise guidance of church leaders and a number of dedicated LDS emigration agents who provided timely advice. These men in motion had propelled the church forward into the twentieth century and left a great legacy of service until Castle Garden closed down.

It is estimated that over sixty-five thousand Latter-day Saint immigrants came through Castle Garden between 1855 and 1889. In 1889 Castle Garden, along with its records, was destroyed by fire, with the Ellis Island immigrant receiving station taking its place.[63]

# 8

## LDS Emigration through Missouri by River and Rail (1838–68)

As noted, on October 27, 1838, Missouri governor Lilburn W. Boggs had issued a decree that stated, "The Mormons must be treated as enemies and must be exterminated and driven from the state, if necessary for the public good." This infamous extermination order caused thousands of Latter-day Saints to flee the state and seek refuge in Illinois, across the Mississippi River.[1] Throughout the harsh winter of 1838–39, many Latter-day Saint families fled western Missouri to its eastern border (a distance of as much as two hundred miles for some) by carts and wagons and on foot.

This chapter examines the Saints' experience as they emigrated through Missouri during the three decades following the extermination order. Disclosing the events of these decades is important as the coming of the transcontinental railroad would virtually put an end to the LDS migrant experience in Missouri, which is a neglected period in Latter-day Saint history.

The forced exodus during this frigid winter had deeply embittered the Saints against Missourians and had continued to fester long after they gathered to the Salt Lake Valley a decade later, as evidenced by LDS emigrant accounts recorded in the mid-nineteenth century. The injustices and cruel treatment of the Saints at the hands of the western Missourian mobocrats during the 1830s was deeply etched into their memories. LDS narratives demonstrate that these memories, coupled with recollections of a just vengeance predicted by the LDS prophet Joseph Smith, lingered in the minds of the Saints as they encountered bleached bones strewn across the overland trail heading west. Yet Joseph Smith had publicly prayed, "Have Mercy, O Lord upon the wicked Mob, who have driven thy people . . . if repentance is to be found."[2] He also boldly warned, "Let the government

23. Lilburn W. Boggs. Missouri Historical Society, St. Louis.

of Missouri redress the wrongs she has done to the Saints, or let the curse follow them from generation to generation."[3]

## Attitudes toward and Avoidance of Salt Lake City

The certainty that God's awful wrath would be heaped upon the Missourians was widespread among the Saints. Apparently, this widely held view deterred westbound Missouri emigrants, who were hesitant to enter the city of the Saints. On July 2, 1849, James H. Humphreys of Hannibal, Missouri, wrote, "Having some fear of going through Salt Lake on account of the ill feelings they the Mormans had against the Missourians, we concluded to take the Serblets [Sublette's] Cut Off."[4] Reports like Albert King Thurber's may have also reached the ears of Missourian migrants heading west:

24. Albert King Thurber, ca. 1880. Church History Library, PH 1700 120.

"Arrived in G. S. [L.] City July 19 (1849). I was riding along the street [and] spoke to an aged man. Well, says he, we are glad to see you if you did not drive us out of Missouri, which was all Greek to me as I knew nothing of Mormons or their history."[5]

One Missourian who traveled to California the following year wrote, "I went north of Salt Lake City as the Mormons [were] down on Missourians generally."[6] Another emigrant wrote, "We arrived at Salt Lake in the early part of August [1849]. . . . I was told that he [Brigham Young] said that there were people coming and skulking through that place on the way to California, who had taken part in driving them out of Missouri, and if he could catch them, he would send them to Hell Across Lots. There were some Missourians who became alarmed and started on as soon as possible."[7]

Although this resentment seemed to pollute the migrant plains, LDS converts (mostly from Europe and the eastern United States) continued to cross Missouri borders by steam and rail during the next three decades, when the extermination order was still officially in effect.[8] Knowing what Utah Saints generally thought of passing migrant Missourians, what did the LDS emigrants encounter during this tumultuous period of the mid-nineteenth century when they crossed between Missouri borders? What challenges did they face?

### St. Louis: An Oasis for Saints Who Were Respected by Local Citizens

Though most Saints fled the state of Missouri at the time of the extermination order, some found refuge on the eastern edge of the Missouri border in the metropolis of St. Louis, although as previously noted, apostates posed a threat to the passing Saints headed for Nauvoo (1840–46). This thriving city also served as an inland transmigration port for about eighteen thousand European LDS converts who crossed the Atlantic and traveled up the Mississippi, with most heading west on the Missouri River to the Salt Lake Valley.[9] St. Louis was considered an important juncture for steamboat travel on the Mississippi and Missouri Rivers and had become an important temporary gathering place for the Saints and an oasis of tolerance and safety following the extermination order a decade earlier. By 1855 the LDS periodical *St. Louis Luminary* explained, "This city has been an asylum for our people from fifteen to twenty years.... There is probably no city in the world where the Latter-day Saints are more respected."[10]

### LDS Emigration on the Missouri River (1848–55)

After Brigham Young and the vanguard company of Saints reached the Salt Lake Valley in the summer of 1847, a new gathering place emerged. Church leaders then selected various outfitting posts each year at which the incoming emigrants could assemble before crossing the plains to Salt Lake City. Changes in outfitting posts and routes were influenced by concern for the incoming converts, and arrangements were made according to the safest and most economical routes possible on the Missouri River.

Although it appears the Missourians were not an obstacle along the "Big Muddy," the Saints feared another enemy—cholera—which is attested in a number of LDS emigrant journals. Another potential threat was the fear of a boiler explosion, such as the one that claimed the steamboat *Saluda* in the spring of 1852. However, this event seems to have carried a silver lining in the relations between Saints and Missourians, as evidenced by Missourian acts of compassion that may have helped atone for the mobocracy witnessed on the western Missouri border in the 1830s. In what some historians consider the worst steamboat disaster in Missouri River history, the *Saluda* blew her boilers on April 9 (Good Friday). Twenty-six Latter-day Saint emigrants were killed and many others injured at a river bend near Lexington, in western Missouri. Lexington citizens, modern-day Good Samaritans, quickly hastened to the dismal scene and rendered needed aid. Not only did they raise money to bury the Latter-day Saint dead, but they also gathered funds to help the survivors continue their journey to Utah. The local townspeople created an orphan fund, and some even adopted the destitute Latter-day Saint children.[11]

Latter-day Saint Abraham Smoot, an eyewitness to such compassion, wrote, "I shall never forget the kindness of the citizens of Lexington in caring for the living and burying the dead. The Lord certainly inspired them to do all that sympathy and benevolence could suggest in aid of the afflicted."[12]

### LDS Emigration on the Northwestern Border of Missouri

Once the exiled Nauvoo Saints reached the Missouri River (which also served as the western border of Missouri), they benefitted from what LDS historian Richard E. Bennett called "an uneasy truce" as they temporarily settled on the border of Iowa and Missouri near the "Big Muddy" (1846–50). Here, in the Council Bluffs region, they crossed the border and found refuge in St. Joseph and in other settlements in northwestern Missouri, where they sought trade and employment so they could purchase necessary provisions to continue their journey west to the Great Basin. Bennett has persuasively argued that "Missouri became the lifeline to the exodus. Had it not been for this Missouri trade [and employment,] most would not have gathered sufficient means to migrate to the valley of the Great

25. Abraham O. Smoot, ca. 1890. Photo by C. R. Savage.
Church History Library, PH 1700, 2805.

Salt Lake. Once their inveterate enemy, Missouri became provider, supporter—in a word, their economic salvation."[13]

Although it certainly appears that at times both the Saints and the citizens of Missouri were a bit uneasy with the relationship, Hosea Stout wrote that as 1847 dawned "the most opposition [the Saints had] in Missouri [was] in consequence of the stories of the dissenters otherwise the Missourians [were] very friendly."[14] This report is most interesting, as this desire for cooperation rather than conflict is also attested in St. Louis on the eastern border of Missouri. At the same time, however, in both cases, the apostates were stirring up problems for the Saints on the Missouri borders.

## Rerouting the Saints by Rail through Missouri

Beginning in the spring of 1855, Latter-day Saint immigration was rerouted to the East Coast due to the threat of deadly disease on the Mississippi River.[15] During the nineteenth century, New York LDS emigration agents such as George Q. Cannon usually met the incoming voyages and arranged for the groups to continue on their journey. Cannon also suggested that the LDS emigrants use the Hannibal and St. Joe Railroad to pass through Missouri when it opened in 1859.

During the period of 1859 to 1866, an estimated eighteen thousand LDS immigrants crossed the Atlantic and the Mississippi River (via Quincy, Illinois, and Hannibal, Missouri) to gather in the Salt Lake Valley and used the Hannibal and St. Joe Railroad. When the LDS emigrants left Quincy and traversed the Mississippi, they left not only a larger, more refined community but also a city that had matured in tolerance, influenced no doubt by the large number of European immigrants there. However, as they entered the Hannibal region, they encountered different demographic circumstances as well as a tumultuous environment influenced by past and current episodes of discord. National and local newspapers also played a significant role in fueling local prejudices. The conflict between the Latter-day Saints and Missourians, the recent Utah War, and the advent of the Civil War all sparked a smoldering enmity in the press.

## Crossing Missouri on the Hannibal and St. Joe Railroad during the Civil War

Unpredictable guerilla warfare during the Civil War (1861–65) made the rail journey through Missouri challenging.[16] Andrew Christian Nielson, who passed through this turbulent region in 1864, wrote, "In Quincy, Illinois we stopped several days and then had to take cattle cars for St. Joseph through Missouri. We had some trouble in getting through the wars. Here was the ruins of whole towns as had been laid waste by the terrible struggle."[17]

An emigrant from an 1863 LDS pioneer company related, "All of the passenger cars had been burned [so] they locked us up in cattle cars which had straw floors. There were no seats. We passed a soldiers' camp and it was here we ran into a place where logs had been placed to disrail the cars.

I happened to be standing up when the cars struck the logs and the jolt threw me head foremost to the other side of the car among the women and children. Everyone was crying and screaming. A few were hurt."[18]

Although the cattle cars were at times dangerous, they were actually safer than the passenger cars that carried Union soldiers and were thus the constant target of Confederate attack. Yet the passage through the "North" (consisting of a rail route usually from New York to Chicago) did not carry the threat of warfare that was prevalent in Missouri.

Not only were the emigrants consigned to cars fit only for beasts, but the roads were of very poor quality. One passing emigrant remarked, "We had a rough ride through the State of Missouri. The H. & St. Joseph's Railroad was new but not finished. Appeared to be the most uneven road for a railroad I ever traveled on."[19] At times the threat of destruction to the tracks posed an additional challenge. One passing migrant wrote, "To Quincy. Got over the Mississippi River to a grove of trees and laid there to the 11 of June 64. (All the cars was in the South with the soldiers.) Then to Palmyra [just north of Hannibal], we saw 1000 of soldier. They tore the track."[20] One emigrant remembered a close call, especially for those who chose to ride in the passenger cars during their trip through war-torn Missouri:

> Just before we arrived in St. Joseph, Missouri, the rebels, or bushwhackers, fired two cannon balls through our train, one shot went through the passenger car exactly eight inches above the people's heads and the other through the baggage car destroying a great amount of baggage. We stayed three or four days, afraid to go on because of the rebel soldiers being all throughout the country. While we were there, some fifteen rebel soldiers were taken prisoner, right from among [meaning near] our company, by the northern soldiers. Two companies of Union soldiers surrounded the depot and made the rebels surrender or they would have killed them. I can truly say I saw a little of the war between the North and the South.[21]

Latter-day Saint emigrants also feared that the soldiers would abduct them. For example, in 1864 Mary Ann Ward Webb learned of a young Dutch LDS woman passing through St. Joseph, Missouri, who had been stolen by the soldiers and later rescued.[22] The year before, Thomas Henry

White also reported that a girl in their company had been taken by soldiers.[23] White further wrote of his company's encounter with soldiers while crossing Missouri: "At every station the soldiers would ask, 'When are those Mormons coming through.' The emigrants were in danger, especially the boys of being drafted into the army."[24] Despite the danger, the Saints continued their march to the Salt Lake Valley.

By the time the transcontinental railroad had crossed America in the spring of 1869, it appears LDS emigrants had come to believe in a revelation Brigham Young delivered on the banks of the Missouri River in the winter of 1847: "Fear not thy enemies; for they shall not have power to stop my work.... Fear not thine enemies, for they are in mine hands and I will do my pleasure with them" (D&C 136:17, 30).

# 9

## LDS Frontier Outfitting Posts

After they were forced to leave Nauvoo, Illinois, in early 1846, the Saints crossed the Mississippi River in the dead of winter and slowly made their way across Iowa Territory. Due to lack of resources, organizational challenges, and poor weather conditions that bogged down wagon travel, Brigham Young decided to set up temporary headquarters near the Missouri River, not far from modern-day Omaha, Nebraska. He named the place Winter Quarters. Although several thousand gathered at Winter Quarters with the main body of the Saints, thousands of others were strewn across the Iowa plains reaching all the way back to the Mississippi River. Brigham Young led a vanguard company into the Salt Lake Valley in the summer of 1847, but most Saints in the Winter Quarters area remained (1846–48), eventually creating settlements on both sides of the Missouri River.

Church leaders established other frontier outfitting posts over the following two decades at various places along the western plains. Such posts changed according to where the Saints would best be fitted out as the years rolled on. After Winter Quarters, Saints were stationed at Kanesville, Iowa, just across the Mississippi (1849–52).[1] The following year a post was set up at Keokuk, Iowa (1853), then in Westport, Missouri (1854), and then in Mormon Grove, Kansas (1855).

To cut the costs of wagon travel, the Saints began traveling with handcarts in 1856. Iowa City, Iowa, served as the trailhead from 1856 to 1858, followed by Florence, Nebraska, from 1859 to 1863. Because of the large number of apostates in Florence, the LDS emigrants were rerouted to Wyoming, Nebraska (1864–66), about forty miles south of Florence. With westbound rail construction on the Union Pacific, the outfitting posts moved farther west to North Platte and Nebraska City, Nebraska (1867), and Laramie and Benton, Wyoming (1868).[2] The following year (1869), the rails were joined at Promontory Point in Utah Territory, ending trail travel for the Saints.

## Winter Quarters (1846–48)

After arriving on the west bank of the Missouri River at Winter Quarters, the Saints had no permanent home. One early pioneer, Isaac Haight, wrote in the early fall of 1846, "Here we are exiled from the United States . . . without a home, dwelling in tents and wagons exposed to the inclemency of weather. . . . Having no abiding city but we are wanderers and pilgrims on earth."[3]

Brigham Young soon negotiated permission for the Saints to temporarily stay on local Native American lands in the Winter Quarters area, which by 1847 had seven to eight hundred houses and about four thousand LDS settlers. The Office of Indian Affairs, however, was not fond of the idea of the Saints settling on tribal lands as they feared potential feuding. Their concern soon became a reality, and the local tribes wanted to remove the Saints from the land.

At this point, the Saints had to choose whether to go on to the Salt Lake Valley with the 1848 migration or move to the eastern side of the Missouri River, if they did not have the means to make the journey. Some went west, which church leaders preferred, but most stayed due to limited resources. They also understood that land in the area had recently been vacated by the Pottawattamie Indians, which raised the prospect of Saints developing western counties in Iowa. These migrating Saints clustered in about forty settlements within a forty-mile radius of the Miller's Hollow area, in the Council Bluffs region of western Iowa. Those who remained in 1848 called this area Kanesville, named after a friend and benefactor of the Saints, Colonel Thomas L. Kane.[4]

## Kanesville (1849–52)

Elder Orson Hyde served as the LDS agent at Kanesville during the years 1849–50 while also serving as an apostle and as editor of the LDS periodical the *Frontier Guardian*. The *Guardian* provided news for LDS emigrants and also benefitted eastern migrants heading west. At the same time that the

26. Orson Hyde, ca. 1860s. Church History Library, PH 1600.

Saints were gathering by the thousands from Europe or the East Coast, tens of thousands with dreams of gold were also heading west, creating a potential hazard for Hyde and the Saints he presided over.

The *Guardian* issued the following account as the steamboat *Mustang* reached the shores of Council Point at the Bluffs in the spring of 1849: "First Boat This Season. . . . She brought some few passengers who are on their way to the gold regions, and a large lot of whiskey. This should go to the gold regions too."[5]

In addition to the potential cultural threat the whiskey-toting boys posed, gold fever also struck Kanesville (both Saint and sinner alike) this same year. The surge of forty-niners who passed through generated an excitement that caused some Saints to believe there was gold in the Kanesville terrain. Nelson Whipple recollected, "Some person . . . found some thing in the bluffs west of Kainsville that had the appearance of gold[;] this raised a grate excitement of corse. Brother Hyde went over to the place with some others and saw it and dedicated it to the Lord. This was all right and in good shape but the stuff turned out to be entirely worthless and no body could tell what it was."[6]

Yet the gold rush also proved to be a blessing to the Saints, as thousands of argonauts poured into the Kanesville area and boosted the economy. Warren E. Foote recalled in May 1849, "We are crowded with 'Gold diggers' as we call them." One farmer reported, "We are busy every day and night grinding and the mill is crowded full. . . . We are making money midling [sic] fast now, but it can't keep this way long."[7] The following year, even more gold diggers made their way west through the area, and with the additional resources, many poor Saints who had been temporarily located in the Bluffs region were able to continue their journey west to the Salt Lake Valley.[8]

The *Frontier Guardian* offered advice to all passing emigrants who journeyed west, including a continual reminder to beware of Indians who might steal their wagons, animals, and other belongings.[9] In light of this apparent danger, the *Guardian* counseled the California-bound companies to travel in "a strict military organization" with fifty well-armed men and fifty wagons.[10] Some groups of non-LDS gold miners joined LDS companies on the trail to increase their numbers. In June of 1849 a group of gold miners heading west joined the Samuel Gully/Orson Spencer Company, agreeing to obey their rules and regulations.[11] Two months later Captain A. W. Rathburn's company, from Cleveland, Ohio, joined the LDS company led by Allen Taylor for protection against Indians on the plains.[12]

In an attempt to sell subscriptions, with tongue in cheek, an article in the *Frontier Guardian* alluded to the idea that the forty-niners would be safer on the plains if they had a copy of the newspaper with them. It also warned, "Should you leave without this pre-requisite, and after you got well out on the plains, should there discover, off in the distance, a war party of Indians, following you up—then think that you neglected to take the

*Guardian.*" The article also reminded the California-bound miners that "the Mormons found the gold there."[13] Finally, the paper noted that the *Guardian* would "even draw out gold where there is no mine at all," adding, "Our circumstances are such that we cannot go to the gold regions ourself, but we would like to have a little gold, notwithstanding, and we know not how to get it, except we say to you, subscribe to the *Guardian.*"[14]

By the time the LDS British converts reached Council Bluffs, Iowa, the Mormon trail that for many had begun in Liverpool was crowded with California-bound emigrants, argonauts, wagonloads of cargo, and clouds of dust.[15] The *Guardian* speculated that about twenty-five thousand emigrants were headed west on the plains by the spring of 1849.[16] First-person accounts indicate that LDS companies passed many gold hunters on their way to California as well as soldiers who had deserted the military.[17] They also tell of many who died of cholera along the way.[18]

Although many LDS emigrants traveled together from the time they crossed the Atlantic until they arrived in the Salt Lake Valley, some did not. Throughout the journey by land and by sea, economics was a key factor in whether LDS immigrants could make their way to Zion in one season. The Perpetual Emigrating Fund (PEF), established in 1849, classified LDS immigrants in one of three categories. The "independent" group consisted of those who could pay their entire way to Utah. The second category included "ordinary" immigrants, those who had enough money to cross the ocean and were then forced to work at a port, city, or frontier post before journeying on. The third group contained the "PEF" immigrants, who were assisted almost entirely by the Perpetual Emigrating Fund.[19]

With help from the PEF and the strong encouragement by church leaders to come to Utah, most Saints who had lived in the Council Bluffs, Iowa, region had completed their journey to the Salt Lake Valley by 1852. An epistle issued by the church's highest council that year had influenced converts on both sides of the Atlantic. The message was clear that conversion and the gathering to Zion went hand in hand: "When a people or individuals, hear the Gospel, . . . it is time for them to gather, without delay to Zion. . . . The longer they wait the more difficult it will be for them to come home."[20]

## Keokuk (1853)

As previously noted, LDS agent Horace S. Eldredge arranged for Keokuk, Iowa, to serve as the frontier outfitting post for the 1853 emigrating season. Located just a dozen miles south of where the Saints had abandoned Nauvoo in 1846, Keokuk was uniquely designated an Iowa LDS emigration frontier outfitting point for only one year. The emigrants' route was temporarily changed to avoid the hazards of the Missouri River after the 1852 explosion of the *Saluda*.[21] The post was only active for a year because it took an extra three hundred miles of wagon travel across Iowa to arrive there, making the change in route rather unappealing.

Upon reaching the encampment on the outskirts of Keokuk, the Latter-day Saints were placed under the competent charge of the local LDS emigration agent, Isaac C. Haight, and his assistant, Vincent Shurtleff, who had made the necessary arrangements for the incoming migrants.[22] Still other Latter-day Saints willingly volunteered to help the incoming emigrants reach the LDS encampment from the Keokuk levee, although they were probably not officially assigned to aid in emigration matters. One emigrant recalled, "Brother Locke and others brought their teams and [helped] the Saints to bring their luggage to the camp of Israel. A sight which gladdened my heart to behold."[23]

### LDS Descriptions and Experiences at the Keokuk Encampment

On reaching the encampment, Christopher Jones Arthur, a young LDS British baker, remembered, "The camp was lively, scattered over many acres. Some in tents others in wagons."[24] Scandinavian proselyte Christian Nielsen described the encampment as "open air quarters," noting, "In the morning I went out to see our 'open air' lodging place that looked well to me. We came first to the place where emigrants from England were placed, and thereafter to the spot where we Danish emigrants should have our quarters.... We could help ourselves to all the wood we needed."[25] Less than a week later, Nielsen further noted, "Our 'territory' for quarters gets wider day after day. Each day additional wagons loaded with emigrants come to our quarters, and tents are put up to be the abode for the emigrants."[26]

Sometimes the European emigrants faced hardships due to the unfamiliar frontier conditions. Upon arriving in Keokuk, Hannah Cornaby described the encampment, which sat on a hill near the Mississippi River:

> Here we found the wagons and tents. We had just placed our baggage in the wagons; some were making awkward attempts at erecting tents while others were trying to place the covers on the wagons, some of which obstinately refused to reach over at both ends, when we were struck by a furious storm of wind and rain, accompanied by thunder and lightning such as we had never heard or seen before. The storm raged with such fury that we feared the wagons would be upset, and after the wind subsided, the rain poured down incessantly three days and nights, our luggage and bedding becoming thoroughly soaked, and the camp ground ankle deep with mud. Under these circumstances, my second child was prematurely born.[27]

Stephen Fosdick further described the Keokuk encampment: "The Mormon Camp consisted of a long street with wagon[s] on each side. We were shown our camp, which consisted of about twenty empty wagons, equipped with bows. As we belonged to the ten pound company, we were told to divide ourselves into groups of ten, and each ten to take possession of a wagon."[28] However, sometimes migration plans needed to be modified once the emigrants reached Keokuk. One emigrant who departed from Liverpool understood that upon reaching Keokuk, his ten-pound company would have ten people to a wagon and would be allowed one hundred pounds of luggage. Yet he noted, "We had to take twelve in a wagon and consented to reduce our extra luggage to seventy-five pounds and if possible to fifty. There was no way to hire out extra luggage taken to the valley so we burned our boxes and extra weight."[29]

During the several weeks when Latter-day Saints made preparations for their overland journey, there was a little time to explore the surrounding area. Some took time to see the dilapidated Nauvoo Temple and to visit the mother of the martyred prophet Joseph Smith (Lucy Mack Smith) and also Smith's wife, Emma.[30] Though most were very busy with their preparations, they enjoyed socializing with one another.

In the camp, the European Saints joyfully reunited with acquaintances from their homelands on American soil. At Keokuk, James McNaughton

27. Hannah Last Cornaby. Daughters of the Utah Pioneers, Salt Lake City.

penned, "Here we had the unspeakable pleasure of being in the camp of Brothers Barnes & Allen, from Hull and of seeing their families. What a meeting!"[31] McNaughton also provided insight into weekly Sabbath services, writing, "Meetings were held for public worship at the camp ground."[32] A week later, he noted, "These were good times on both Sabbaths. The Lord truly blessed us."[33]

Convert Frederick Piercy provided a vivid description of the encampment through the eyes of a young, gifted British artist: "I sallied out in search of the Camp, which, after climbing a steep bluff on the edge of the river, I found most picturesquely situated on top of a hill, surrounded by wood, and commanding a view of the country for miles around. The situation was admirably chosen, as there were good drainage and an abundance of wood and water combined."[34]

Piercy also described the social conditions of the European converts:

> The emigrants from each nation had wisely been placed together, and those who had crossed the sea together were still associated as neighbours in Camp. I heard no complaints of sickness, and I was told that the general health was good. The Elders in charge seemed thoroughly competent, and Elders Haight and Eldredge were incessant in their labours. I particularly noticed the generosity with which Elder C. H. Wheelock volunteered the use of his teams for the public good. They were constantly engaged in transporting the luggage of the emigrants from the river to the Camp, which saved many a poor person's scanty means, and rescued many a poor family from a dilemma, for as yet there were a very few oxen in the Camp, and most persons were unwilling to run the risk of their animals being worn out before the commencement of the journey.
>
> The Camp was in excellent order, and the emigrants informed me that when the ground was not muddy they would as soon live in a tent as in a house. I saw few idlers—indeed, rather than remain unemployed until the trains moved off, those who could not get work in the town of Keokuk at their trades took advantage of the opportunity which [was] offered of working on the roads. By this means they saved what little money they possessed, and in many instances added to their stock, and were thus enabled to obtain many little comforts which they must otherwise have gone without.... Before leaving Keokuk I made [a] sketch of the Camp, showing the arrangement of the wagons and tents, which, with their white covers, looked extremely picturesque amidst the spring foliage of the country.[35]

### Descriptions of LDS Emigrants by the Local Keokuk Press and Public

The *Keokuk Dispatch* reported on the arrival of the Saints, including the following article:

> Two hundred Mormons arrived here on Friday last on board the steamboat Hindoo on their way to Salt Lake, several hundred more are lying at St. Louis and two or three ship loads expected daily from New Orleans. Those who have arrived have gone into camp above the city incorporation. They are all native of England and Wales and left the port of Liverpool on the 18th of February last for New Orleans, where they arrived safely and in good health, having lost but one of their number on the way. The whole train when it is made up, it is expected will number two thousand persons. They intend making Keokuk their starting point. Farmers having stock or cattle fit for the yoke will here find a ready market.[36]

Just one week later, the *Dispatch* added, "Two hundred more of the Mormon faith arrived at this place on last Sunday. They have also gone into camp awaiting the arrival of about two thousand more who are expected here soon."[37] By the end of May, the *Dispatch* reported, "Some eight hundreds [sic] Mormons have left and some three hundred have arrived at the camp ground. About 3000 have already reached this port and about 800 more are expected. The Mormons have behaved in the most peaceable and courteous manner during their stay here and have won the respect and confidence of the community with their orderly and law abiding behaviour."[38]

The Saints earned some of that respect by providing physical labor to improve the city of Keokuk. The *Dispatch* reported on April 26, 1853, "A large number of Mormons are now employed in grading the streets of our city. Each man is a 'full team' behind a pick and shovel. A pile of dirt before a dozen or two of these hard fisted, strong fellows, is 'nowhere.' The rough places of our city are rapidly becoming smooth and if the Mormons remain here awhile longer, our streets will present quite a different appearance from what they have presented heretofore. We are not sorry to see this improvement going on. Nothing needs improvement worse than the streets of our city."[39]

Besides grading the streets, the Saints also found temporary work in town at their trades. And a few capitalized on their skills quite creatively. One British convert observed, "Many of the brethren obtained employment. Our Scandinavian brethren, with characteristic industry and forethought,

28. William K. Belknap, ca. 1860. Library of Congress, Brady-Handy Photograph Collection, LC-DIG-cwpbh-00590.

purchased trees from the owners of the neighboring forests, from which they manufactured a variety of useful articles. . . . All were busy preparing for the journey."[40] Some of the women found work cleaning the homes of the locals in Keokuk. William Belknap noted in a letter to his sister that he and a local named Mrs. Van Antwerp were going "up to the [Mormon] camp this afternoon as she wants to find some women to clean her house."[41]

Concerning his visit, Belknap, who would later serve as a major general in the Civil War and as secretary of war to President Ulysses S. Grant, told his sister Clara, "Yesterday was Sunday & I wish you had been here to go up to the Mormon Camp with me. They had preaching at three stands in three languages—English, German & Danish. They sing—especially the Danes—very sincerely & are perfectly enthusiastic. It is a strange, strange mystery & if you were here you'd be astonished. There are nearly 3500 here now and 'still they come' by every boat & some of them are genteel and many of the girls very pretty. . . . The Mormons are mainly honest, earnest & sincere."[42] Thus, the passing emigrant Saints did not go unnoticed in Keokuk.[43]

### Westport, Missouri (1854)

As previously noted, Keokuk served as an emigration outfitting post for only one year, as the three hundred miles of extra wagon travel across Iowa, and the added costs, made the change in route unattractive. Thus, church leaders changed the route back to the Missouri River and designated Westport, on the Missouri-Kansas border, as the outfitting post for the 1854 emigrating season. Westport was an established trading center about four miles south of the Kansas City steamboat landing, and the Saints found a place for their outfitting post just on the outskirts of town.

River travel on the Missouri had its advantages over land travel across Iowa, but it posed its own problems, especially the occasional outbreaks of cholera that infected emigrants along the way. The history of Jackson County, Missouri, also had to be considered. The Saints maintained that Jackson County was the center place of Zion, though they had been exiled from the state by Governor Boggs's infamous extermination order in 1838. Debate over the passage of the Kansas-Nebraska Act in the spring of 1854 further heightened tensions, reopening the question of slavery in the U.S. territories and also encouraging a sudden rush of settlers to the free state and proslavery Kansas region.

The Saints were part of a large body of westbound emigrants primarily looking to improve their temporal conditions, but they were chiefly motivated by religious reasons. Historian John Unruh Jr. estimated that during the 1854 overland season, six thousand emigrants headed for Oregon, another twelve thousand for California, and just over three thousand for Salt Lake City.[44]

While he was stationed in England as a missionary in December 1853, William Empey was assigned to shepherd the Saints through St. Louis to Westport. He promptly crossed the Atlantic and arrived in St. Louis on February 7, 1854. Empey was no stranger to emigration as he had been a member of Brigham Young's vanguard company that entered Utah in 1847. Not only did Empey arrange for steamboat travel, oxen, cattle, wagons, and provisions for the Saints, but sadly he was also responsible for buying coffins for the many emigrants who died of cholera along the Missouri River.

Empey's diary entries from early spring of 1854 mention several occasions during which he came into contact with victims. On April 9 he noted, "Many of the saints were dying with the Chollery. I was oblige[d] to git coffins for them." The following day he wrote, "This day I visited the sick & behold thoes that were dying with the collery." On April 20 Empey recorded, "Oh the awful scene to behold to see the children or a husband mourning for his affectionate wife & see a woman lamenting for her husband. It would cause the stoutest man to drop a tear. God be merciful to us & save us from the grasp of distruction."[45]

In 1854 the *Millennial Star* reported an average of 207 deaths a week from cholera in St. Louis during the month of July.[46] The epidemic also traveled along the Missouri River to the Kansas border. The *Liberty Weekly Tribune* noted that during this same month there was "a good deal of cholera on the route [and among] some of the trains, particularly the Mormons suffered severely from this disease." Earlier in May, the *Weekly Columbia Missouri Statesman* had proclaimed, "This scourge is again on the river, in some of the towns. We have heard of a number of deaths on different boats among the Mormon emigrants."[47]

This plague struck the LDS Scandinavian immigrants most severely, but so did another malady. Christian Emil Nielsen recalled that he nearly died when "measles broke out" among the Scandinavian Saints encamped near Westport.[48] Svend Larsen noted that more than two hundred of the seven hundred Scandinavians, including four of his family of seven, died from illness on the way to Utah.[49]

The earliest account of the LDS campground near Westport comes from LDS missionary Dorr P. Curtis, dated April 11, 1854. Curtis recorded that "he had selected a sheltered spot, about a mile from Kansas, with plenty of wood and water, for a camping place." He further noted that eight in his company had died since leaving St. Louis and that the cost of "fare and freight were . . . very high." In his letter, Curtis added, "The inhabitants at Kansas appeared to be quite friendly, and ready to render assistance to the Saints."[50]

Curtis assisted Empey with several financial emigration transactions during this time, including purchasing goods for the emigrants before they headed west. An April 13, 1854, receipt shows that Empey had purchased more than three thousand pounds of bacon and fifteen hundred pounds of beans from St. Louis and then had the goods shipped on a steamboat to the port of Kansas near Westport. Empey's account book also contains hundreds of financial transactions for supplies, provisions, livestock, and more. He also kept receipts for lodgings, including some from the Union Hotel in Westport, where he apparently assisted with securing temporary housing for some emigrants.[51]

In late June Empey wrote a letter to Brigham Young summarizing the 1854 emigration season and providing information about wagons and companies. He reported, "There has been considerable mortality among the Saints this season, about 200 have died."[52]

Despite these devastating losses, some good also resulted from the Westport experience, including new associations and trusted connections. One such connection was the long-lasting relationship Empey formed with local businessman Elijah Milton McGee, who offered Empey a part of his property to house the LDS emigrants just below the landing at the Kansas levee where steamboats came and went. Their business relationship turned into a friendship, which they maintained after Empey left the area. Evidence of such comradeship is apparent in a letter McGee wrote to Empey in Utah the year following the Westport emigration season: "Dear old friend the Long looked for [letter] came to hand yesterday[.] I was verry glad to hear that you all got home safe and that you found your family all well [as] you seartainly are deserving of much and to take so many given people across the plains. . . . You will be rewarded for your enterprise[;] god will if man does not[.] I am always glad to hear from you. Brother E, M, McGee."[53]

It is noteworthy that McGee added "Brother" to his name, as he was likely not a Latter-day Saint. This friendly term of sincere affection is espe-

29. Elijah Milton McGee, 1870. Missouri Valley Special Collections, Kansas City Public Library, Kansas City, Missouri.

cially remarkable considering the fact that just two decades earlier, McGee had taken an aggressive stance against the Saints living in Jackson County.[54]

This scenario suggests that as the Saints marched in and out of this Missouri-Kansas border region near Westport, they were focused on their destination, not on the past conflict in Jackson County. The enemy in 1854 was not the nearby Jackson County citizens or the western Missouri mobocrats but rather the deadly cholera that devastated the Missouri River valley. Although the 1838 Missouri extermination order was technically still in effect, it was not being enforced, and there is no evidence of any overt conflict between the Saints and the people in the Westport area during the 1854 emigration season.[55]

## Mormon Grove, Kansas (1855)

The following year, in 1855, church leaders moved the frontier outfitting post less than sixty miles northwest to Mormon Grove, which was less than five miles west of Atchison, Kansas. Both Atchison and the Saints had something the other needed: Atchison wanted to attract business and settlers, and the Saints needed a temporary settlement where they could find employment to help them purchase overland supplies. Their brief time together proved to be mutually advantageous. For Atchison, the influx of Latter-day Saints jump-started commerce and provided labor to build streets and make other necessary improvements. And for several thousand passing converts in 1855, Mormon Grove on the outskirts of Atchison was a temporary haven and aid to them as they made their way west.[56]

In late August 1854, Brigham Young directed Milo Andrus, an LDS leader residing in St. Louis, to find a place on the western frontier where the incoming European emigrants could safely and temporarily settle before continuing on to Utah. He specifically named Kansas as a possible settlement and outfitting location. On February 17, 1855, Andrus and forty others left St. Louis bound for the western Missouri River frontier. Some were looking for employment, and others were assisting in gathering stock, but most importantly, they wanted to make final preparations for the spring emigration season.[57]

Before mid-March, Andrus and his search party publicly announced that "after mature deliberation," they had chosen Atchison to be the general outfitting place for the 1855 LDS emigration season. Instructions were quickly conveyed to leaders of incoming groups of emigrants to ship for and land at Atchison. On March 20, the LDS agent wrote that he had located four claims comprising 350 acres in a hickory grove approximately four miles west of Atchison that could be used for a general camping ground. He praised it as being a "healthy location" on a high prairie that included two hundred acres of open land for farming.[58]

This "mature deliberation" about Atchison had its genesis in the fall of 1854, in discussions between influential Utahns and Atchison businessmen.

30. Milo Andrus, ca. 1890. Wikimedia Commons.

These discussions, enhanced by Elder Snow's visit to the Kansas region, caused the Saints to decide to outfit at Atchison at least as early as January 1855—with the understanding that the Atchison Town Company would prepare for the LDS emigrants. Two weeks before Andrus left St. Louis to finalize plans for the spring emigration season, "extensive preparations" were reportedly underway in Atchison "for the accommodation [sic] of the Mormon emigrants." Large warehouses were being constructed, and merchants were enlarging their stores to stock more goods and supplies.[59]

Andrus and his associates evidently went to Atchison to make sure preparations were progressing as promised and to finalize Mormon Grove business. When Andrus found that the necessary improvements were in process and that land had been secured on which the emigrants could temporarily live, he gave final approval for Atchison to be "the outfitting point." It wasn't until then that the Saints officially approved and announced that Atchison would be the place of assembly and outfitting for the 1855 emigration season.[60]

Jane C. Robinson Hindley was one of more than two thousand European LDS converts who spent about two months at the Mormon Grove post in 1855. Some work had already been done to prepare the Mormon Grove camp, but three simple sentences in Hindley's diary indicate the reciprocally advantageous relationship between Atchison and the Saints:

> May 23rd we have just arrived at Mormon Grove it is a delightfull place.
>
> May 24th went to see the farm was very much pleased with it.
>
> May 28th went to town and bought some More provision for the plaines.[61]

When Saints such as Hindley disembarked from their steamboats in 1855, Atchison was little more than a bend in the river. After the town was surveyed in the fall of 1854, a number of lots were sold, but very little building construction had begun. Most of the lots had been purchased by the principal businessmen in the Town Company for real estate speculation. One Scottish LDS emigrant arriving in Atchison remembered, "There was then but few inhabitants in this part of the west[;] there was only some three houses in the town."[62] Even by the spring of 1856 Atchison only "contained probably forty houses."[63] The influx of thousands of LDS emigrants into the area in 1855 dwarfed the permanent town population, which didn't even reach five hundred until about 1859.[64]

In actuality, Atchison was little more than a promising "paper town" until the Saints made it their outfitting place and freighters made it their supply post.[65] The size of the river town was likely a key factor in the Saints' decision. Atchison was small and undeveloped and hadn't yet attracted the kind of people or enticements that would prematurely halt the travel of the Utah-bound faithful.

31. Jane Charters Robinson Hindley. Daughters of the Utah Pioneers, Salt Lake City.

Atchison was also a hotbed and de facto territorial headquarters for proslavery advocates. U.S. senator David Rice Atchison's reputation as a rabid Missouri proslavery man attracted people with similar desires to see Kansas become a slave state. The Saints were detached from the national slavery controversy.[66] They posed no threat to either pro- or antislavery factions who were assembling in the territory. Their intention to make their stay in Kansas Territory temporary was sufficient to garner acceptance by both political factions. Even the LDS practice of polygamy was not an issue for the proslavery advocates in Atchison. They recognized that both polygamy and slavery, the "twin relics of barbarism," were being targeted by powerful national forces. At issue was the sovereign right of a people in a state or territory to determine and protect their own vested cultural practices: polygamy for the Saints and slavery for the South.[67] An editorial article in Atchison's newspaper admonished its readers not to join the national crusade against polygamy: "Let us but once join in the attack upon the Mormons, then farewell to the rights of the south."[68] The people of Atchison, sympathetic to the plight of the beleaguered Saints (if not to their polygamous beliefs), were willing to tender the Saints an earnest welcome.

The local trade for cattle and oxen and other outfitting supplies boomed. The demand for cattle exceeded the supply, as the local newspaper reported: "Immense droves of work cattle have been driven and sold to the emigrants and merchants for Salt Lake and yet more are wanted."[69] Atchison businesses had not anticipated that the demand for their goods would be so great. The local newspaper reported, "The emigrants as a general thing, purchased their supplies here and none of our merchants had goods sufficient to meet the demand."[70] Despite these positive reports, LDS converts purchased some essential items before arriving at Atchison. An old settler recalled years later that the Latter-day Saints "brought their wagons on the steamboats and also brought their oxen to move... out to the Grove. They had their boxes to haul their goods in, made to fit their wagons."[71]

Other goods and supplies were also purchased at Atchison. At this early stage of Atchison's development, there were very few merchants. In the fall of 1854, the George T. Challiss Store was the only merchandising establishment open for early squatters and passing emigrants.[72] Newspaper advertisements informed travelers about outfitting and brought trade to businesses like Challiss's store. In the *St. Louis Luminary,* an LDS advertisement counseled each emigrant "to have, when they leave Atchison, one hundred pounds breadstuffs, and a few pounds bacon or dried beef, and as much sugar, tea, coffee, and dried fruit as they calculate to eat during a three month's journey over the Plains."[73]

The Atchison Town Company was intricately involved in arranging for temporary quarters for the Saints. According to nineteenth-century Kansas historian William G. Cutler, "The town company sold the Mormon Immigrant agents a section of land which had been purchased from squatters."[74] This parcel of ground was described in the local Atchison newspaper as being "just back of town" when in actuality it was four and a half miles west of Atchison.[75]

In May 1855 Milo Andrus arrived at Mormon Grove with 550 head of oxen and cows that would be used to cross the plains. He found that church members had already built a small cabin, in which they intended to store provisions. A vegetable garden was planted next to the cabin. The day after his arrival, Andrus "started the hands to ditching in the farm," noting that there was "nearly one mile of the ditch and sod fence completed."[76] This sod fence later attracted the attention of a reporter for the *New York Daily Tribune* who stopped at Mormon Grove during his travels in early 1856. He initially "had no intention of stopping, but something in the appearance of the place arrested [him]," the newsman said. He was particularly fascinated by the neat sod fence, which he said looked as if it had been constructed "on a more scientific plan" than usual fences of that sort.[77] The Saints also plowed and "planted about five acres of corn, potatoes, and garden vegetables."[78]

After the emigrants arrived at Mormon Grove, they were divided according to nationality (British, Scandinavian, and American) and then by overland company. The camps were organized with rows of tents framing streets and alleys between them, the whole arrangement presenting "a city-like appearance."[79] These camps were also grouped into ecclesiastical branches over which church leaders presided. Andrus reported that the health of the camp was "remarkably good though in some instances among so vast a crowd [they had] some sickness."[80]

The sickness referred to was likely cholera, which afflicted the LDS emigrants at Mormon Grove. Some even died along the four-and-a-half-mile stretch on the way there from Atchison. One local observer wrote, "I saw several of the Mormons die of the cholera in their wagon beds before they got started for the Grove."[81] Cholera decimated the LDS emigrants in 1855. The *Deseret Semi-Weekly News* reported that "in that season, as many as sixteen persons were buried in one grave at this same Mormon Grove."[82]

Most of Atchison's residents were friendly toward the Saints, even if the primary motive was economic. One LDS observer was happy to report, "The citizens who are interested in the welfare of the town, and who have invested capital for its improvement, are friendly towards us." He mentioned that the Town Committee in particular was in favor of the Saints' presence in Atchison. The few citizens who were "hostile" to them held little influence. The Saints didn't want their brief stay to be marred by troubled relations with the local settlers and hoped to ensure this peace "by minding [their] own business, and letting theirs alone."[83]

Public perception of Latter-day Saints at the time had been influenced by negative press and inflamed by anti-Mormon rhetoric. The citizens of Atchison were surprised when the Latter-day Saints proved amicable and pleasant. The Atchison newspaper complimented the Saints for the way "they [had] conducted themselves," attesting, "We have [not] the first dispute or quarrel to hear of, and no bad feelings between the citizens and these people have taken place." The article credited "the good behavior on the part of the Mormons, and their strict attention to their own business, [which] gave no room for misunderstanding."[84]

The concentrated LDS presence in the Atchison area lasted from February through July of 1855. As companies with several hundred people in each were readied, they moved out onto the prairies to begin their march westward. The annual LDS immigration statistical report for 1855 indicates that 8 companies, 2,030 emigrants, 337 wagons, 2,433 oxen, 319 cows, 86 horses, and 8 mules had journeyed from Mormon Grove to Utah.[85] Deaths at Mormon Grove were considerable and continued to rise even after these companies moved onto the plains. Before reaching Utah, these 8 companies tallied 120 deaths after departing from Mormon Grove, at least 50 of which were attributed to cholera.[86]

Kansas historians have recognized the important role the Latter-day Saints played in Atchison's early history. William G. Cutler attested that the LDS emigrants' trade was so constant "that Atchison derived as much benefit from the adjacent town [Mormon Grove] as though it had been permanently a portion of her own corporation." He noted that the "actual outfitting was all done in Atchison and this fact first established her business career."[87] Peter Beckman concurred: "A small but significant Utah trade gave Atchison its first real growth in 1855."[88] In Walker D. Wyman's view, Atchison's rise "was due more to the patronage of overland freighters than to outfitting emigrants, but the latter nevertheless furnished a significant segment in its economic history."[89]

### Iowa City, Iowa (1856–58)

The shift to the Eastern Seaboard as a place of disembarkation for LDS immigrants due to the threat of yellow fever and cholera on the Mississippi River was timely. America's rail lines were quickly extending, and by 1856 Iowa City boasted the farthest-west railhead—a development Brigham Young was determined to take advantage of.[90] During the years 1856–58, thousands of European Latter-day Saint converts poured through the ports of Philadelphia, Boston, and New York and onto booked railroad cars. After disembarking in Iowa City, they secured handcarts or wagons and were assigned to an overland trail company.[91]

While Elder John Taylor was stationed at New York as a presiding church leader and LDS emigration agent, he kept an observant eye on immigrants entering other eastern ports and, through careful negotiation, arranged the best rail travel for them that he possibly could. For example, in the early spring of 1856, Taylor wrote the following to Brigham Young:

> I have been appointed to superintend the Emigration in [to] the West. . . . A ship load of passengers is expected here shortly. They come by way of Boston. I have been enabled to make better arrangements for their conveyance to Iowa City by the New York R.R. than by the Boston line; they will therefore come to New York. This may bring the Bostonians to terms another time. I have managed to keep up opposition between the railway companies thus far and wish to continue it. The New York & Erie R.R. Co. bring our emigrants from Boston and thence to Iowa city for 50 cents less per head than the Boston company will take them direct.[92]

Thus, during the 1856 emigration season, European converts were routed from Boston through New York and then carried by rail to Iowa City. The previous year, in 1855, the Chicago and Rock Island Railroads had decided to push their lines as far as this midwestern city.[93] In its Thirteenth General

Epistle, the LDS church's First Presidency not only specified the route for 1856 but also initiated what appeared to be the most economical travel means—the handcart: "[Let] them pursue the northern route from Boston, New York or Philadelphia, and land at Iowa city or the then terminus of the railroad; there let them be provided with hand-carts, on which to draw their provision and clothing, then walk and draw them, thereby saving the immense expense every year for teams and outfit for crossing the plains."[94]

## Rail Travel

After the westward-bound Saints sailed across the Atlantic, they faced the next transportation hurdle: rail travel.[95] Andrew Smith recalled, "It was very rough traveling upon the railways in this country. It is nothing strange to be knocked out of your seat and frequently to pass heaps of cars and engines all smashed up by collision or otherwise. . . . The road from Devon Point [Davenport, Iowa] to Iowa City is awful . . . the rails laid quite crooked."[96] Elizabeth White Steward remembered the rail ride from Boston to Iowa City as "a very unpleasant journey," saying, "We were put in cars that had no seats and we had to sit on our trunks and baggage with no room to lie down at night."[97] George Harrison, who had crossed the Atlantic with Elizabeth and other Saints aboard the *Horizon*, echoed a similar view, noting, "The cars were so crude and the railroad so rough we were all tired out when we arrived in Iowa City."[98] Peter Howard McBride explained, "From Chicago, we had to ride in cattle cars and freight cars."[99]

## Reports from the Press

As LDS emigrants traveled by rail from the East Coast through various cities, a number of newspapers gleaned information about their westward migration to Salt Lake City, where it was well known that the Latter-day Saints were practicing polygamy.[100] The notice of their passing certainly had repercussions as evidenced by both private and public records. The press on both sides of the Mississippi River in Rock Island, Illinois, and Davenport, Iowa, generally reported a one-sided, negative view of the passing Saints as they traveled west by rail toward Iowa City in 1856–57. One female emigrant seemed to get the best of a reporter by facetiously telling him that she had several husbands. The reporter not only included in his article that the woman had "no less than four husbands" but added that "she [was] said to have been an intelligent individual."[101]

In Iowa City the press was also aware of LDS emigration during the spring and summer of 1856. The *Iowa City Republican* ran multiple articles in the same issue regarding the Saints' movement. One reported, "We understand that quite a number of Mormons started last week from their camp two miles west of this city, on their way to serve as 'working bees' in the hive of Deseret." This article and others suggest that the reporters viewed the emigrants as naive, having been beguiled by LDS church leaders.[102]

The fact that the Republicans launched their 1856 campaign against the "twin relics of barbarism"—slavery and polygamy—certainly helps explain why a number of newspapers in Iowa City and on both sides of the Mississippi River would report unfavorably about the Saints passing through.[103]

### Emigration Agent Assistance

Upon reaching Iowa City, emigrants were met by LDS agent Daniel Spencer in 1856 and agent James A. Little in 1857. In Liverpool, Franklin D. Richards had authorized Daniel Spencer "with power to contract & use his name in all matters" pertaining to emigration business for the Saints.[104] Soon thereafter Spencer and Chauncey G. Webb (Webb was asked to assist Spencer with making handcarts) and two other elders, John Van Cott and John Goodsall, left Liverpool for Boston. They disembarked from the *Canada* at Boston on March 30, 1856.[105] The following day Elder Spencer wrote, "Called upon 'Enoch Train' &c. . . . was kindly entertained by Mr. Twain [Train] and all interested with him." On this same day Spencer also wrote, "Called upon Mr. Twichel, president of the Boston & Massachusetts Limited Railroad Company. Mr. Armstrong accompanied me by request of Mr. Twain [Train]." Elder Van Cott, writing the same day, noted, "31st—Spent in company with Brother Spencer in making inquiries as to the prospect of forwarding our passengers on the railroad west."[106]

The next day Spencer wrote, "Spent the day making inquiry price of passage of emigrants to Iowa City. Left proposal with Mr. Twichel for answer which is promised by Saturday next. In the evening called on another office on the subject of emigration agent named R. R. Randall who took my conditions."[107] Spencer sought the very best rail price he could find.

Just one month later, over five hundred Saints disembarked from the *Enoch Train* at Boston and reaped the fruits of Spencer's labor and collaboration with Mr. Train & Company. Soon after arriving in Boston, the Saints were forwarded to Iowa City via New York at the price of $11.50 for passengers fourteen or older and $5.75 for youth ages four to fourteen, while those under four traveled free of charge.[108]

### Iowa City and Its Reception of LDS Emigrants

Throughout the years 1856–58, regardless of the port of entry used or the tracks the Saints traveled on, the farthest railhead west terminated in Iowa City. The town flourished during the years of LDS emigration through the area—mainly thanks to the railroad. In January of 1856, the first train of passenger cars entered Iowa City, whose population was about 3,500. However, in just one year, the population swelled to about 8,000.[109]

A fine location for an emigrant campground lay about two miles west of Iowa City, selected in early May 1856. William Woodward, writing to LDS church leader Heber C. Kimball, described the site as being "on a rising point of land ... a good location & was selected by Bro. D. [Daniel] Spencer," the LDS agent assigned to oversee the westward migration through Iowa City for the year.[110]

Woodward wrote the following entry in his journal when he arrived in Iowa City on June 2, 1856: "Several of the brethren were at the railroad depot waiting our arrival. ... I drove a team from the depot to the camp of the Saints, about two miles west of Iowa City. ... I received a kind welcome from Daniel Spencer. ... A good feeling existed in the hearts of the Saints that were in camp previous to our arrival. Our company swelled the number of the camp to about 1400."[111]

Mary B. (Brannigan) Crandell, who arrived in Iowa City on June 1, 1856, exclaimed, "Oh what a sight met my gaze! Tents pitched, men working at the handcarts, women cooking outdoors, every person busy as a bee. I thought I had got into the hive of Deseret sure. ... Everyone was so kind to me when they found I was alone that I soon dried my tears and went around the camp to see what was going on, everything was so new and strange."[112]

The following year another emigrant recalled the Saints' kind assistance upon her arrival at the Iowa City rail depot. She noted that teams waiting for her company's arrival transported the emigrants to the campground, where a stream of water ran through a grove of trees. "We had no money," she recalled, "so we went to the captain of the camp, James A. Little, and told him of our plight. He furnished us with something to eat.... He also gave permission to get work in Iowa while preparations were being made for the trip across the plains."[113]

Little, who had arrived from St. Louis the night before, was just in time to receive those who had crossed the ocean on the *George Washington* and were on westbound trains. Busily engaged in gathering tents, wagon covers, and provisions in St. Louis, Little worked to prepare for the incoming Saints, and upon their arrival, he quickly oversaw the erection of tents as well as the use of wagon covers for temporary bedding.[114]

Having gathered to the campground where the main body of the Saints were assembled, a decision was made when individuals and companies would depart, one based on the readiness of companies' handcarts and emigrants' assessment of whether or not they had the necessary funds for travel across the plains. Quite a number of the Saints chose to obtain temporary employment in Iowa City, whether they had means for the full journey or not. Most sought the extra money and did not want to squander their time waiting to depart with their homemade handcarts.

### Working While Waiting in Iowa City

Some who worked for a few days in the Iowa City region were tempted to delay their journey onward to the Salt Lake Valley due to the high wages they were offered. Priscilla Merriman Evans, who crossed the ocean on the *S. Curling* in 1856, remembered that she and her family spent three weeks in Iowa City waiting for their handcart to be completed. She explained, "We were offered many inducements to remain there. My husband was offered ten dollars per day to stay and work at this trade of iron roller. But money was no inducement, as we were anxious to go to Zion." Evans also noted that those who remained to improve their circumstances "died of cholera and many apostatized from the church."[115]

Others also ran into misfortune. Elizabeth Sermon, who passed through Iowa City in the summer of 1856, wrote, "We arrived in Iowa and a number of us rented a house at twenty dollars per month.... My husband ... got some work to do at $1.00 per day."[116] Louisa Mellor fared a bit better. She recalled, "We remained in Iowa City from July 8 to July 28, 1856, where my father secured work, and with the means was able to buy two handcarts and some food and clothes to make the journey across the plains."[117]

About this same time, Mary Brannigan Crandell recollected, "While waiting for the handcarts to be finished, three or four of us went to Florence [Iowa,] a beautiful little place, about six miles from Iowa City, to see if we could get some sewing to do.... A lady by the name of Johnson engaged me at five dollars a week, and my board, the other girls got more.... I cut and made dresses for the lady and taught one of her boys to write." Mary soon made friends with the Johnson family, who, Mary noted, "treated [her] like their own daughter." Eventually Mrs. Johnson asked her, "What will you do hauling a handcart across the plains? Why your hands will be blistered the first day, and you have never been accustomed to hard work." Mary responded, "Dear lady I know you are interested in me and I feel grateful for your kindness, but I shall try it."[118] She did, as did nearly three thousand others. In all, ten companies left with handcarts from Iowa City or later from Florence between 1856 and 1860, and of the ten, eight had successful journeys. The fourth and fifth handcart companies would meet with tragedy: about two hundred Saints departed late from Iowa City in 1856 because they hadn't been able to obtain ships in Liverpool earlier in the year, and they perished as the winter set in.[119]

### Florence, Nebraska (1859–63)

In 1859 Florence, Nebraska, served as the frontier outfitting post for the emigrating Saints. A dozen years earlier the Saints had gathered near Florence, at Winter Quarters, and Florence would become the point of emigrant land travel from 1859 to 1863. Trail historian William G. Hartley noted that during these years, "Florence became a busy outfitting center each May, June, and July for crowds of LDS travelers. The Florence story involves nearly ten thousand Saints, thousands of tons of supplies, at least fifty-five skillfully organized wagon companies, one thousand wagons, thousand[s] of cattle, corrals, LDS boweries, stores, storage, river docks and steamboat arrivals."[120]

Florence replaced Iowa City as the outfitting point in 1859 when LDS emigration agents realized that traveling by train and steamboat through Missouri upriver to Florence was less challenging than traveling nearly three hundred miles across Iowa.[121] By April 1861, the same month that the American Civil War began, Florence was bustling. About two weeks after Confederates had fired on Fort Sumter, Jacob Gates arrived in Florence, where months earlier he had been appointed as the emigration agent. Gates, along with Nathaniel V. Jones, East Coast LDS agent, had negotiated railroad contracts in New York. Then Gates had traveled to Chicago and ordered 111 wagons at about $65 apiece from Peter Schuttler, and purchased other supplies prior to his arrival in Florence.[122]

The 1861 emigration season was unique not only because it was launched at the beginning of the Civil War but also because it saw the beginning of the "down and back" program, which church leaders instituted due to a surplus of oxen in Utah. The three main purposes of the program were "(1) to bring west poor immigrants at low cost, (2) to bring west goods purchased cheaply in the East, and (3) to move surplus Utah oxen and flour east to Florence to be sold or traded for good[s]."[123] It is estimated that a combined total of nearly four thousand immigrants from Europe and Saints from the eastern U.S. made their way through Florence to Utah during the year.[124] These migrant Saints were assisted by about two hundred "down and back" wagons traveling from Utah to the banks of the Missouri River with needed supplies.[125]

Thousands of Saints passed through Florence during the 1862 and 1863 seasons, and the "down and back" wagons continued to provide assistance. During the Florence emigration years (1859–63), Andrew Jenson noted, "Florence was a flourishing and growing town . . . but being so close to the new city of Omaha, the city of Florence . . . had to yield to Omaha as a commercial center, and . . . in due course of time became part of Omaha."[126]

### Wyoming, Nebraska (1864–66)

When Latter-day Saint Amos M. Musser passed through Florence in the late 1850s, he reported, "Apostates are becoming as thick in this country as the lice were in Egypt in the days of Phareoh [sic]."[127]

By 1864 the outfitting post had been moved from Florence to Wyoming, about forty miles south of Florence.[128] The number of LDS apostates

32. Amos Milton Musser, ca. 1890. Church History Library, PH 327.

near Florence who tried to dissuade the incoming European emigrants from going to Utah presented one valid reason for moving the post. H. N. Hansen reasoned:

> In previous years the starting point had been Florence, Nebraska about 40 miles farther up the river, and about four miles from Omaha. Perhaps the principal cause for this change was the fact that this latter place having so long been on the line over which the mormons . . . traveled, . . . many of the citizens of Omaha and Florence were apostate mormons. Some having refused to journey any further having become weak in the faith before reaching the mountains, and others after having gone there had become disgusted and returned and located at these places. It was not desirable by the leaders of

the mormon emigration to take the people where they would be so close in contact with these apostates, as they might bring them such information as would not be desirable for them to obtain, thus leading perhaps others to apostatize.[129]

Other practical reasons existed for moving the frontier outfitting post. By 1864 the transcontinental railroad tracks had moved farther west, and the distance to Wyoming was shorter for river steamers that departed from St. Joseph.[130]

Joseph W. Young, nephew of Brigham Young, served as the Wyoming emigration agent in 1864, providing welcome relief to the weary travelers. As one convert noted, "Immediately on our arrival at Wyoming we received provissions from the church agent, consisting of flour, pork, dryed apples, rice, sugar, and also soap for washing."[131]

Despite the hospitality he showed the Saints, Joseph Young, for practical reasons, was eager for them to move on. Elder John T. Gerber noted that by late June 1864 "about a thousand Scandinavian Saints and one or two hundred Saints of other nationalities" were encamped at Wyoming.[132] Soon thereafter, on July 4, Joseph Young wrote a letter to the LDS agent in New York, stating, "Gen. McClelland's [voyage] company came up last night, and oh! my soul and all that is great, ain't we rather busy and noisy today. I shall send these people off regardless of everything else. They will eat us up here in three weeks."[133] Young did last, and over 2,600 LDS emigrants left Wyoming, Nebraska, for Utah during the 1864 emigration season.[134] Thousands more on their way to the Salt Lake Valley passed through Wyoming during the 1865–66 seasons in hundreds of wagons.[135]

### Emigration at Union Pacific Railroad Towns in the Late 1860s

Railroad towns erupted mile by mile as the Union Pacific rails moved west. Historian John K. Hulmston observed:

> For three years following the Civil War, Mormon departure centers followed the path of the Union Pacific Railroad as it was built westward. By 1866 workers had extended it into the heart of Nebraska Territory to North Platte. In the final year of the church trains (1868)

33. Joseph W. Young, ca. 1860s. Church History Library, PH 1700 3400.

Mormons utilized two departure points. The railroad builders, moving swiftly across the broad, level plains of southern Wyoming Territory, reached the young city of Laramie by the spring of 1868. The Mormons organized wagon trains here for three months. Pulling up stakes in Laramie, the Mormons next moved their terminal even closer to the Salt Lake Valley, and for the remaining nine months of 1868 the railroad town of Benton City, Wyoming Territory, served as the departure point for Utah-bound immigrants.[136]

### The Saints and the Completion of the Union Pacific Railroad

By 1868 three thousand European Saints had arrived in Salt Lake City, and many were ready to go to work on the Union Pacific (UP) Railroad;

some had even provided labor for the UP before they arrived in the Salt Lake Valley.[137]

Brigham Young could see the advantage of the rails and had outlined where track should be laid when he crossed the plains in 1847, over two decades before the track reached Utah and united with California. Brigham Young recalled:

> I do not suppose we traveled one day from the Missouri here, but what we looked for a track where the rails could be laid with success, for a railroad through this Territory to the Pacific Ocean.... When we came here over the hills and plains in 1847 we made our calculations for a railroad across the country.... We want the benefits of the railroad for our emigrants so that after they land in New York they may get on board the cars and never leave them again until they reach this city.[138]

Latter-day Saint emigrant and later church leader George A. Smith added,

> We started from Nauvoo in February, 1846, to make a road to the Rocky Mountains. A portion of our work was to hunt for the railroad. We located a road to Council Bluffs, bridging the streams, and I believe it has been pretty nearly followed by the railroad. In April 1847, President Young and one hundred and forty-three pioneers left Council Bluffs, and located and made the road to the site of this city [Salt Lake City]. A portion of our labor was to seek out the way for a railroad across the continent, and every place we found that seemed difficult for laying the rails we searched out a way for the road to go around or through it.[139]

In April 1847 Brigham Young chose Jacob Weiler to travel with him to Utah in the vanguard company. Weiler noted, "Many times when gathered around the camp fire we would plan and talk over the future of our dreary wastes through which we were traveling. I remember more than once the possibility of a railroad to the Pacific was spoken of as being in the near future."[140]

Brigham Young was also one of the first to buy stock in the UP Railroad. By 1852 he had asked Congress for a transcontinental railroad. By 1863 he

34. Jacob Weiler, ca. 1880s. Church History Library, PH 1700 168.

was named a member of the UP board of directors, and by the late 1860s he had arranged with the UP to bring incoming church members onboard their trains at the lowest fares possible.[141] By 1868 he had contracted with UP officials for thousands of Saints to help with grading in Utah Territory for 30 cents a cubic yard.[142]

The following year, on May 10, 1869, the UP and the Central Pacific linked at Promontory Point, and the transcontinental railroad was complete. The Saints had made a significant contribution to the grading in Utah. In fact, historian Stephen E. Ambrose even included a chapter about their contribution, "Brigham Young and the Mormons Make the Grade," in his book about the building of the transcontinental railroad.[143] The completion of the transcontinental railroad allowed the Saints to cross the plains in about a week instead of several months. It was a tremendous blessing to the LDS emigration operation and to many other travelers in the late nineteenth century.

# 10

## LDS Emigration and Military Posts

Just as emigrating Saints took advantage of LDS frontier outfitting posts during the decades between their vanguard journey to Salt Lake City and the coming of the transcontinental railroad (1848–68), they also benefited from the military posts aiding westbound emigrants at Fort Laramie and Fort Bridger.

LDS wagon teamster Zebulon Jacobs, heading west to Utah in 1862, wrote, "Fort Laramie ... half way to our mountain home."[1] Fort Laramie was not only the halfway point for Latter-day Saints on the overland trail but was also considered the most important stopping place for emigrants headed to Oregon, California, or Utah and is recognized as America's first inland trade center.[2] Named for the obscure French trapper Jacques La Ramie,[3] the fort functioned as a vital center for basic provisions, communication, and commerce. It also served as a central cultural connecting point for Native Americans and French traders, U.S. soldiers and government surveyors, argonauts and artists, Christian missionaries and Latter-day Saint emigrants, travelers, and others.

Although a view of Fort Laramie from each group's perspective merits scholarly investigation, this chapter focuses on LDS emigrants' descriptions of life in the vicinity of Fort Laramie between 1847 and 1868. These accounts, recorded in documents covering the two decades the overland trail was used before the completion of the transcontinental railroad (1869), capture a kaleidoscope of human activity at or near the fort during the mid-nineteenth century. After the discovery of gold in California, the massive amount of westbound travel on the overland trail beginning in 1849 astonished the nation. That same year the U.S. government purchased Fort Laramie, which served as a military post for the next four decades

35. Fort Laramie. Drawing by Frederick Piercy. In James Linforth, *Route from Liverpool to Great Salt Lake Valley, Illustrated with Steel Engravings and Woodcuts from Sketches Made by Frederick Piercy* (Franklin D. Richards, 1855).

(1849–90).[4] Due to the heavy emigration stimulated by the gold rush, the primary function of the military units stationed at the fort was "to protect the emigrants and the transcontinental communications which followed the Oregon Trail."[5] For the most part, U.S. soldiers did not need to interact much with the self-sufficient LDS emigrant trains, but occasional exceptions to this pattern arose. The most significant occurred in 1854 when a Danish LDS emigrant lodged a complaint at the fort about the theft of one of his lame cows, which ultimately resulted in what became known as the Grattan Massacre.

This slaughter occurred on August 19, when at his own request Brevet 2nd Lieutenant John L. Grattan led a volunteer military company of twenty-nine men into a Sioux settlement to arrest the suspect who had stolen the cow and bring him back to Fort Laramie. In hindsight, it appears the military could have been instrumental in restoring the value of the lost property, mediating justly between both parties and preventing the conflict. Instead, Lieutenant Grattan, a young, hot-headed Irishman, newly arrived from West Point and eager for promotion, made a mountain out of a molehill, which cost him and his company their lives. The ambitious frontier lieutenant foolishly precipitated his own slaughter by attempting to dictate to, rather than negotiate with, Conquering Bear, chief of the Sioux, through an intoxicated, antagonistic French interpreter named Augusta Lucia.[6]

Members of several LDS companies who passed by the scene of carnage provided a description of the massacre. Job Smith, a company captain who learned about the slaughter a day after it occurred, explained that the Native American, on finding the lame cow, "killed her and took the meat to the Indian camp." Smith further noted that "the emigrant, on going back after the cow, not finding her, went straight to the Fort and complained of the Indians for stealing his cow, whereupon the commander at the Fort ordered out a posse ... to go and make claim for the cow ... [and] whiskey was dispensed."[7]

John Allen Sutton, a nine-year-old member of Smith's company, recalled that soldiers from Fort Laramie were sent to the scene with a cannon and an interpreter.[8] He also recollected that "while parleying with the Indians there was a misunderstanding between the chief and the interpreter. The captain ordered one of the men to shoot the chief, which he did, and in less than twenty minutes the Indians killed all the company, broke their cannon, and threw it into the Platte. The emigrants greatly feared that the Indians would take Fort Laramie."[9] Watkin Rees noted that soon after the soldiers were killed, a courier arrived at their camp who "was going east for reinforcement, while the people at the fort had shut themselfs up in fear lest the Sues [Sioux] whould return and kill them all."[10]

Robert L. Campbell provided a vivid description of the soldiers' burial place, located about eight miles from James Bordeaux's trading post: "They are buried close by the road, I have Visited the grave & some of the mens heads are not even covered. it was the Settlers that buried them as the remainder of the Soldiers could not leave the fort being few in Number. . . . Several Military gloves were lying ... close by."[11] Twenty-three-year-old Elizabeth Graham MacDonald, an emigrant traveling in the LDS Daniel Garn Company, added, "We saw the signs of the fatal contest; it had been so recent that some of the fires of the camp were still burning."[12]

During the years 1857–58, the Saints were more hesitant to come to Fort Laramie due to the Utah War. This conflict arose following a misunderstanding between church members in Utah Territory and the U.S. government, when President Buchanan and his administration incorrectly surmised that the Utah Saints would resist the replacement of Governor Brigham Young. As a result and without proper investigation, 2,500 soldiers were sent to Utah under the direction of Colonel Albert Sidney Johnston.[13]

Correspondence sent to Brigham Young from points on the overland trail reveals the Saints' concerted efforts to discover the military expedition's intentions. One letter noted, "We shall endeavor to learn all we can about the Troops and report as often as expedient. Bro. N. V. Jones informs us that on the 16th he had conversation with Reshaw who had just arrived from Laramie from whom he learned . . . he had orders to remove our stations from the line."[14] The following year, Latter-day Saint Isaiah Coombs recorded, "We intend passing the fort under the cover of night that we may escape observation. There is but one co. of soldiers there & of course we do not fear them but if they should see us they would send an express to Col. Johnston informing him of our movements which might result in our capture. We wish to pass along unobserved."[15]

## Beyond Kindness

Yet years earlier there was no need for passing LDS migrants to conceal themselves while traveling near Fort Laramie. In fact, in the fall of 1849 Major Winslow F. Sanderson had shown great kindness to LDS missionaries traveling east from the Salt Lake Valley. Elder John Taylor, headed to France to initiate church proselytizing there, told of the excellent order observed at the post by some of his companions who had passed through Fort Laramie the previous summer on their way to Utah. Taylor's glowing description of Fort Laramie's remarkable transformation from a commercial trading post to a fully operational U.S. military outpost was certainly a tribute to Major Sanderson's excellent leadership and the hard work of those under his command.

Taylor noted that the members of his traveling company were "astonished at the great improvements which [had] been made [there] in a few months' time. There was an air of quietness and contentment of neatness and taste, which in connection with the kind reception given by the polite and gentlemanly commander, Major Sanderson[,] made us feel as if we found an oasis in the Desert."[16] Elder Erastus Snow, on his way to open missionary work in Denmark, noted, "Maj. Sanderson and his officers received us kindly and supplied us with such articles as we needed at the original cost."[17] Such interaction continued to affect ongoing LDS emigration.

At times the soldiers and the officers went beyond kindness and demonstrated an unwelcome interest in the welfare of the young LDS women. While encamped one mile from Fort Laramie, Mary Hammer recalled that the captain of her company, Andrew H. Scott, wanted the group to rest for a day while the soldiers inspected the company's guns and wagons. The soldiers, however, apparently had additional things on their mind to inspect. Mary claimed, "Some of the soldiers became very familiar with the young girls of the company and [our] Captain fearing trouble ordered the company to leave early the next morning before the soldiers were up."[18]

Agnes Caldwell Southworth recalled another incident during which one of the officers at the fort tried to seduce a young Scottish woman, Christina McNeil, a member of the ill-fated James G. Willie handcart company.[19] Agnes noted, "The officer used the time in trying to persuade Christina to stay there, proposing to her, and showing her the gold he possessed, telling her what a fine lade [lady] he would make of her." When he was unsuccessful, the officer "tried discouraging her, telling her how the handcart company would never reach Utah, because of the severe cold[;] they would die of exposure and hunger. . . . She told him in plain language she would take her chance with the others even though it may mean death." Finally, when the officer knew he could not persuade her to desert neither her company nor her beliefs, he showed his admiration for her faith by giving her "a large well cured ham and wish[ing] her well in her chosen adventure."[20]

## Interaction with Native Americans

Just as the nature of the Saints' interaction with the military at Fort Laramie varied, so did their experiences with the local Native Americans in the fort region. Furthermore, it appears that some LDS pioneers may have taken more time to interact with the Indigenous people than did other West Coast–bound emigrants, especially those who were seized by gold fever in the mid-nineteenth century.

Margaret Gay Judd Clawson recalled of her journey to Salt Lake City in 1849, "The California emigrants traveled much faster than the Mormon emigrants."[21] In addition, the Saints did not have as far to travel as the California emigrants did, and they traveled in a consistent, organized manner. They journeyed as a religious community concerned with the individual welfare of each member of an ordered company, whereas the argonauts appear to have generally hurried with not as much thought about the needs of those with whom they were journeying.[22]

Taking a bit more time to cross the plains provided some interesting cultural contact for the Saints. One amusing incident occurred in the life of twenty-seven-year-old Christopher Jacobs when he crossed the plains in 1847.[23] Jacobs recalled that while trading at Fort Laramie, some of the boys in his company proposed that he turn somersaults for the entertainment of about five hundred Native Americans who were assembled: "They were amazed. They stood on the ground and jumped up and down on it to see if it would spring with them. Finding that the ground was solid they came and felt of my legs . . . much surprised that such a thing was possible."[24]

Just as the Native Americans couldn't figure out the magic behind the somersaults, the LDS pioneers couldn't predict the behavior of the Indigenous people. Although pioneer accounts reveal that most were friendly to the passing Saints, the Native Americans, particularly the Sioux, posed a continual threat to their livestock. In 1852 Ann Rogers Snow remembered that the Sioux frequently made contact with their emigrant company camp near Fort Laramie. She noted, "They were well dressed in their buckskin suits which were all trimmed with beads. One day there were several rode past our train and tried to stampede our cattle, but we were blessed and the cattle were not frightened. Thus the Indians were unable to carry out their designs."[25]

Other accounts reveal that the Native Americans at times considered the young LDS women more desirable than livestock and were even willing to barter their cherished horses for them. In 1848 Mosiah Hancock noted that when his company neared Fort Laramie, "[they] just about got into some trouble with a large company of Sioux Indians. John Alger started in fun to trade a 16-year-old girl to a young Chief for a horse. But the Chief was in earnest! [They] got the thing settled, however, and were permitted to go without the loss of Lovina."[26]

Six years later, thirty-seven-year-old Thomas Ambrose Poulter recalled a similar incident when he witnessed thousands of Sioux Indians camped outside Fort Laramie, waiting for their government rations to arrive. He remembered, "The young bucks came out to trade for a wife. They offered three ponies for a wife. Some of the girls for the fun of it made a trade which nearly ended in a fuss."[27]

In 1856 a young brave proved a bit more persistent in attempting to purchase Kezia Giles from her father, William. The young Indian rode up to a campfire at Fort Laramie and fixed his eyes on the sixteen-year-old girl.[28] He communicated to the company that he wanted to purchase Kezia and offered her father his own "squaw" and his best pony in exchange. Rebuffed in his attempt, the young brave left the campfire disgruntled and angry. This encounter created apprehension throughout the company, and Kezia was warned to never lose sight of the camp.[29] Other overlanders had similar experiences with Native Americans on their journey west. Such cultural misunderstandings could become flash points that resulted in conflict.

Fortunately, LDS companies rarely became involved in these direct hostilities. The most notable exception occurred near Fort Laramie on September 22, 1865, when the Minor G. Atwood Company was attacked by Native Americans.[30] Twenty-eight-year-old Danish convert Francis Christian Grundvig recorded the tragic account of seeing his beloved wife, Jensine, kidnapped during the assault.[31] While the company was camped near the fort, a band of local Native Americans began stealing their cattle, and some of the men in the company were sent to look for their livestock. Francis described the terrible events that followed, which left an excruciating memory he carried throughout his life:

> My wife became very tired, we got behind the train[.] our boy stayed with the wagons[.] the train finally reached a creek[;] their [sic] was lots of thick brush along it. A lot of Indians were hid in the brush. When the boys drove the cattle to water[,] five of them were wounded by the Indians; then every man in camp came out with their guns and frightened the Indians away. At that time my wife and I were about ½ a mile from camp and some of the Indians came to-wards us and with a big yell started to shoot at me while one Indian took my wife on a horse and rode away with her. I was hit by four or five

arrows the last one hit in my right hip. I pulled it out and dropped it thinking it was all out, while the whole arrow head was left in the hip bone. It left a running sore. The Indians thought me dead so they left. I crawled to camp on my hands and knees with out assistance. I carried the arrow head in my side for a year and eleven months.

He further remarked, "All the bodily suffering passed through for nearly two years was but small compared with the Anguish and sorrow for the loss of my wife. I have often stood by the workbench with the tears running down my cheeks."[32]

As noted, such tragedy was the exception. LDS–Native American relations on the trail west were more often than not harmonious. Joel Judkins Terry wrote that after a Sioux war party determined that the approaching Latter-day Saint emigrants were not the Crow Indians, their enemy, they "commenced shaking hands with [them] . . . [and] gladly escorted [them] to Laramy."[33]

Ann Gregory Wilkey, traveling in the Joseph W. Young Company in 1853, recalled that two of her male relatives became lost on their way to obtain provisions at Fort Laramie. She wrote, "Thinking to get there quicker they crossed the mountains and got lost. They traveled on and on and got into a cactus bed. As it was night they could not see. After a while they came to an Indian camp, the Indians were friendly to them."[34] Henry Pugh, the company clerk, recorded that after setting up camp near Fort Laramie and caring for the cattle, the Saints began to sing, and "the songs of Zion were heard throughout the camp." He further noted, "We were visited by several Indians, all of who behaved themselves courteously and honestly."[35]

One amusing incident occurred when some Native Americans experienced what appears to be their first encounter with the peculiar handcarts the Saints used on the plains.[36] Mary Powell Sabin explained, "At Fort Laramie there was an encampment of sixteen thousand Indians, they were holding a treaty. They were camped for a distance of thirty miles up the river. We camped near the river that night but without a fire. The next morning we met five hundred Indians on the road. They were on their way to the treaty. Father presented some of them with beautiful peacock feathers.

This pleased them very much. They stopped and looked at our handcarts. 'Little wagons, little wagons,' said they. How the squaws laughed."[37]

## Trade with Native Americans

The desire for trade often led to contact between the Saints and the Sioux. In late August 1849, Jesse Morgan described his company's interaction with three Native Americans who escorted them five miles to a camp to trade. Morgan wrote, "Sioux is a new trading post, fifteen miles east of Fort Laramie; they received us with friendship; we stopped some four hours and traded with them, giving flour, meal, powder, lead and cloths, for buffalo robes and moccasins."[38]

In 1851 the Levi Hammon Company spent two hours at Fort Laramie, where they encountered "many Indians at and near the Fort [and] all was Frindly."[39] That same year Ossian F. Taylor recorded, "Indians are camped all about the fort, and up and down the river. They come about our wagons as thick as bees about a hive, to beg some serga [sugar] [and] buisea [booze?] and to sell moccasons [sic] &c. but they seem to be very friendly."[40]

Two years later Hannah Cornaby recalled the unexpected generosity of one "squaw": "Reaching Fort Laramie, we made a short halt when many Indians visited our camp; the squaws being particularly anxious to exchange their commodities for groceries, &c. I remember one squaw in particular, who took quite an interest in our dear little daughter; measured her foot, and next day returned with a very tastily embroidered pair of moccasins which she placed upon her feet, refusing to take anything in payment."[41]

Throughout the following decade, trade between the Latter-day Saints and Native Americans remained active. In mid-August 1862, a few miles east of Fort Laramie, Jens C. A. Weibye wrote that his company "passed in front of 100 Indians who had lined up on the roadside for the purpose of trading. They were friendly and had their camp near the road."[42]

## Wagon Repair and Animal Purchases

The abundance of trade opportunities with Native Americans and others on the trail no doubt lessened the need for Latter-day Saints and other westbound emigrants to visit Fort Laramie for supplies. Historian John

36. Jens C. A. Weibye, 1872. Church History Library, PH 1700 2381.

D. Unruh Jr.'s monumental work *The Plains Across* describes in detail the multitude of private entrepreneurs who set up shop along the overland trail, offering a variety of services.[43] In addition, when Latter-day Saints needed repairs, they often had men in their own companies who had the supplies and skills to make them.

In 1853, when British artist Frederick Piercy began a sketch of Fort Laramie, he noted the self-sufficiency exemplified by his company's captain. On August 23 he wrote that the road near Fort Laramie "became the roughest [they] had had," saying, "We broke one wheel, one axle, and one tongue, which Elder [Daniel A.] Miller fixed as usual. He is really a model of a captain, and deserves great credit for the masterly manner in which he managed everything, and the good-humored energy with which he surmounted every difficulty."[44]

Still, a visit to Fort Laramie often proved not only useful but also necessary for church wagon trains. In 1853 William K. Sloan wrote, "Arriving at Laramie we remained there two days shoeing some cattle and repairing wagons."[45] Fort Laramie also provided the Saints the opportunity to exchange their weary cattle and oxen for fresh animals needed for the journey to the Salt Lake Valley, an invaluable service. As early as 1847, Perrigrine Sessions wrote, "[At Fort Laramie,] we bought several yoke of Oxen, repaired our wagons, set tires, &c."[46] Some chose to avoid the fort and purchased trail animals at nearby trading posts. In 1855 Henry Sylvester Earl wrote that at a "small trading post" near Fort Laramie, "[they] bought 10 yoke of oxen at one hundred dollars, four yoke."[47]

French traders conducted quite a business near Fort Laramie, purchasing worn trail animals and then selling them after the stock had sufficiently recovered. In 1847 Jesse Wentworth Crosby explained that the French merchants "buil[t] for dwellings a kind of fort built of unburnt brick that does well," and noted, "As some of our cattle gave out we exchanged with the traders for fresh ones, they sell and buy cattle."[48]

Some LDS emigrants believed that these traders, in league with Native Americans, had resorted to cattle theft to enhance their profits. Andrew Jackson Shupe wrote that same year, "Men was detached to go to laramy in perSuit of Som Stolen horses. on the evening of the 15th 2 of those men returned to the camp with news that they had found Some of the horses in the posseshion of Some frenchman and they refused to gav them up."[49]

Traveling through the area a decade after Shupe, Henry McCune noted that when his company arrived at Fort Laramie, "[they] found some French traders who had a big herd of cattle, supposed to be cattle stolen from other companies by the Indians, with whom they were in league. [McCune's] father purchased a yoke of oxen of them, to replace the yoke that was run off by their emissaries, the Indians."[50]

Two years later Thomas McIntyre, a member of the George Rowley Company, told of the company's good fortune on a venture to obtain a wagon wheel from the fort. On July 27, 1859, he wrote, "Two of our boys are dispatched to the Fort to trade for a wagon wheel to fill the place of the one which was broken on the 11th." On their way to the fort, they found a wagon wheel in the river, "which answered the purpose very well."[51] Most emigrants were not as lucky—the prices were generally very high or no supplies were available for purchase.

### The Absence or High Cost of Provisions

With few or no options to resupply, the Saints worried about the lack of provisions at the fort. One such case is illustrated by a disappointed William Holmes Walker, who upon reaching Fort Laramie in 1847 wrote, "We were out of provisions and could not get but a small supply, indeed, at any price."[52] William K. Sloan also recalled that Fort Laramie was short of provisions during his migration in 1853, a situation that appeared "rather gloomy": "[We] were disappointed in not getting a sufficient quantity of supplies, the commissary claimed to be short themselves, having had to furnish others who were ahead of us, more than was expected. We had to be content with two barrels of mushy pickled pork three sacks of flour and one sack of beans."[53]

The lack of provisions became especially critical for the James G. Willie handcart company, which met with disaster in the fall of 1856.[54] Amasa Christian Linford recalled, "On reaching Fort Laramie, no provisions were found, making another reduction in rations necessary. The beef supply was entirely cut off."[55]

Even when provisions were available, the Saints often had to purchase them at exorbitant prices. "Provisions very high," wrote Luke Gallup in 1850. He then proceeded to give a detailed list of the cost of several items: "Flour $18, pr. hund. Bacon $18, sugar & coffee 50 cts pr. lb.—other things in proportion. Iron is worth almost nothing, yet Blacksmith work is very high. Shoes for a yoke of oxen will cost $8. Nails 75 cts pr doz or over $13 a yoke besides the labor of setting them on."[56] The following year, in 1851, Alfred Cordon recorded, "Went to the fort to get Supplies and they Charged us any price they had a minde."[57] In 1860 Charles R. Savage added, "Several of the Brethern went to Laramie to get shoes, nails, &c—none to be got, prices very high for every thing."[58]

### Accidents and Medical Assistance

As the only site for medical aid between Fort Kearny and Fort Hall, Fort Laramie also handled the accidents and medical emergencies of the Latter-

37. Thomas McIntyre, ca. 1860s. Church History Library, PH 200.

day Saint travelers and other emigrants.[59] One serious incident occurred in 1852 when the steamboat *Saluda*, noted earlier, exploded on the Missouri River near Lexington, Missouri. Thirteen-year-old Ira Brown was severely injured in the explosion, and eventually his leg had to be amputated at Fort Laramie. The surgery was a success, and later that year he arrived in the Salt Lake Valley with other surviving members of his family.[60]

Three years later another amputation proved to be less successful. While the Richard Ballantyne Company were encamped near Fort Laramie, an LDS boy accidentally shot a woman in his company named Ann Palmer. The ball shattered her knee. Charles Ramsden Bailey recalled, "The Poor woman was taken back to [Fort] Lareme And She Suffered terrible[.] they

Cut her leg of [off] above the Knee but they had to Cut above again And again And She finealey died[.] this Caused a Sad feeling in the Company as She was a beautiful Singer And the life of the Camp."[61]

Eight years later Norwegian convert Lorena Jacobson was run over when she leaned out of her wagon to give her baby to her husband. Her daughter, Elizabeth Isabelle, recalled that because of the accident, her father had to seek employment at Fort Laramie, which brought this Norwegian family into contact with Native Americans. Elizabeth wrote, "They carried mother into an old log house which had no doors or windows and large cracks in the walls. Mother was helpless, the baby was ill, and I was left with a family of seven to care for, although I was only twelve years old." She further noted, "Father had to work at the fort for our bread. The Indians were very friendly with us and often came in to see what they could do for us."[62]

### Trading at Fort Laramie for Needed Provisions

Latter-day Saint overlanders visited Fort Laramie for diverse reasons, including to stock up on a variety of provisions. Samuel Woolley, who stopped at the fort on July 15, 1856, recorded the services and supplies he purchased as well as their cost: "I got the watch fixed I carry, paid $1.50[,] bot 1 lb raisins for .50[,] tin cup 10[,] candy 10[,] Hair Pins 25."[63] Others visited simply for food. In the fall of 1849, William Appleby recalled, "I visited the Fort . . . purchased twenty eight pounds of Bacon at ten cents per lb. and carried the same on my back to camp some two miles."[64]

Some of the LDS emigrants opted to trade rather than purchase needed supplies. Miles Romney, a member of the 1850 Edward Hunter Company, wrote, "The Company stopt at the fort 3 days to trade for Provissions."[65] Albert Jones, a member of the ill-fated 1856 Edward Martin handcart company, recorded, "I sold an extra over-coat at Laramie to one of the cooks for some dried Peaches, apples, and a little bacon and some flour, which made me feel, if not the richest man in the camp." Both the food and the coat were needed to withstand the frozen, snow-covered plains of Wyoming.[66]

Hannah Lapish apparently could not wait to obtain food at Fort Laramie. In 1860, barely surviving on a daily half-pound ration of flour, she and other members of the Daniel Robinson Company were forced to reckon with the scarcity. She traded her expensive British jewelry for seven hundred pounds of flour at a trading post just east of the fort. One member of her company gratefully recalled, "This so greatly increased our food supply and lasted us until we were met by a relief party at Green River [Wyoming]."[67]

## The Magnetic Pull of the Mail

The desire for correspondence caused many emigrants to cross the irregular Platte River from its north side to visit the fort, thus enabling them to receive news from home and send letters to loved ones.[68] A number of journals and diaries attest to the importance of mail at Fort Laramie and along the overland trail. In the summer of 1850, an official postal service was established between Fort Laramie and Salt Lake City. Samuel H. Woodson received a contract and salary of $19,500 to carry the U.S. mail each month from Independence, Missouri, to the "Mormon Mecca" and back, on a thirty-day schedule.

The following year this mail line was divided into two, with Fort Laramie serving as the midway point between Independence and Salt Lake City. The mail from each of these cities was to be delivered to the fort on the fifteenth of each month.[69] However, as winter set in in 1852 and the mail service hadn't arrived, Brigham Young wrote to the Utah delegate in Congress, "So little confidence have we in the present mail arrangements that we feel considerable dubiety of your receiving this or any other communication from us."[70] However, late or not, the mail did arrive at Fort Laramie, as did eager LDS emigrants and other overlanders anxious for a letter.

The following year LDS captain John Brown wrote, "At Larime I got a letter from home[;] all well."[71] That he noted receiving a letter at all indicates a sense of relief and satisfaction in this one brief sentence.[72] Several years later Samuel Woolley visited Fort Laramie and wrote, "Mailed the 4 letters I wrote.... I received a letter from my Dearly Beloved Catherine[.] I was truly pleased to hear from her & that her & the children were all well, & it caused my heart to rejoice to read the sentiments of affection & confidense, reposed to me & that all things move on well at the home of the Saints. & that crops are generally good."[73]

At times the Saints became frustrated when there simply wasn't time to put a pencil to paper. On July 28, 1855, John Parson recorded, "Arrived at Fort Laramie at 3 o'clock. The mail from the [Salt Lake] Valley was in and about to start, so that we had no time to write, but posted the letters we wrote at Plum Creek to Elders Snow and Ballantyne."[74]

Parson's account further reveals that correspondence also served to communicate the trail experience to church leaders. In fact, the Elder Snow mentioned by Parsons was likely church apostle Erastus Snow, and Richard Ballantyne, as noted earlier, was the captain of an 1855 company that brought an injured woman to Fort Laramie just over two weeks later.[75] Documentary evidence also exists of correspondence between company leaders and Brigham Young. One LDS trail leader, Homer Duncan, wrote from Fort Laramie to President Young on August 5, 1861, reporting his company's progress and mentioning, among other things, that they spent some extra time on July 24 at Ash Hollow, celebrating the anniversary of the first LDS company to reach the Salt Lake Valley in 1847.[76]

Evidence also exists that in 1861 several LDS companies were preoccupied with and passionate about the mail at the fort. However, because the Platte River had to be crossed to get to Fort Laramie and it lay about two miles from the trail, LDS captains sometimes sent men from their companies to pick up and deliver mail on behalf of the group. Captain Samuel Woolley, who presided over one company, wrote on August 19, 1861, "Sent 3 men to Larramie to mail letters & get some things for Co. I had one mailed to my wife & Received one from her & my son S.W., I was glad to hear from them."[77] The following year Henry Stokes also recalled a mail assignment he received from his company leader, Henry W. Miller: "Wrote out list of names for the Captain of all those who expected to receive mail at Fort Laramie as the Captain was sending over the river to inquire at the post office."[78]

In retrospect, the demand for medical attention, wagon repairs, fresh overland livestock, and basic provisions made Fort Laramie a vital service center on the overland trail. Situated at the confluence of the North Platte and Laramie Rivers, this unique stopping place absorbed a flow of cultural activity based on necessity as well as the attraction of trade and the desire to send or receive mail. Such pull factors brought distant Latter-day Saint emigrants into intimate contact with U.S. soldiers, Native Americans, and other travelers bound for the western frontier.

38. Jim Bridger. American Heritage Center, University of Wyoming.

### *Latter-day Saint Emigration and Connection via Fort Bridger (1847–68)*

Like Fort Laramie, Fort Bridger also served as an important stopping point for many emigrants in the mid-nineteenth century, including the Latter-day Saints.[79] Named for famed mountain man Jim Bridger, it stood next to Fort Laramie in importance to westbound sojourners who needed supplies.[80]

The Latter-day Saints' first encountered Bridger on June 28, 1847, when the LDS vanguard company journeyed to the Salt Lake Valley. Here, overlooking the Great Basin less than a month later, Brigham Young would declare, "This is the place." Wilford Woodruff wrote, "Met Mr. Bridger of the fort on way with two other men going to fort Laramie. He was expecting us & was to have an interview with President Young & the Twelve And also we wished to interview with Him. . . . We met in Council & spent some hours in conversations. We found him to have been a great traveler And a great knowledge of nearly all Oregon & Calafornia. . . . He spoke . . . highly of the great Salt Lake for settlement."[81]

## Trade at Fort Bridger (1847–49)

Wilford Woodruff lamented the high prices he encountered at Fort Bridger: "I went to Bridgers House & traided off my flint lock rifle for four Buffalo robes. The robes were large & nice will taned or dressed. He Called the gun $20 & the robes $5 each. The Articles generally at Bridgers fort were at least one third or one half higher than at any other traiding post in America that I ever saw."[82]

Erastus Snow, also in the Brigham Young vanguard company, provided another view of trade at this time: "We traded some with the Traders of the Fort; and with the French and Indians that were camped near there; but we found that their skins and peltry were quite as high as they are in the States, though they allowed a liberal price for the commodities we had to exchange."[83]

Later, Benjamin Ashby recalled, "When we got to Fort Bridger, I traded some powder for some antelope skins, from which I made me some moccasins."[84] Lorenzo Brown, who journeyed with Ashby in the Brigham Young Company of 1848, wrote about trade at Fort Bridger, where his brother was employed: "This morning bought an Elk shirt of a mountaineer for a Hickory shirt worth 25cts. Homer my only brother stops here to work for Bridger & Vasques the proprietors for a year at $15.00 per month. At this I felt to grieve."[85] Thus, Brown determined that the owners of the post had taken advantage of his brother. Likewise, John Pulsipher perceived that the local Indians who had settled by the fort had been cheated by these white traders who had taken wives from among these Natives.[86]

Although the trappers apparently got the best of the Native Americans they lived among, the Indians appear to have gotten the best of some of the

39. Howard Egan, ca. 1865. Church History Library, PH 4966.

more vulnerable LDS emigrants. Isaac Russell recalled this experience: "Well we traveled on and in due time we reached fort bridger where we camped for a few days to recruit our teams and do some washing and trading with the indians and there I got my first and last pair of skin pants. They done quite well and was a novelty until I got them wet then they shrank so as to reach about half way to my knees and made me look like a great greenhorn that got up too early and ran his legs to[o] far through his pants."[87]

Like Russell, Howard Egan also crossed the plains in 1848 and attested that the Native Americans got the best of some of the passing emigrants at the fort: "[There were] Indians and white men all dressed in buckskin clothes. . . . It was here that Father traded for the same pistol he had held in his hand and dropped, when shot, in the fight at the Horn River. It had passed from Indian to Indian and arrived at Bridger long before we did."[88]

## Changes That Affected Emigrants

By 1852 Latter-day Saint emigrants were receiving support from fellow church members from the Salt Lake Valley, which must have been a welcome relief to the Saints who were paying high prices at Fort Bridger. Philip De La Mare wrote, "At Fort Bridger more assistance was received. Abraham O. Smoot brought from Salt Lake City a load of flour. Flour at this time was selling for $50.00 pr 100 pounds. After a few days rest Mr. Smoot began his return journey taking with him several of the emigrants."[89]

The following year a notable account from British artist Frederick H. Piercy provides evidence that the Latter-day Saints (as well as other passing emigrants) were not wanted at Fort Bridger. Piercy described the fort as "merely a trading post," adding, "The fort is built in the usual form of pickets, with lodging apartments opening into a hollow square. A high picket fence encloses a yard into which the animals . . . are driven for protection. . . . Mr. Bridger has erected a board on which was written a request for emigrants to keep a mile away from his place."[90]

Concerning Bridger's sign, historian Fred Gowans asked, "Had Bridger completely withdrawn in 1853 from any trade with emigrants? . . . The majority of the emigrants passing the fort were Mormons, which at this point could explain the sign. Possible, too, Bridger was concerned about his pastures which could have been overgrazed by letting the emigrants' stock overrun them."[91]

## Conflict between Jim Bridger and the Latter-day Saints

Of the friction between Bridger and the Saints, Gowans wrote, "Difficulties between Jim Bridger and Brigham Young reached a climax in the late summer of 1853 when the Mormon leader became convinced that the mountain man was engaging in illegal trade with the Indians as well as stirring up enmity between the natives and the Mormons." This conflict had been fueled by tension between Bridger's mountain men and LDS ferry men, who were both trying to control the process of ferrying emigrants across the Green River.[92]

Because of the lawlessness of the situation, Utah territorial governor Brigham Young sent an LDS posse to arrest Bridger in August 1853. Isaac C. Haight described meeting this posse on the way to the fort: "We met a large posse going out to arrest Bridger and some of his gang that resisted the authorities of Utah. They have stirred up the Indians to commit depredations upon our people and some of our people have been killed."[93] The arrest was not to be, as Bridger escaped.

### The Saints Purchase and Control Fort Bridger in 1855

By the summer of 1855, LDS emigrants were passing by Fort Bridger at a steady pace, and tension with Bridger had subsided, largely because Bridger had sold the fort to the church on August 3, 1855.[94] Just three weeks later, Latter-day Saint William Knox wrote, "Setterday we got to Fort Bridger about 2 oclock PM here there was two waggons from the Velly with Flour for sail A ox was Killed for this company at 8 and 12 Cents per pound at neight there was A Dance at the Fort."[95]

Two months later Thomas Evans Jeremy noted as he arrived at Fort Bridger, "Here I met many of the Valley Brethern with whom I was acquainted. They are here in consequence of some disturbances with the Indians.... We staid here until noon. We leave 5 head of cattle here with some of the Valley Brethern to take care of and bring on when fit for use."[96]

### Church Members at Fort Bridger Assist Fellow Saints with Handcarts in 1856

Although the handcart plan launched in 1856 saved money, it cost many lives for two of the handcart companies who left late in the emigration season. Evidence shows that emigrants in the ill-fated James G. Willie and Edward Martin handcart companies were most grateful to get rid of the carts at Fort Bridger before proceeding on to the Salt Lake Valley in wagons. One account from a member of the Willie Company reads, "When we reached Fort Bridger (one hundred twenty miles from Salt Lake City) we didn't have to use those two-wheeled man-tormentors anymore, and anyone who felt the need could get a ride."[97] Another narrative from a member of the same handcart company reads, "On the third day, supplies arrived, and the lives of the remainder of the company were saved. Those who were sick and helpless were now able to ride. The remainder walked as before until they reached Fort Bridger. Here they were met by a large number of wagons, and all were able to ride."[98]

One member of the Edward Martin handcart company expressed his relief when he heard that help was coming from the Salt Lake Valley: "Nearly 60 horse teams on the road load with flour and was going to take in all the people. I immediately came to the conclusion to roll back to the Fort leave my wagons and oxen and go in with the horse teams. Dec 7 [1856] Sunday.... I went to the Fort took dinner with bro. Lewis Robison, the brother that owns the Fort."[99]

In the same emigration season, Robison would witness the relief of the suffering endured by not only the handcart companies heading west via Fort Bridger but also by the distressed and disillusioned apostates heading east who had left Salt Lake Valley. Writing to Brigham Young, Robison noted, "If a person wishes to hear the distresses of the inhabitants of the valleys they would only have to be on the road [to] hear and listen to the tales of those who have got Enough of Mormonism and ar[e] Hell bound for the States."[100]

The following year Robison continued to supervise the operations of the fort. In a letter dated July 12, 1857, to LDS church leader Daniel Wells, Robison provided a glimpse of his busy schedule handling emigration affairs: "This is Sunday all though it does not seem much like it here.... [It] has been quite a busy day as there has been emigration passing through everyday."[101]

## U.S. Military Occupation of Fort Bridger (1857–60)

Because of the threat of 2,500 U.S. soldiers coming to Utah Territory to depose Brigham Young as governor, the Latter-day Saints abandoned Fort Bridger, and Lot Smith and his LDS raiders burned it to the ground in late September 1857. This defensive move prevented military occupation of the fort buildings at the beginning of the Utah War; however, the military took command of the charred property under the direction of Colonel Albert Sidney Johnston.[102]

The following year a few LDS emigrants trickled past Fort Bridger, one of whom provided a glimpse of the situation at the fort: "On arriving at Fourt Bridger we learned that the difecuty was settled; Soon we met the peece commishiners Comeing down to Bridger in conveyances, this aforded us great relief of mind, we have 1,10 miles more to make Salt L, City and our animals are much faded, we shall now drive more moderate, as the blow to be struck is stayed, thank god for all his goodness, and his protecting care over his honest and much abused people."[103]

By 1859 the U.S. military was supervising affairs at Fort Bridger. The soldiers were struck by the novel sight of the Saints with their handcarts, as well as the sight of women in a region where they were few and far between. LDS emigrant Thomas McIntyre, who traveled in the George Rowley handcart company, wrote, "August 28 [1859] We start at 10 and in two hours we are marching in close order through Fort Bridger, all the soldiers are turned out to see the novelty to see 250 persons pulling handcarts over a wild country of a thousand miles and all for a religion in which they have implied faith confidence. A few of them try their persuasive wiles so to prevail on the sisters to go no further but it is no go."[104]

On this same day another emigrant in the company noted the soldiers' attempt to persuade the LDS women to remain at the fort and mentioned an additional intrusion to the party: "Some of the Soldiers try to induce the Sisters to go no further as Salt Lake is a poor place to live in but it was no go." He also noted that their camp had been disturbed "by a man Shooting off a revolver and riding into Camp bareheaded like a mad man saying that some... Mormon had demanded his horse." The company later learned that "he was the only person of that stamp around, an Apostate."[105]

Even though the military irritated the Saints by preying on the women, evidence shows that the soldiers extended kindness to members of the John P. Taylor Company in 1860. Annie Taylor Dee recalled:

> When we reached Fort Bridger some of the families were getting short of food supplies. We met a section of Johnston's army, returning from Utah. Father and some of the other men went to try and buy supplies from the army. They saw the officer in command. He took them to the commissary and told the storekeeper to let them have supplies enough to last the train until they reached Salt Lake, and to have the cattle, that needed it shod and fixed for the journey to Utah.
>
> All this they did without charge. The Captain afterwards came to our camp and met my grandmother. He was very much impressed and said she put him much in mind of his own mother. He went

back to his camp and brought her some special dainties, wished her goodbye and good luck.[106]

### LDS Emigration at Fort Bridger during the Civil War

The following year, in 1861, the Civil War broke out, and the California and Nevada Volunteers were sent to watch over Fort Bridger during this tumultuous period. In 1862 Colonel Patrick E. Connor sent some of his California Volunteers to the fort. At the end of the year, Captain M. G. Lewis, with Company I, Third California Volunteers, took over for Connor's men. They were followed by various companies of volunteers during the remaining years of the war.[107]

The passing Saints encountered a variety of challenges during the war years, including searches for gunpowder and weapons. Sally M. Porter recalled, "When we arrived at Fort Bridger, Wyoming, which was a military camp, we were detained by officers who inspected everyone that came into Utah. They were searching for anything that might have a United States mark or stamp on it. One of the boys from [U]tah had a revolver and he asked one of the young ladies to wear it under her dress until they left the camp."[108]

Lorenzo Hadley, a member of the 1863 Thomas E. Ricks Church Train, wrote, "At Ft. Bridger about ten soldiers came up on horseback and asked at every one of our seventy wagons if we had any powder. I don't know if they got any or not but we didn't have any extra."[109] When Elijah Larkin's company strayed from the main trail route, the military required that they return to the Bridger Road: "Friday 25th Sept 1863. A day long to be remembered by bouth Trains, as the folowing will show. This morning at half past seven oclock, A compy of Armed Mounted Men Calling themselves, U.S. Soldiers, which they turned out to be, wrode into or rather between the two Camps & d[e]manded the Capns to take their trains to Bridger & reprimanded our Capn for not going the Bridger Road."[110]

Along with enduring the inspections for ammunition and the routing requirements, the emigrants were also forced at the fort to swear an oath of allegiance to the Constitution. James Mills Paxton, an eighteen-year-old traveling in the 1863 Daniel D. McArthur Company, wrote, "At Fort Bridger a company of soldiers made us go back twelve miles to take the

Oath of Allegiance."[111] William McLachlan, age twenty-three, who crossed the plains in the 1863 John W. Woolley Company, recorded:

> Wednesday 23rd September 1863. . . . A company of Brethren were Sent out by President Young to Green river to meet the trains that had powder, as a Company of U. S. Soldiers were Stationed near Hams Fork to Search the trains as they Passed. . . .
>
> Friday 25th September 1863 This morning as we were driving up our Cattle[,] 25 U.S. Soldiers made their appearance and requested both aliens and citizens to take an oath of allegiance to the Constitution of the United States, which we did[.] He afterwards caused our Captain J. W. Woolley to take an oath that he had no Powder or Ammunition in his possession only that necessary for his own protection and those under his charge.[112]

Two years later, the Civil War ended. On July 25, 1868, Wyoming was established as a territory, and the eighteen years during which Fort Bridger resided in the boundaries of Utah Territory came to an end. This also marked the last year of LDS emigrant traffic on the overland trail; as previously noted, the transcontinental railroad took its place in 1869.

In retrospect, Fort Bridger, situated on the northeastern corner of Utah Territory (1847–68), served as a significant point of contact for LDS emigrants. There they encountered a cultural collage of French trappers, shrewd traders, Native Americans, and U.S. soldiers as they purchased needed provisions and supplies. The intersection of Fort Bridger and the Mormon Trail was a unique meeting place in the American West—the last abode of "Babylon" before the Saints traveled onward to the headquarters of Zion.

# 11

## Arrival at the Final Post

The European Saints who crossed the Atlantic were undoubtedly excited to arrive on the southeastern or eastern coast of America, but reaching their final destination in Utah was even more thrilling. We are often left to wonder how the new converts were assisted as they reached the final terminus at Salt Lake City.

The moment these emigrant converts arrived in the city was for most the high point, the culmination of their journey.[1] Having left the boundaries of "Babylon" and reached the core of Zion, the Saints often felt a flood of emotions as they faced the challenge of assimilation. Although assisted in most instances by trustworthy missionaries returning home from their fields of labor, or by skilled teamsters on the plains, these new arrivals were on the threshold of a new life in an unfamiliar territory.

What were their thoughts when they entered the city of the Saints and their journey came to an end? How did they change throughout the latter decades of the nineteenth century during the trail years (1847–68) and the transcontinental rail decades (1869–90)? Who met the emigrants at those junctures? What did the church do to aid assimilation? This chapter explores these questions and offers an overview of what most Latter-day Saint converts likely experienced upon arriving in the Salt Lake Valley in the latter half of the nineteenth century.

### Arrival at the Old Fort (1847–49)

During their first two years in the Valley, many early LDS sojourners first contacted the Old Mormon Fort, and a number of them also found lodging in or near there.[2] One major reason this fort had been built in such a desolate region was to protect the early pioneers from Native Americans. One week after Brigham Young arrived in the Salt Lake Valley, vanguard camp historian William Clayton noted that Elder Heber C. Kimball proposed that a corral (or fort) be erected and "that the houses form a stockade or fort to keep out the Indians that [their] women and children be not abused, and that [they] let Ute Indians alone."[3]

Less than a week later, the Quorum of the Twelve Apostles issued the following epistle: "We are also laboring unitedly to build a stockade of houses around a ten acre block. This also will be a greater blessing to others." They further noted, "We are engaged in other improvements here in like manner, but when we come here with our families and the inhabitants begin to spread abroad in the city, we expect that every family will have a lot on which they may build, plant and also farm, as much land as they can till, and every man may be a steward over his own."[4]

Several accounts provide a glimpse of the life of the pioneers as they arrived in the Great Basin between 1847 and 1848, received the help they needed, and soon thereafter prospered. J. C. Ensign recalled, "I drove the first Ox team into the valley under the direction of Daniel Spencer landing on the grounds of old Fort square. September 23rd. 1847."[5] Apparently Ensign, whose journey had very humble beginnings, reached out to others who found themselves in the same situation or worse. His circumstances a year later are described in an account by Rachel Emma Woolley Simmons: "We went to Brother Ensign's who kindly offered us the hospitality of their one room until we could do better."[6]

Other early pioneers, not so fortunate upon arrival, found themselves needing to make a rental payment. Ann Cannon Woodbury wrote, "Uncle Taylor rented a room of the old fort from some of the Mormon Battalion boys who got to the valley ahead of some of the pioneers. They buil[t] some houses in the pioneer fort and rented them to some of the folks that came later. We got into the fort on October 6, 1847."[7]

When Daniel Davis entered the valley the following year, he noted, "Went down towards the fort or temple Block & as We drew near the Saints came out to meet us with cheers[.] Bro Brigham Met us to bade Welcome[,] also Parley P Pratt & Bro Jediah [Jedediah] M. Grant."[8] Aroet Lucius Hale remembered that as he came into the Valley the same year, "[the emigrants] camped around the Old Fort that the Poyneers [pioneers] of 47 built." Further, "In the fawl [fall] of 48 all the Saints had liberty to Scatter out . . . and Settle on their City Lots."[9]

### Arrivals at Union Square (1850s)

Journals written during the 1850s frequently mention arrivals at Union Square, or Public Square, as it was called.[10] William Goforth Nelson wrote, "We reached Salt Lake City, Sept. 9, 1850, and camped on the public square for two days."[11] Peter McIntyre recalled, "We arrived in Salt Lake City on Sept. 22nd 1853 and camped on the Public Square."[12] One distinctive group that entered Union Square during this decade was the Abraham O. Smoot Company, arriving in early September 1852.

Isaac Brockbank remembered feeling joy and gratitude when he arrived in Salt Lake City: "On first taking a view of the city, our hearts were filled with gratitude to God that we had been enable[d] to complete our journey. . . . This being the first company that had arrived direct from Europe under the auspices of the Perpetual Emigration Fund Co., considerable interest was taken by the Saints of the City in visiting the company on their arrival on Union Square. Pres. Brigham Young, Heber C. Kimball, and others of the leading authorities of the Church visited and counseled the new arrival[s]."[13]

William Woodward recalled his experience of receiving help and guidance from a new acquaintance he met shortly after his arrival in September 1851: "How beautiful Salt Lake City appeared after crossing the plains. Here we met acquaintances and were greeted with kindness. I was now looking for something to do. After my arrival in the city I met an acquaintance on Main Street, who asked what I was thinking of doing." The man said, "'Come across the street and see our Bishop.' This was N. [Nathaniel] V. Jones, of the Fifteenth Ward. He introduced me to Brother Jones and told my business. Said Brother Jones, 'My brother-in-law, Robert Burton, wants a hand.' This brother took me to Brother Burton's and I engaged to work for him, and went there the next day."[14]

Two years later Ann Gregory Wilkey would give birth to a baby girl shortly before reaching the Salt Lake Valley. Although Ann was tired and hungry, the teams and provisions sent from the valley enabled her and her company to successfully reach their destination. Ann wrote, "We were then

40. Brigham Young, ca. 1870. Church History Library, Brigham Young Portrait Collection, box 1, fd. 9, PH 598.

placed on the public square in Salt Lake City, with no shelter, but the blue sky above us and the ground beneath[,] no home and nothing to eat and in October. My baby was then ten days old. I was very sick and tired and very weak having had not much food and being sick . . . but dear friends came. Bro. and Sis. Theabald took us to their home. They had been in Utah two years. We remained with them a few weeks."[15]

This same year, Joseph W. Young led a company into the Valley. Hugh Pugh, who served as the company clerk, serves as an example of what must have taken place many times as various companies were dismissed from

Union Square. Pugh noted that the company had arrived there at 5:00 p.m. on October 10, 1854. The following morning the sound of a trumpet awakened the company, and soon Brigham Young welcomed them, gave an inspiring message to teach the arrivals what was essential for their "future destiny," and "blessed the people in the name of the Lord." He was then followed by others who offered helpful counsel.[16]

Ann Lewis Clegg, who reached the Salt Lake Valley in 1854, recalled her memorable entrance into the city of the Saints and expressed gratitude for the splendid reception she and her company received on the public square. There Clegg camped along with hundreds of other emigrants for several weeks until they could find housing. She was grateful to make the valley in time for the fall general conference and noted, "The square was full of people to welcome us in. Brigham Young was there first and gave us a hearty welcome. . . . Some were expecting their loved ones in the company and I tell you it was a grand reunion, a time of rejoicing together . . . but I was very lonesome for awhile."[17]

Though it was not uncommon for family and friends to meet the incoming emigrants, some, like Clegg, had no one to meet them. Watkin Rees and his wife were one such couple who entered the valley in 1854 at conference time. Rees recorded, "Here on the Public Square many of the emigrants ware met by friends[.] Others had places to go to and it was not long befor[e] the whole camp was disposed of[;] it happened that I and the wife and baby was left till last and we felt somewhat Lonesome without money without friend and all gone but us[;] it looked blue."[18]

During most of the handcart years (1856–59), Union Square served as the arrival point for the Saints, and church leaders continued to welcome arriving emigrants to their main gathering place. John Crook, who journeyed overland in the Philemon C. Merrill Company in 1856, expressed elation when entering the valley: "There was the scene before us that we had long looked for, and read and sung about, the city of the Saints. Oh what a joy filled each bosom at the sight. About noon the 15th of August we rolled into Salt Lake City and went into camp on Emigration square."[19]

Wilford Woodruff wrote that he was particularly impressed with the behavior of the leader of the first handcart company, Edmund Ellsworth, when Ellsworth returned to Salt Lake from a mission to England with his cart in hand on September 26, 1856. According to Woodruff, "Brother Ellsworth . . . passed by his lovely home and saw his wives and children standing in his door, he made no halt, only gave a passing salute, continuing with his company until he reached the public square and saw them all comfortably encamped and fed." Woodruff further recalled, "I felt that his position was far more honorable and lovely in the eyes of God and Angels and good men, than it would have been, had he been mounted upon the best steed that ever trod the earth, clothed with ermine and gold."[20]

Mary B. (Brannigan) Crandell, who arrived the same day as Ellsworth but in the Daniel D. McArthur handcart company, recalled, "Bands came out to meet us, and the First Presidency came. What a beautiful sight met our eyes after our long journey. . . . What cheering and shouting as we came. . . . The streets were thronged with men, women and children. . . . When we got to the Public Square there were plenty of victuals cooked up for the two companies." She added, "We were the second company and Brother Edmund Ellsworth's was the first; but we came into the Valley at the same time."[21]

Such assistance was also provided in individual ways, as attested by Robert McQuarrie, who journeyed across the plains in the same year that Johnston's army was headed for Utah. McQuarrie came into view of the Salt Lake Valley in the early fall of 1857 and recorded the following entry in his journal on September 12: "Robert Baxter met us on the top of the little mountain, we went into Salt Lake City and camped on the public square at 2 O'clock. bro Baxter took us (my fathers family) to his house and kindly entertained us for one week. during which time I went to Ogden and bought a farm of R.G. Golding for $1000.00."[22]

### Arrivals at Eighth Ward Square (1859–65)

Beginning in 1859, during the latter part of the handcart era, emigrants often first gathered and camped on what is referred to as the Eighth Ward Square, Washington Square, and Emigration Square.[23] Ellen Wasden, then age ten, remembered the flood of emotions she experienced upon arrival:

> When we came into Salt Lake City, it was a small "city" then, we camped on 8th Ward Square, where the City and County Building

now is. We drew our wagons into a circle and the Saints hailed our coming by the band playing, "Home, Sweet Home." . . . I shall never forget how my tired and weary body and soul responded to that song. We had reached our goal, worn and hungry, with nothing but the strength of a mighty purpose to support us. There were no comrades we had known before and the solemn primal curse, "Earn thy bread by the sweat of thy brow," was upon us.[24]

Robert Bodily wrote, "[We] finally arrived on the 5th day of Oct. 1860. We camped on the lot where now stands the City & County Building S L City. The next day we went to Conference and heard that great man President Brigham Young and other good men whom we had never heard before. . . . After Conference my father bought a place in the 6th Ward."[25]

In subsequent years, converts continued to record their arrival in the valley. For example, in 1861 convert Eli Wiggill finally reached Salt Lake from a distant South Africa. He recollected, "Found an old acquaintance from Africa by the name of Charles Roper, who lived in the Seventh Ward. . . . Stay[ed] at his house untill our Company came into the City who came in the Next day and we campted on the Emigration Square."[26]

In 1862 Hannah Harrison crossed the plains with the James Wareham Company and recalled, "After 13 long weeks on the plains we reached Salt Lake City, September 30, and camped for the night on what was then known as Immigration Square. This was then the camping ground of all immigrant trains."[27] Arriving the following year, Charles Henry John West remembered, "We arrived at Salt Lake City on the camping grounds of the 8th Ward Square. The friends and relations of different ones would come and take them away to their homes."[28]

Although new arrivals were often met by family and friends, many also needed assistance from church leaders, and of course all appreciated the support of their fellow church members, especially on the day of arrival in the city of the Saints. World traveler and celebrated British writer Richard F. Burton, an eyewitness to one handcart company's arrival in 1860, described from an outsider's point of view the impressive way the Saints rendered immediate support and assistance to the joyful newcomers at the public square: "We saw the smoke-like column which announced the emigrants were crossing the bench-land; and people were scurrying from all sides to greet and get news of friends. Presently the carts came. . . . All the new arrivals were in clean clothes, the men washed and shaved, and the girls, who were singing hymns, habited in Sunday dresses. The company was sunburned, but looked well and thoroughly happy."

In addition, Burton provided the observant detail that "when the train reached the public square . . . of the 8th ward, the wagons were in line for the final ceremony. . . . On this occasion the place of Mr. Brigham Young was taken by President [Edward] Hunter, a Pennsylvanian, whom even the most fanatic and intentionally evil-speaking anti-Mormon must regard with respect.[29] Preceded by a brass band."

Finally, Burton observed, "In a short time arrangements were made to house and employ all who required work, whether men or women."[30]

The *Deseret Weekly News* published a most impressive report of the emigrants' arrival in the late fall of 1864. A lengthy extract of this article, "Home Items," is provided here for its rich detail and keen observations concerning the Saints' arrival in downtown Salt Lake City and their assimilation into the community:

> The last of this season's emigration has arrived, mostly in good health and fine spirits. Cap. Wm. Hyde's train, which reached the Public Square on the afternoon of the 26th ult; was unusually well provided for by the donations of the people through their Bishops. Early on that day brother Jesse C. Little, one of Bishop Hunter's counselors, Bishop John Sharp, together with those appointed at the regular Bishop's meeting . . . got some tents from the General Tithing Store and put them upon the 8th Ward Square preparatory to the reception of the company.
>
> Immediately on the arrival of the train, the brethren and sisters came forward with soup, beef, potatoes, pies, sugar and coffee, to supply the wants of those who had just come in from their long and tedious journey across the plains. . . . They also provided for the sick, and had them made comparatively comfortable in the 8th Ward School House. Sister Sluce was on hand to wait upon the sisters, several of whom were in a delicate state of health. Dr. Hovey was called

41. Edward Hunter. Church History Library, item 6, PH 5202.

in to give medical advice and to administer such remedial agents as could best be applied; and, from the arrival of the train to the time that all found places to go to, the best that could be done was done, to alleviate suffering, to comfort, to bless and render happy the poor of God's chosen people, and in this none seemed remis [sic] in their duty to God and their brethren and sisters.

It has always been customary for the Saints to assist the incoming emigration, but this season has seemed to call for an extra and additional effort, because of the lateness of the season before the last two companies got in. This call for assistance, therefore, was made upon every Ward in the city, and, to their praise be it spoken, every Ward, and almost every family freely responded to the Bishops' call. . . . We think great credit is due to Bishop Hunter and his assistants for the promptness and energy with which they have carried out the wishes of our President in providing food and homes for these large companies of Saints. This is the way the Latter-day Saints treat their poor brethren when they come here from distant nations, ignorant of our manners and customs, ignorant of our mode of procuring the necessities of life, and many of them ignorant of the language we speak. Can this be the result of fanaticism? or is it the fruit of that pure and undefiled religion of which the apostle speaks? We ask, can the Christian world show its equal? Our religion teaches this maxim, "By their fruits ye shall know them."[31]

Yet admittedly, not all Saints wore halos, and some incoming converts had high expectations that at times went unmet. Therefore, the *Millennial Star* warned converts, "We have known Saints who, in going to the Valley . . . have enumerated the names of Elders who had been on missions from Zion in their midst, whom they had entertained at their homes and calculated confidently on meeting a warm reception from them and being invited to live with them until they could do better. In some instances, [those] who indulge in such expectations have them gratified; but more frequently are disappointed."[32]

### *Tithing Yard (1866 to the End of the Nineteenth Century)*

By 1866 incoming emigrants were often temporarily housed at the Tithing Yard, located at the northeast corner of South Temple and Main Street, where the Joseph Smith Memorial Building now stands. A *Deseret News* article titled "Commendable" announced, "There is a very comfortable structure erected in the yard of the General Tithing Store, for the incoming immigrants, with other accommodations for their use. Bishop [Edward] Hunter and Counsel have been energetically preparing for their comfort. Bishop J. [Jesse] C. Little aiding, counseling, directing and laboring with his accustomed zeal."[33]

Yet when Hans J. Zobell arrived in Salt Lake City three years later, the Saints were coming in rapidly on the transcontinental railroad. Evidently the hospitality he longed for in the city of the Saints was lacking. Despite this initial discouragement, he found inner contentment, as surmised from this penetrating account:

> We therefore arrived in Salt Lake City on August 11, 1869 and were dumped out in the tithing yard, and made our bed on the ground with high heaven for roof. So this was Zion. We all felt to praise our God for our safe delivery but it seemed that it was Zion in name only, because there were none to welcome or give us a brotherly handshake; no one paid the least bit of attention to us.
>
> We soon found out that we were to be more or less upon our own resources and the familiar words of the song came to me when I was pondering over these things, namely: "Think not when to Zion you arrive that your troubles are over" and so on. I realized at once that my troubles had come to an end—the first end, because I had left a goodly home, with a roof over it to shelter me, a nice soft bed to rest myself, and plenty of food to eat; and here I am in Zion, with no home, no bed, and no food. But still I was happy and my very soul went up in praise to my Heavenly Father because I stood here in Zion, under the stars, with empty hands, a mother, two sisters and a betrothed sweetheart to look after, in a strange land, strange people and customs, and no work of the kind that I was trained in. And still I knew within my heart that I had obeyed the voice of the one who had said: "Get ye up out of Babylon and get ye to the tops of the mountains, where you can walk in my paths and keep all of my statutes," so I felt an assurance that if God had given me the call to come here, he would not leave me here to starve, and to be without shelter. So I was satisfied with my lot.[34]

With the transcontinental railroad finished, a number of incoming Saints got off the train at various locations before reaching the Ogden railway station and later the Salt Lake Valley. By the 1880s the valley was filling up with Saints, and thus a number of converts had dispersed to expand the periphery of Zion's core. For example, in 1882 William George Davis wrote, "We arrived at Evanston [Wyoming] in the afternoon and at Echo about dusk. Several of our company left us at these places, they having friends who met them and took them to their homes." He later noted, "We arrived in Ogden about midnight. . . . Many of the Saints left us at Ogden and went with friends who came to meet them. . . . We arrived in Salt Lake City about noon and found the depot crowded with friends and old acquaintances."[35]

Arriving at the edge of Utah's border in the fall of 1885, Samuel R. Bennion recorded, "Quite a number got off at Evanston."[36] Anthon H. Lund, who presided over this company, observed, "At Evanston 14 emigrants left our train." Another Scandinavian convert wanted to be dropped off soon thereafter, as "he did not like to be oxen." Still another was asked to leave the train at Uintah.[37]

During the late nineteenth century, newcomers found improved facilities in Salt Lake City.[38] In the spring of 1873, the *Millennial Star* issued an article titled "For Emigrants," which announced the following: "A new and substantial building is in course of erection in the Tithing Office yard [Salt Lake City], which is to be used for the accommodation of emigrants arriving here without any home to go to, until they are in a position to provide for themselves. The building will be 43 by 20 feet, two storeys high, and will have a porch on the south side."[39]

Just a few months later, Jens A. Weibye, on his arrival in Salt Lake City in late September, wrote, "The Saints scattered to different places. Some of us to the Emigrant House in the Tithing Yard."[40] About this same time, William Kilshaw Barton recalled, "The Saints who had no relatives or particular friends, went [to] the Tithing yard where they stayed until homes were provided for them in Salt Lake City or in the other towns south."[41] One company had no one to meet them when they arrived one fall night in 1880, because news had gone forth that the train would arrive the following morning. James Samuel Page Bowler explained, "We passed the night in the tithing house as best we could, but even that was better than thousands of others who came to this country in early days."[42]

The Tithing Yard was not just a place of dispersion and dwelling where incoming converts temporarily lodged at the Emigrant House; it also served as a place for instruction, and such timely tutorials proved invaluable, especially to those vulnerable foreign converts who did not speak English. In 1874 company leader Peter C. Carstensen reported, "A meeting was held in

42. Tithing Office and Deseret Store, ca. 1870–75.
Church History Library, item 1, PH 9228.

the tithing yard, in the afternoon, when Brother [Erastus] Snow gave many good counsels and instructions to the newly arrived Saints, and spoke in the Danish language. After meeting was closed the company separated, the Saints going with their relations and friends to their homes."[43]

During the following decade, Latter-day Saint emigrant accounts reveal that the incoming Saints continued to gather to and disperse from the Tithing Yard. James Hansen, who reached Salt Lake City in 1882, wrote, "A great many people was at the station to meet their friends and teams came to take all the emigrants up to the Tithing Yard where some provisions were brought for them."[44] Andrew Christian Nielson arrived the following year and later recalled, "Got to Salt Lake City, stopped in the Tithing Yard, and emigrants scattered."[45] The front page of the *Deseret Evening News* for November 12, 1883, carried the headline "Immigrants Arrived." The editor explained, "Those who came down to the city were met, as usual, by their immediate friends and relatives, conveyed by the teams provided by the Bishops to the Immigrant House in the Tithing Yard."[46]

Other articles from the *Millennial Star* provide evidence that the Tithing Yard was frequently used to temporarily house the incoming converts throughout the 1880s. For example, in 1885 C. J. Arthur explained in the *Star*, "Most of the company have left, a few only remain, and they will soon find some friends who will provide them labor and a home for the time being. At present they remain in the Emigrants' Home, in the Tithing Yard."[47] The following year Edwin T. Woolley reported, "Our company went forward to their various destinations without delay, and by nine o'clock of the morning following our arrival in Salt Lake City but very few were left at the emigrant quarters in the Tithing Yard."[48] This same year C. F. Olsen recounted his experience when his company arrived in Ogden in mid-July: "Those going north remained in Ogden over night, and those bound for Salt Lake City and the south proceeded to the city the same evening, where many received a hearty welcome and warm greeting from their friends and relatives, while those who were going still further were made comfortable at the Tithing Yard."[49]

In 1889 John William Craven wrote of his company's safe arrival in another *Star* article: "We went to the Tithing Office, and were very soon enjoying the good things which are temporarily provided free of expense to all members of the Church. Before going on to our destination we stayed one week, visiting former friends whom we knew in England."[50]

### *Temporary Lodging in the City of the Saints*

Emigrants arriving in the late nineteenth century not only visited friends but on many occasions stayed with fellow Saints until they could find permanent housing. Charlotte Ann Bates, who entered Salt Lake City in the summer of 1871, vividly remembered, "We arrived in Salt Lake City about the 20th of July. It was in the evening after dark. I remember passing on South Temple and looking down Main Street. They had boardwalks and a small ditch on each side of the street with water running down it. They had lamp posts with lamps lit up all the way down the street." Bates further recalled with gratitude, "Milford Bard Shipp [a missionary] took us to his home for a day or two until we could get located some place. The next day some friends of father's and mother's named Smith came to see us and said they had a house we could live in as long as we wanted it. There was a log room and a lumber room, so we moved in."[51]

Other Saints were also filled with a profound sense of thanksgiving as they entered the holy city of Zion. One such was Alma Ash, who arrived in Salt Lake City in 1885. As Ash reflected upon this sacred occasion, he remembered with great intensity:

> Never shall I forget how our hearts throbbed gratitude filled with emotion as we peered all around us to catch a glimpse of the place and the people as silently our little company trudged [a]long South Temple Street towards the tithing yard where we expected to stay until morning. Oh, how reverently we regarded everything and everybody and so sacred did everything appear to us. . . . We wondered almost how people could be rude or light-minded in such a sanctified city. We gazed up at the temple . . . with the towers just commenced and silently in our hearts we resolved to begin a new life with new ambitions. . . . We spoke in a quiet manner, I may say in a whisper, for fear of appearing boisterous or in any manner unbecoming.

While Ash's company was being kindly fed at the Tithing Yard, he received a message from a friend who had emigrated six years before and desired to take him to his home. Upon arriving at the home of his friend's parents, Ash was surprised by the family's prosperity as they comfortably conversed while reclining in their rocking chairs. On this occasion, Ash recalled, "We were received kindly and were soon answering questions about the folks in [the] Birmingham [England] Branch. . . . They invited us to sleep outside and [we] readily consented. . . . This was the first time in my life that I had slept outside. Of course such a thing would hardly be possible in England except upon very rare occasions when a dry spell would occur in the summer time." Ash then concluded, "I confess that I enjoy the novelty of sleeping outside in the open air the first night in Zion. . . . My prayer was that I would or might be faithful to God and his people."[52]

### Church Leaders Meet Rail Pioneering Saints and Assist with Assimilation

Like the Saints who crossed the plains by handcart or covered wagon, the Saints who journeyed by rail also enjoyed visiting with friends and were impressed with church leaders who greeted them as they entered Utah. As noted, Elder Erastus Snow met the Danish Saints and provided needful guidance in their native tongue to help them assimilate, and visits from other church leaders no doubt helped with the transition into Zion.

The month after the completion of the transcontinental railroad, Thomas Meikle Forrest met President Young shortly after arriving at the railroad terminus in Ogden, Utah: "Saturday, June 26, 1869.... We had the privilege of seeing Brigham Young this morning at 4:30. He shook hands with all who were awake." Forrest described Young as "a fine looking man, heavy and tall with gray whiskers."[53]

Just eight months after the completion of the transcontinental railroad, the Utah Central Rail, which ran from Ogden south to Salt Lake City, was finished. Beginning in 1870 church leaders met incoming converts on this route before they even reached Salt Lake. For example, John MacNeil wrote to his family in Scotland, "When we were about half way to the City we had shunt to let a train past that came from the City. When they were passing they stopped and let out Brigham Young, George A. Smith & Daniel H. Wells. They stepped into our train and went right through shaking hands with everyone as they went along through the cars."[54]

About six weeks later, another company of incoming Saints traveling by train was blessed to meet prominent church leaders. Jesse N. Smith recalled this memorable event: "At Kaysville we were met by the First Presidency of the Church and some others.... The brethren passed through the cars shaking hands with the passengers. At Woods Cross we were met by Bishop [Edward] Hunter.... Our train was the largest that had ever come to the City there being in all eleven passenger and five baggage cars."[55] George Goddard recalled meeting the Brethren once his party reached the City of the Saints: "We arrived in Ogden after dark, and remained in the cars until morning.... [In Salt Lake City,] we found Presidents [John] Taylor and [George Q.] Cannon, and a host of warm hearts and cheerful faces, to welcome us as we met them in the street or visited them in their offices."[56]

### Employment for Newly Arrived Emigrants

The cost to get to the Salt Lake Valley and settle was significant, especially for the Europeans who had borne the high expense of crossing the Atlantic before their journey across the plains. However, for most the cost was worth it, and as already noted, church leaders had established the Perpetual

43. *Reunion of the Saints* in Salt Lake City by C. C. A. Christensen, 1878.
Daughters of the Utah Pioneers, Salt Lake City.

Emigrating Fund, which provided temporary assistance to many of the poor. All who partook of the aid knew that they would need to repay this revolving loan as soon as possible after reaching the Salt Lake Valley—the word *perpetual* served as a constant reminder that the fund needed to be replenished for others. Yet some emigrants took advantage of the system, and others did not fulfill their obligations. Although some were not able to repay their loans or chose not to do so, many did through a variety of employment opportunities, including labor on public works within the boundaries of Salt Lake City.[57]

Other Saints would have opportunities to launch immediately into various colonies. Determining which emigrants would be sent was influenced in many cases by the skills of the emigrants and the needs of the colonies. For example, Silas Richards, writing from Union, Utah, to President Young in 1860, noted, "As the immigration will begin to arrive soon . . . I wish to employ a Tanner and currier, and a boot and shoemaker that are first-rate workmen. I also want a farmer with a small family that has not the necessary means to carry on the business himself." Richards further noted that "there [were] a number of small tracts of land on the creek for sale of good quality . . . also houses and lots in Union very low from one hundred to six hundred dollars. This would be a good location for a black Smith [blacksmith]; common laborers can get employment."[58]

Despite these opportunities, many incoming converts struggled to find employment to match their skills, as well as to know how best to live. Church leaders were keenly aware of such challenges, which continued over the remaining decades of the nineteenth century, but over time the Saints grew stronger as they established colonies and extended Zion's borders in several directions.[59]

### *Finding Zion from the Inside Out*

The phrase "knowing how to live" seems to symbolize whether the converts who entered the Salt Lake Valley and vicinity ever really found Zion, as it appears Hans J. Zobell and Alma Ash did, as previously noted. Zion is defined in Latter-day scripture as both a spiritual state and a temporal or actual dwelling place. Not only did Zion comprise the places where the Saints gathered, such as Kirtland, Ohio (D&C 38:31–32); Independence, Missouri (D&C 57:4); Nauvoo, Illinois (D&C 124:25–27); and the Salt Lake Valley, but it was also the abode of "the pure in heart" (D&C 97:18)—a people who "were of one heart and one mind, and dwelt in righteousness; . . . [with] no poor among them" (Moses 7:18).

Some emigrants discovered this concept of Zion, whereas others did not. Zion was certainly to be understood not only with the eyes but also with the heart—something that was not just talked about but had to be worked for to be fully realized. Joseph Smith had warned incoming converts that "they must not expect to find perfection, or that all will be harmony, peace, and love; if they indulge these ideas, they will undoubtedly be deceived."[60] Some did not abide this counsel and thus never found the Zion they sought, while others found a promised land by making it so.

This concept of creating Zion seems best captured by the experience of a fifteen-year-old Swiss convert named Frederick Zaugg, who asked a penetrating question as he entered the Salt Lake region in August 1885. When he came to the end of his long journey and climbed a hill to view Park Valley, he "drew a long breath" and asked, "Is this Zion?"[61] A wise man named Mr. Hirschi, there to greet and guide him, responded, "Yes, when you make it [so]." Zaugg later wrote, "These words left a deep impression in my mind. 'If you make it' became my mot[t]o. Things we like to live in and enjoy, we have to make. If we want a friend, we must love him. If you want a favor of the Lord, we must serve him and keep his commandments and the blessings will come by going after them."[62]

As the Saints reached the Salt Lake Valley, they were often met by church leaders, family, and fellow members at various locations where the incoming emigrants congregated. Although the lodging was varied and improved as the decades rolled on, whether the Saints traveled by sail, rail, or trail, they encountered a steady flow of caring and accommodation that persisted throughout the latter half of the nineteenth century. Most emigrants assimilated quickly into Salt Lake City and the scattered communities where they found employment. Those who did not secure immediate housing with family or friends found temporary shelter at the Emigrant House or in the Tithing Yard. And although all Saints did not wear halos, most appeared to be kind and hospitable to the newest arrivals. Those who came seeking Zion discovered it by looking in a mirror rather than through a window at the unfinished city of the Saints.

The gathering to Zion is a story of a people who combined their energy and talent to move not only westward but heavenward. And even after gathering to their American Zion, the Saints were willing to extend its borders, launching hundreds of colonies, starting from scratch, regardless of the sacrifices required. To achieve harmony and beauty, the Saints would apply the same principles used to gather to Zion to further build and expand it onward and upward.

# Appendix

## LDS *Emigration Agents (Nineteenth Century)*

### Ports

**LIVERPOOL**

| | |
|---|---|
| Amos Fielding | 1841 |
| Reuben Hedlock | 1845 |
| Orson Pratt | 1848 |
| Franklin D. Richards | 1850 |
| Samuel W. Richards | 1853 |
| George Turnbull (LDS?) | 1855 |

**NEW ORLEANS**

| | |
|---|---|
| Lucius N. Scovil | 1848–49 |
| Thomas McKenzie | 1849 |
| John Brown | 1852–54 |
| James McGaw | 1854–55 |

**NEW YORK**

| | |
|---|---|
| Parley P. Pratt | 1844 |
| Jesse C. Little | 1846 |
| William I. Appleby | 1847–48 |
| John Taylor | 1855 |
| Thomas B. H. Stenhouse | 1858–59 |
| George Q. Cannon | 1858–60 |
| Nathaniel V. Jones | 1861 |
| Thomas Williams | 1861 (assisted Nathaniel V. Jones) |
| Horace S. Eldredge | 1862–63 |
| Ormus E. Bates | 1862 (assisted Eldredge) |

| | |
|---|---|
| William C. Staines | 1863 (assisted Eldredge) |
| John W. Young | 1863 (assisted Eldredge) |
| Joseph A. Young | 1864 (assisted Staines) |
| Thomas Taylor | 1865–66 |
| William H. Folsom | 1866 (assisted Thomas Taylor) |
| Hiram B. Clawson | 1868 (assisted William C. Staines) |
| William C. Staines | 1867–81 |
| James H. Hart | 1881–87 |

**PHILADELPHIA**

| | |
|---|---|
| Angus M. Cannon | 1857 (acting for John Taylor) |

## Posts

**IOWA CITY, IOWA**

| | |
|---|---|
| Daniel Spencer | 1856 |

**KANSAS CITY**

| | |
|---|---|
| William Empey | 1854 |

**ST. LOUIS, MISSOURI**

| | |
|---|---|
| Nathaniel Felt | 1847–52 |
| Horace S. Eldredge | 1853–54 |
| Erastus Snow | 1854 |
| Milo Andrus | 1854–55 |
| James H. Hart | 1854–57 |

**KANESVILLE, IOWA**

| | |
|---|---|
| Orson Hyde | 1849–52 |

**FLORENCE, NEBRASKA**

| | |
|---|---|
| James McGaw | 1856 |
| Jacob Gates | 1861 |
| Joseph W. Young | 1862 |
| Col. Feramorz Little | 1863 |
| Bishop J. G. Bigler | 1863 (assisted Feramorz Little) |
| Mr. Lewis Hill | 1863 (assisted Feramorz Little) |

**WYOMING, NEBRASKA**

| | |
|---|---|
| Joseph W. Young | 1864 |
| N. S. Beatie | 1864 |

**LARAMIE, WYOMING**

| | |
|---|---|
| Horace S. Eldredge | 1868 |
| "Agent Piper" | 1868 |

**OGDEN**

| | |
|---|---|
| Franklin D. Richards | 1869 |
| John Reeves Jr. | 1884 |

# Notes

## Abbreviations

BL      Bancroft Library
CHL     Church History Library
FHL     Family History Library
JH      *Journal History of the Church of Jesus Christ of Latter-day Saints*
LTPSC   L. Tom Perry Special Collections
MS      *Latter-day Saints' Millennial Star*
SLR     St. Louis Record

## Introduction

1. *Webster's Dictionary of English Usage*, 389, s.v. "emigrate/immigrate," notes the following: "Emigrate and immigrate make a case in which English has two words where it could easily have made do with only one. The two words have the same essential meaning to 'leave one country to live in another'—and differ only in emphasis or point of view: emigrate stressing leaving, and immigrate stressing entering." However, to further complicate things, the term *emigrate* is used once an immigrant has arrived in a new country and begins to emigrate, or move to an area within that country. It should also be noted that sometimes the foreign immigrants were joined by Saints who gathered from the eastern coast of America, or they merged with other LDS companies at frontier outfitting posts. These Saints would be properly termed *emigrants*, as would the agents who assisted them. Throughout this work, I have tried to use *immigrate* and *emigrate* as defined here.

2. Though this website has been hosted by the BYU Harold B. Lee Library for many years, it will be moved to the Church History Library in Salt Lake City and merged into what is now known as the Church History Biographical Database (https://history.churchofjesuschrist.org/chd/landing?lang=eng). This database is the result of combining the Pioneer Database and the Missionary Database into one

tool. The Saints by Sea Database will also be added to provide a more thorough and comprehensive degree of research.
3. The Church of Jesus Christ of Latter-day Saints' tenth Article of Faith states, "We believe in the literal gathering of Israel and in the restoration of the Ten Tribes."
4. Joseph Smith Papers. Discourse, 11 June 1843–A, as Reported by Wilford Woodruff, accessed November 12, 2022, https://www.josephsmithpapers.org/paper-summary/discourse-11-june-1843-a-as-reported-by-wilford-woodruff/1. Current church president Russell M. Nelson echoed this message to Latter-day Saints in the talk "The Temple and Your Spiritual Foundation" in a worldwide general conference in October 2021: "The ultimate objective of the gathering of Israel is to bring the blessings of the temple to God's faithful children." See https://www.churchofjesuschrist.org/study/general-conference/2021/10/47nelson?lang=eng.
5. Stegner, *Gathering of Zion*, 8.
6. Jane C. Robinson Hindley, Journals 1855–1905, vol. 1, 11–14, CHL.
7. Most did not mean all. Though first-person accounts reveal that LDS converts gathered to America primarily for spiritual reasons, there were certainly temporal advantages to consider, and admittedly some took advantage of church resources to immigrate to America. For a treatment of economic motives for British converts in the nineteenth century, see Taylor, "Why Did British Mormons Emigrate?," 249–70. See also Taylor, *Expectations Westward*, 26–29, wherein Taylor correctly observes that missionaries would occasionally exaggerate the temporal advantages of Zion, creating problems that had to be addressed by church leaders in Salt Lake City. Taylor's argument is bolstered by a sermon delivered in the Salt Lake City Tabernacle on September 24, 1854, by Jedediah Grant, a counselor in the church's First Presidency, titled "Instructions to Newcomers," in *Journal of Discourses*, 3:65–69. President Grant notes, "Some of the Elders have told the Saints in England that the first two weeks after they landed here all they would have to do would be to contemplate the beauties of Zion, and be furnished two weeks' provisions. The imaginations of some Saints have been so exalted by the elders who preached to them, that they suppose that all our pigs come ready cooked, with knives and forks in them, and are running round squealing to be eaten" (65). For the best overall treatment of nineteenth-century LDS economic history, see Arrington, *Great Basin Kingdom*.
8. For further information on the Council of Fifty in general, see https://www.josephsmithpapers.org/articles/administrative-records-council-of-fifty-minutes. For a discussion of the Council of Fifty as it pertains to the LDS emigration west, see Bennett, "'We Are a Kingdom to Ourselves.'"
9. Coman, *Economic Beginnings*, 2:184.

## 1. Early Church Beginnings

1. "Facts and Statistics," The Church of Jesus Christ of Latter-day Saints, accessed November 11, 2022, https://newsroom.churchofjesuschrist.org/facts-and-statistics.
2. "Facts and Statistics," accessed November 11, 2022.
3. D&C is an abbreviation for the LDS book of scripture known as the Doctrine and Covenants of the Church of Jesus Christ of Latter-day Saints (Salt Lake City: The Church of Jesus Christ of Latter-day Saints, 1981). LDS church members believe it contains revelations received in the nineteenth and twentieth centuries to guide the Church of Jesus Christ and its members.
4. Because of their belief in the Book of Mormon, Latter-day Saints have been nicknamed "Mormons," and the church is sometimes referred to as the "Mormon Church," though the church continues to emphasize the importance of using its full name, the Church of Jesus Christ of Latter-day Saints.
5. Nelson, "Gathering of Scattered Israel."
6. Nelson, "Let God Prevail."
7. Nelson, "Gathering of Scattered Israel."
8. This material was culled and modified from Woods, "Latter-day Saint Gathering," xv–xxvi.
9. For an account of the journey of these branches to the Ohio, see Porter, "Ye Shall Go," 1–25.
10. See Allen and Leonard, *Story of the Latter-day Saints*, 63–64. The LDS missionaries were Peter Whitmer, Oliver Cowdery, Ziba Peterson, and Parley P. Pratt (see D&C 30:5–6; 32:1–3). They were sent specifically to preach to the Native Americans living in what was then known as the Indian Territory, just west of the Missouri River. On the way, Pratt was prompted to visit his friend Sidney Rigdon, and although they baptized many in the Ohio region, they did not convert a single Native American in the Indian Territory, as they immediately ran into serious problems because they did not have a license to preach.
11. *Scraps of Biography*, 68.
12. Porter, "Ye Shall Go," 19.
13. Jared Carter, Autobiography, typescript, 2–3, CHL. This account is singular in that it appears to be the first known LDS reference to divine intervention during a maritime migration, a theme that will also be discussed when addressing ocean crossings.
14. Smith, *History of Joseph Smith*, 204–5.
15. "Mormonism," *Niles Weekly Register XL*, July 16, 1831, 352; Porter, "Ye Shall Go," 18. The article "Opening of Navigation," *Buffalo Journal & General Advertiser XVL*, May 11, 1831, 3, notes that the steamer the Fayette Saints were aboard when the ice

broke was the *Niagara*, whose captain was Captain Blake. Blake had previously captained another vessel owned by General Stephen Mack, brother of Lucy Mack Smith. See Porter, "Ye Shall Go," 17.

16. "Mormon Emigration," *Painesville Telegraph*, May 17, 1831, 3.

17. Fifteen vessels and a number of captains have now been identified as having transported Latter-day Saints to and from Fairport Harbor as they gathered to Kirtland or left on missions to gather others to Ohio. These fifteen vessels have been identified mostly from first-person narratives. The names of the captains, culled from local Lake Erie newspapers and LDS emigrant accounts, are listed here alongside the vessel they commanded in alphabetical order: *Buffalo* (Levi Allen); *Charles Townsend* (Simeon Fox); *Columbus* (Captain Walker); *Commodore Perry* and *Daniel Webster* (Captain Taylor or Tyler Morris); *Erie* and *Great Western* (Captain Walker); *Illinois* and *Monroe* (Captain Whittaker); *Niagara* (Captain Blake); *Robert Fulton* (Captain Hart); *Sandusky* (T. J. Titus); *Uncle Sam*, *United States*, and *William Penn* (John F. Wright). For a more complete account of the LDS gathering to Kirtland via Lake Erie, see Woods, "Mormon Migration on Lake Erie," 291–305, from which segments were selected for this chapter.

18. In D&C 20:2–3, Joseph Smith and Oliver Cowdery were designated by revelation as the first and second elders of the Church of Christ, later known as the Church of Jesus Christ of Latter-day Saints.

19. Backman, "Warning from Kirtland," 30, estimates that about 13 percent, or 50 out of 475 families, left the church at this time in the Kirtland region. Yet he also notes that about 40 percent of this number later returned to the church.

20. Smith, *History of the Church of Jesus Christ of Latter-day Saints*, 2:489.

21. Whitney, *Life of Heber C. Kimball*, 103–4. The uneducated Kimball, initially overwhelmed by the thought of going to the learned country of England to preach, was determined to carry out what he perceived as the will of heaven.

22. Joseph Smith Papers, History, 1838–1856, volume B-1 [1 September 1834–2 November 1838], https://www.josephsmithpapers.org/paper-summary/history-1838-1856-volume-b-1-1-september-1834-2-november-1838/34.

23. Allen, Esplin, and Whittaker, *Men with a Mission*, 53. Elders Kimball and Hyde left England on April 20, 1838.

24. For more information on the mission of the Twelve to the British Isles, see Allen and Thorp, "Mission of the Twelve," 499–526; and Allen, Esplin, and Whittaker, *Men with a Mission*.

25. Smith, *History of the Church of Jesus Christ of Latter-day Saints*, 4:119. By this time the total membership of the church in the British Isles was reported as 1,631, including 132 priesthood leaders. See Whitney, *Life of Heber C. Kimball*, 278.

26. Joseph Smith Papers, History, 1838–1856, volume C-1 [2 November 1838–31 July 1842], https://www.josephsmithpapers.org/paper-summary/history-1838-1856-volume-c-1-2-november-1838-31-july-1842/1.

## 2. By Land and Sea

1. Ellsworth, "History of Mormon Missions," 257–58.
2. Jenson, LDS Biographical Encyclopedia, 1:614.
3. Many elders volunteered to serve missions without being officially appointed to serve. Quite often they chose to proselyte in areas where they had once lived.
4. Henry Boyle, Autobiography, typescript, 3, 5, 10–11, LTPSC.
5. Brown, *Testimonies for the Truth*, 18–19, Americana Collection, LTPSC.
6. Lorenzo Brown, Reminiscences and Journals, typescript, 6, LTPSC, notes, "April 21st [1839] Started on our westward journey to gather with the saints, but where to go we hardly knew as this winter past the brethren were expelled from Missouri, and there was now no particular location[.] Our company was composed of my Father with two teams, Grandfather Mumford and Charles with one Enoch Crowel in one drawn by a single horse, and John and Jesse Crosby, who joined us two days after with a three-hors[e] team. We were altogether fifteen in number."
7. Jesse Crosby, Autobiography, typescript, 5, LTPSC. Brown, *Testimonies for the Truth*, 20–24.
8. Berrett, "Southern States Mission," 192, notes that missionary George W. Brandon reported that he had created the Charity Branch in Benton County, Tennessee, in April 1842. The following month, eight of its eighteen members emigrated to Nauvoo, while a few moved to other locations. The branch was thus left with four women (three of whom had unbelieving husbands) and only one male who was a young boy.
9. Berrett, "Southern States Mission," 208. Berrett (217–18) points out that 1842 and 1843 were peak years for missionary work in the South and that 150 Saints emigrated during this period. In his appendix (296–99) he provides an annual summary of southern LDS emigrants who gathered to Nauvoo between 1839 and 1846. In addition, Berrett includes the names of the missionaries, the states they served in, and the branches and number of converts.
10. Benjamin Ashby, Autobiography, holograph, 7, LTPSC.
11. Smith, *History of the Church of Jesus Christ of Latter-day Saints*, 6:318–19. A *stake* is a Latter-day Saint church unit that usually consists of several thousand church members from smaller ecclesiastical units referred to as *wards*, which generally have several hundred church members. An even smaller church unit is called a *branch*.
12. Ellsworth, "History of Mormon Missions," 266–67.

13. Ellsworth, "History of Mormon Missions," 273–74.
14. "Epistle of the Twelve," *Times and Seasons* 5 (August 15, 1844): 619.
15. Smith, *History of the Church of Jesus Christ of Latter-day Saints*, 7:305–7.
16. Piercy, *Route from Liverpool*, 2.
17. Richard Rushton, Journal, January 30, 1842, CHL. Several British emigrant accounts from the mid-nineteenth century also mention their rail travel to the Lime Street Station in Liverpool before they transported their belongings to the docks. For example, Daniel Spencer wrote, "Started from Leeds for Liverpool, . . . went to Lime Street Station" (see Daniel Spencer, Diary, March 12, 1856, CHL). Richard Egan recalled the same station and LDS assistance: "At noon I went down to the Lime Street Station to meet the Birmingham Saints. Found they had arrived ok & were well. I hired . . . cabs to take their luggage down to the Princess landing stage for ten schillings" (see Richard E. Egan, Journal, July 27, 1869, CHL).
18. Smith, *History of the Church of Jesus Christ of Latter-day Saints*, 4:134.
19. "Autobiographical Sketch of Hugh Moon," 2, CHL. For easier access, see "Autobiographical Sketch of Hugh Moon," accessed November 12, 2022, https://saintsbysea.lib.byu.edu/mii/account/161. Other ocean and river narratives for the Nauvoo period that might also be found throughout this chapter are paralleled in the Saints by Sea website: https://saintsbysea.lib.byu.edu/. Such support was also provided on subsequent voyages destined for Nauvoo. See, for example, William Clayton, Diary, 73, CHL; and Thomas Callister, Reminiscences and Autobiographical Notes, 8, CHL.
20. Francis Moon, Letter to the Editor, MS 1, February 1841, 253.
21. MS 1, February 1841, 254–55.
22. "Emigration," MS 1, February 1841, 263.
23. Smith, *History of the Church of Jesus Christ of Latter-day Saints*, 4:186.
24. Jenson, "Church Emigration," 441. While my research generally parallels Jenson's research, a notable exception is that he lists only one LDS voyage from Bristol in 1841 when in fact there were three voyages. Jenson accurately lists 181 Saints who embarked from Bristol on what he refers to as an unnamed ship in February of 1841. This ship was the *Caroline*. It is also probable that the *Caroline* brought another group of about 100 Saints in August of the same year. The ship *Harmony* also carried a group of approximately 50 Saints across the Atlantic in 1841. The 1846 unknown voyage that Jenson refers to may be the *Windsor Castle*, which embarked from Liverpool on February 17, 1846.
25. Jenson, "Church Emigration," 441. M. H. Cannon, "Migration of English Mormons," 441, maintains that from 1840 to 1846, 4,733 British Saints out of the 16,241 who were baptized in the British Mission gathered to Nauvoo. LDS immigration historian Richard L. Jensen, "Transplanted to Zion," 77–78, estimates that at least

4,600 church members immigrated between 1840 and 1846 and that 90 percent of them gathered to Nauvoo before the martyrdom of Joseph and Hyrum Smith on June 27, 1844.
26. Allen and Leonard, *Story of the Latter-day Saints*, 160, most likely following the research of M. H. Cannon, "Migration of English Mormons," 205n61, also accept the figure of 4,733 British Saints who gathered to Nauvoo before her exile, which thus boosted the population over 25 percent. Black, "New Insights Replace Old Traditions," 12, indicates that 26 percent of LDS church membership from 1830 to 1848 originated in England. She also notes that her statistics parallel those of Cannon, "Migration of English Mormons," 441, who estimates that 25 percent of the British Saints who had immigrated to Nauvoo between 1837 and 1846 had been baptized in England before their departure to America.
27. Ward, *Winter Quarters*, 60.
28. Thomas Callister, Reminiscences and Autobiographical Notes, fd. 1, 1; Autobiographical Notes, fd. 2, 8–9, CHL.
29. Carter, *Our Pioneer Heritage*, 16:505.
30. "[Reminiscences] of Priscilla Staines," in Tullidge, *Women of Mormondom*, 288.
31. For more information, see Piercy, *Route from Liverpool*; and Taylor, *Expectations Westward*.
32. Robert Pixton, Autobiography, 19, CHL.
33. [Journal of George Cannon], in Cannon, *George Cannon*, 110.
34. Robert Crookston, Autobiography, 5, CHL. Babylon, once a cosmopolitan city in the ancient world, became a symbol to Latter-day Saints of the world and worldly influence. See, for example, D&C 1:16.
35. Sonne, "Liverpool and the Mormon Emigration."
36. "Epistle of the Twelve," MS 1, April 1841, 311.
37. As noted previously, the names of the ships that voyaged from Bristol, England, to Quebec were the *Caroline* (embarking February 1841, with a second voyage embarking August 8, 1841) and the *Harmony* (embarking May 10, 1841).
38. The names of the three ships disembarking in New York were the *Britannia* (41 Saints, departing June 6, 1840), the *North America* (201 Saints, departing September 8, 1840), and the *Rochester* (130 Saints, departing April 21, 1841). These three combined voyages carried a total of 372 Saints.
39. Of the thirteen voyages that did not travel with an LDS company, twelve disembarked in New Orleans and one in Philadelphia. In 1845 the Forsyth family of four voyaged on the *Susquehanna* before making their way up the Delaware to Philadelphia. (See "History of John Irwin Forsyth," 1, unpublished manuscript, compiled by Grace Meldrum Smith, copy in the author's possession.)
40. Smith, *History of the Church of Jesus Christ of Latter-day Saints*, 4:230.

41. "Epistle of the Twelve," MS 1, April 1841, 311.
42. For a comparison of general maritime travel as compared with the Saints' Atlantic crossing, see Hansen, *Atlantic Migration*, and compare with Taylor, *Expectations Westward*.
43. Jenson, "Church Emigration," 12.
44. Robert Reid to Brother Ward, March 15, 1843, MS 4, May 1843, 15.
45. Mary Ann Weston Maughan, Journal and Autobiography, May 10–12, 1841, CHL.
46. *Wilford Woodruff's Journals*, 2:98.
47. Alexander Neibaur, Journal, 6, LTPSC.
48. William Clayton, Journal, 77, CHL.
49. William Clayton, Journal, 78–79, CHL.
50. Alfred Cordon, Reminiscences and Journal, 163, CHL.
51. "Extract of a Letter from Elder William Kay," MS 4, April 1844, 202.
52. Ward, *Winter Quarters*, 61.
53. Cannon, *George Cannon, the Immigrant*, 111–12.
54. *Wilford Woodruff's Journals*, 2:97, 100–101.
55. For an excellent article on the LDS experience in New Orleans during this era, see Buice, "Saints Came Marching In," 221–37.
56. *Deseret News 1997–98 Church Almanac*, 159–61. For more information on New Orleans as a port for LDS immigration, see Buice, "Saints Came Marching In," 221–37.
57. Sonne, *Saints on the Seas*, 69.
58. Church leaders issued an epistle to the British Saints on November 15, 1841, directing them to use the port of New Orleans, rather than Montreal, New York, or Philadelphia, because it was the least expensive option and also provided the convenience of water travel (JH, November 15, 1841, 3, CHL). Several years later, LDS Liverpool emigration agent Reuben Hedlock again reminded the Saints that fares to the East Coast ports were higher than fares to New Orleans. See "Conference," MS 5, no. 10, March 1845, 155.
59. In a letter from Brigham Young to Franklin D. Richards dated August 2, 1854, "Foreign Correspondence," MS 16, October 28, 1854, 684, Young stated, "You are aware of the sickness liable to assail our unacclimated brethren on the Mississippi river, hence I wish you to ship no more to New Orleans, but ship to Philadelphia, Boston, and New York, giving preference in the order named." However, again for economic reasons, the port of New York became the primary port on the East Coast until the close of the nineteenth century.
60. Conway, "New Orleans," 79. The earliest mention of the Balize occurs in a letter by Phineas H. Young, JH, December 14, 1842, 2, CHL, wherein Young describes the arrest of John Snider by the boarding officer at the Balize. Snider was the

LDS company leader of the ship *Henry*, which came into port in New Orleans in 1842. A year later Thomas Bullock, who voyaged on the *Yorkshire*, indicated that he came in sight of the Balize on May 8, 1843 ("27th Quorum 70's Record," in Thomas Bullock, Autobiography, 14, CHL).

61. Conway, "New Orleans," 79–80.
62. James Palmer, Reminiscences, 66, CHL. See also Richard Rushton, Journal, 9–10, CHL, which relates that in this same year, another group of immigrating Saints aboard the ship *Hope* were towed with another vessel up the Mississippi.
63. George Whitaker, Autobiography, typescript, 7, CHL.
64. George Whitaker, Autobiography, typescript 7, CHL.
65. Lucius N. Scovil to Parley P. Pratt, December 15, 1848, MS 11, March 1, 1849, 72.
66. Whitney, *History of Utah*, 4:117.
67. Jean Rio Baker Griffeths, Diary, transcript, 9, CHL. Baker voyaged to America on the *George W. Bourne* in 1851.
68. Whitney, *History of Utah*, 4:117.
69. Alexander Neibaur, Journal, typescript, 8–10, LTPSC.
70. For an excellent article on this topic, see Enders, "Steamboat *Maid of Iowa*," 321–35. Dan Jones and Joseph Smith Jr. co-owned this vessel.
71. William Adams, Autobiography, typescript, 4, CHL.
72. "[Reminiscences of Priscilla Staines]," in Tullidge, *Women of Mormondom*, 289.
73. Dan Jones was the most influential LDS missionary sent to Wales. He also owned half of the steamboat *Maid of Iowa*, of which Joseph Smith owned the other half. Tullidge, *Women of Mormondom*, 290–91.
74. William Adams, Autobiography, typescript, 4, CHL.
75. Jenson, "Church Emigration," 445.
76. Alexander Wright, Journal, March 1839–January 1843, 398–99, CHL.
77. Jenson, "Church Emigration," 445–46.
78. Jenson, "Church Emigration," 446.
79. Pratt, *Autobiography*, 285.
80. Jenson, "Church Emigration," 450. Matthias Cowley had indicated the previous year that his father, James, was offered ten dollars per day to stay and work in St. Louis. His father emphatically refused, saying, "I started from home to go to Nauvoo, to see the Prophet of the Lord, Joseph Smith, and I'm going, bless your souls. I would not stop here for all of St. Louis." Matthias Cowley, Reminiscences, 1, CHL.
81. However, Stanley B. Kimball, "Saints and St. Louis," 489–519, presents a broader picture of St. Louis in recounting that the city served as an LDS refuge in spite of the 1838 extermination order issued by the governor of Missouri. He also points out that many Saints fled to St. Louis following the Nauvoo exile (1846) and

demonstrates how this inland city was an important stop for poor LDS emigrants, who after receiving needed employment continued their journey west on the Missouri River from 1846 to 1855. Slaughter, "'Meet Me in St. Louie,'" 49–108, provides a useful resource for a study of the Saints in St. Louis during the mid-nineteenth century.

82. Hiram Clark, Journal, LTPSC; excerpt quoted in MS 4, February 1844, 147.
83. Wrigley, "[Autobiography]," 5:496.
84. Wrigley, "[Autobiography]," 5:497.
85. Joseph Fielding to Parley P. Pratt, January 1842, MS 3, August 1842, 77.
86. Joseph Fielding, Journals, vol. 5, 2, CHL.
87. W. Rowley, Letter to the Editor, January 25, 1844, MS 4, April 1844, 193–94.
88. Hiram Clark, Journal, 147, LTPSC.
89. Alexander Neibaur, Journal, typescript, 12, LTPSC.
90. Whitney, *Life of Heber C. Kimball*, 312.
91. James Burgess, Journal, 65, CHL.
92. Robert Crookston, Autobiography, 6, CHL.
93. Joseph Smith Papers, History, 1838–1856, volume D-1 [1 August 1842–1 July 1843], https://www.josephsmithpapers.org/paper-summary/history-1838-1856-volume-d-1-1-august-1842-1-july-1843/284.
94. William Adams, Autobiography, typescript, 4, CHL.
95. Tullidge, *Women of Mormondom*, 291.
96. William Clayton to Edward Martin, November 29, 1840, typescript, 1, CHL.
97. Allen and Leonard, *Story of the Latter-day Saints*, 210.
98. The first group of Saints commenced to depart from Nauvoo on February 4, 1846. Remarkably, on the same exact date, unbeknownst to either party, about 230 eastern Saints left New York City for what was to become San Francisco on the ship *Brooklyn* to establish an LDS gathering place in the West. For more information on this six-month voyage under the ecclesiastical direction of Samuel Brannan see Hansen, "Voyage of the *Brooklyn*," 46–72.

## 3. In and Out of Liverpool

1. MS 2, April 1842, indicates the change in publication from Manchester to Liverpool. This move certainly made it much easier for church leaders and LDS agents to supervise emigration affairs, which were often tied in with news from the *Star*.
2. Parrish, "Beginnings of the *Millennial Star*," 135–39. Parrish further notes that the *Millennial Star* was "published as a monthly, biweekly, or weekly publication for 130 years, . . . the longest continuous publication in the history of the Church,

terminating in 1970, along with *The Improvement Era, The Instructor*, and *The Relief Society Magazine*" (133). It is also of interest to note that the name of the periodical certainly fits the scriptural theme of D&C 29:8, which states that one purpose of gathering the faithful to one place is "to prepare their hearts and be prepared in all things against the day when tribulation and desolation are sent forth upon the wicked," when the millennial era commences. Underwood, *Millenarian World*, 29, notes, "The Mormon doctrine of 'the gathering' served to provide a means of escape from much of the anticipated tribulation of the last days. At the same time, it produced a concentration of the Saints who could be properly prepared for the coming millennium. The gathering, therefore, was the pivotal premillennial event in Mormon eschatology." On the topic of the relationship between the millennium and the gathering in early LDS thought, see also Underwood, "Millenarianism," 50–51.

3. Parley P. Pratt, ed., "Information to Emigrants," MS 2, August 1841, 55–61. On instructions to emigrants for the years 1840–54, see Piercy, *Route from Liverpool*, 19–22.

4. "Emigration," MS 1, no. 10, February 1841, 263.

5. Smith, *History of the Church of Jesus Christ of Latter-day Saints*, 4:186, 5:296; D&C 124:25–27.

6. "Epistle of the Twelve," MS 1, no. 12, April 1841, 311.

7. Cited from the British Mission History, January 16, 1844, in Taylor, "Mormons and Gentiles," 204.

8. "Notice to Intending Emigrants," MS 14, November 20, 1852, 618.

9. Sonne, "Liverpool," 4–5. Yet two vessels did leave the port of London during two of the American Civil War years (1863–64). William Bramall, passenger on the LDS voyage of the *Amazon* (1863), noted, "[It] was not a matter of choice with us but of necessity. We could not obtain a vessel in the port of Liverpool suitable to our purpose—vessels of this description being almost unprecedentedly scarce this spring, and we were, therefore, compelled to go to London." *Deseret News 1997–98 Church Almanac*, 162–63, records the voyages from London during the years 1863–67: the *Amazon* carried 895 LDS passengers from London (1863); the *Hudson*, 863 (1864); the *Caroline*, 389 (1866); and the *American Congress*, 350 (1866). The last two voyages carried a very small number. The *Cornelius Grinnell* transported only 26 LDS passengers (1866) and the *Hudson* just 20 (1867). No voyages left the London docks in 1865. Voyages continued to be launched from Liverpool after this time. For more information on Liverpool as a port of LDS embarkation, see Woods, "Tide of Mormon Migration," 60–86.

10. Van Orden, *Building Zion*, 94.

11. Sonne, "Liverpool," 4. Sonne appears to be culling from Coleman, *Going to America*, 66, in which Coleman notes, "Sailors loved Liverpool, and on long voyages constantly talked about its charms and attractions. It was a sailors' paradise."
12. Aughton, *People's History*, 142–43.
13. Coleman, *Going to America*, 66.
14. Coleman, *Going to America*, 65–66.
15. Hawthorne, *English Notebooks*, 18.
16. Hans Hoth, Diary, December 27, 1853, typescript, translated from German script by Peter Gulbrandsen, BL.
17. Letter from James and Elizabeth Bleak, July 24, 1856, CHL.
18. Hans Peter Lund, Journal, March 15, 1858, CHL.
19. "History of Barbara Sophia Haberli Staheli," 1861, CHL.
20. Thomas Griggs, Journal, June 28, 1876, CHL.
21. Alma Ash, Autobiography, July 31, 1885, CHL.
22. Robert Schmid, Journal, May 17, 1886, CHL.
23. Thomas Atkin, Autobiography, January 18, 1849, CHL.
24. Letter from Andrew Gowan, April 9, 1855, in possession of Daughters of the Utah Pioneers, Salt Lake City.
25. Amos Milton Musser, Diary, March 20, 1857, CHL.
26. Andrew Amundsen, Diary, April 8, 1884, CHL.
27. David H. Morris, Journal, October 19, 1888, CHL.
28. William Davidson, Reminiscences, February 1848, CHL.
29. Letter from Andrew Gowan, April 9, 1855.
30. Garner, *Mormon Rebel*, 10.
31. Thomas Evans Jeremy, Journal, May 18–20, 1864, CHL.
32. George Dunford, Reminiscences and Journal, October 12, 1886, CHL.
33. James Farmer, Journal, January 7, 1853, typescript, 77, CHL.
34. I estimate that of the approximately 85,000 LDS converts who immigrated to Zion in the nineteenth century, about 55,000 were British, 25,000 Scandinavian, and 5,000 Swiss-German. The Swiss-Germans also used Liverpool as the main port of embarkation. Moreover, the total number would be increased by several missionaries returning from their fields of labor in Europe, who often oversaw the needs of their converts and fellow foreign church members. Regarding the LDS German emigration/immigration experience, see Alder, "German-Speaking Immigration." For a brief look at the LDS Swiss immigration experience, see also Alder, "From Beautiful Switzerland," 24–25. Historians Richard L. Jensen and William B. Hartley note that by 1890 LDS European immigration to America had declined, and they estimate that between 1840 and 1910, more than 103,000

European Saints had made the journey to the American Zion. See Jensen and Hartley, "Immigration and Emigration," 2:676.
35. Jenson, "Church Emigration," 181; Mulder, "Mormons from Scandinavia," 237. On the Scandinavian emigration/immigration experience as a whole, see Mulder, *Homeward to Zion*.
36. See Jackson, "Ports," 218–52. During this period, Copenhagen served as the headquarters for the Latter-day Saint Scandinavian Mission. Much of this information has been culled from Saints by Sea, https://saintsbysea.lib.byu.edu/. British and Scandinavian Mission records were also used, as well as customs bills of entry in the City of Hull. For information about vessels carrying LDS Scandinavian converts from Copenhagen, see Anderson, Maness, and Black, *Passport to Paradise*.
37. Jenson, "Sixtieth Company," 458. Jenson further notes that they were delayed fifteen days due to winds and storms.
38. Zaugg, "[Autobiography] of Frederick Zaugg," 25, in the author's possession.
39. Gillett and MacMahon, *History of Hull*, 303.
40. Rasmus Neilsen, Journal, January 7, 1854, typescript, translated from Danish by his son C. E. Neilsen, CHL. Rasmus's calculation of rail travel is about 100 miles off. The trip by rail from Hull to Liverpool was actually about 140 miles. Rasmus never made it to Salt Lake City. After burying his wife on January 26 along the Mississippi River, he recorded his last journal entry: "Lord have mercy on me and my children." His son (who translated the account) then recorded this editorial note: "The next day on the 28th he died." Both appear to have died from cholera.
41. Hans Hoth, Diary, typescript, December 27, 1853, BL.
42. Joseph Hansen, Hansen Family History, December 1852, 7, CHL. For a complete overview of the story of Scandinavian LDS transmigration through the British Isles, see Woods and Evans, "LDS Migration," 75–102, from which segments from this chapter were selected and adapted.

## 4. Shipping the Saints

1. For a succinct account of the mode of conducting LDS emigration, see Jenson, "Church Emigration," 85. In this narrative, Jenson relies heavily on chapter 8 of Piercy, *Route from Liverpool*, titled "Mode of Conducting the Emigrating," 17–19. For a general account of LDS emigration throughout the nineteenth century, see Taylor, *Expectations Westward*; Sonne, *Saints on the Seas*; and Pritchard, "Across the Waves." See also the many sources listed on this topic in Hunter, "Mormonism in Europe," 7–8, https://scholarsarchive.byu.edu/facpub/1389/.
2. Mackay, *Mormons or Latter-day Saints*, 244–45. In addition, although the *Liverpool Mercury* published several negative reports about the Saints during the

early 1840s (October 12 and November 4, 1842, and February 23 and March 22, 1844), one article appearing in the *Liverpool Albion* in September 1842 stated, "The emigration of the Mormons . . . is daily increasing. . . . The class of persons thus emigrating are in appearance and worldly circumstances above the ordinary men of steerage passengers." This article is cited in Armytage, "Gateway to Zion," 39.

3. Richards, "Missionary Experience Recalled by the Death of Queen Victoria," 363. Richards recorded the exact date of the invitation as May 14, 1854: "Received a notice to attend Select Committee of the house of Commons on the 22d—inst." See Samuel W. Richards, Diary, May 14, 1854, CHL.

4. Richards, "Missionary Experience Recalled by the Death of Queen Victoria," 363–65. About a decade earlier, in a previous article, "Missionary Experience," Richards explained, "On the 23rd of May, 1854, in a large and spacious room of the House of Commons of the British Parliament, in the City of London, could be seen tables arranged nearly in the form of a half circle with a committee consisting of fifteen members of the Commons . . . with John O'Connell, Esq., a prominent Irish Catholic defender, in the centre, as chairman."

5. Richards, "Missionary Experience Recalled by the Death of Queen Victoria," 363–65.

6. Richards, "Missionary Experience," 156.

7. Richards, "Missionary Experience Recalled by the Death of Queen Victoria," 366–67.

8. London correspondent of the *Cambridge Independent Press* (May 24, 1854) concerning LDS emigration agent Samuel W. Richards. See Richards, "Missionary Experience," 158–59. Pages 155–59 of this article also contain a firsthand account by Richards himself of this unusual evidence.

9. Sonne, *Saints on the Seas*, 117, 173.

10. This segment on the Guion Line was culled and modified from a previous article, Woods, "George Ramsden," 83–97.

11. "Rise and Fall of the Guion Line," *Sea Breezes* 19 (1955): 190.

12. This regard may be evidenced by the fact that the *Millennial Star* sent out a notice of Guion's death at the age of sixty-six in Liverpool. Among other things, the article notes, "On the announcement of his death flags were hoisted half mast at the Town Hall and police buildings, and also at most of the steamship companies' offices, as a mark of respect to his memory. Mr. Guion was well and favorably known as a man of honor, integrity, and great business capacity. Our own intimate relations with the Guion S. S. Company, in connection with our emigration business, which have been so long extended and mutually pleasant and satisfactory, invest Mr. Guion's death with more than common interest." See

"Death of Mr. Guion," *MS* 47, no. 52, December 28, 1885, 822. His obituary in the *Liverpool Daily Post*, December 21, 1885, notes that S. B. Guion was "a man of stern will, of keen judgment and of daring enterprise.... He was of singularly upright character." The *Liverpool Courier* for this same date, in a notice titled "Death of Mr. S. B. Guion," notes that Guion "may be said to have been one of those pioneers of the steam navigation which has been so perfected and worked such a revolution in ocean travelling as to justify Lord Palmereton's happy remark that we have at last bridged the Atlantic."

13. Chandler, *Liverpool Shipping*, 122–23.
14. Sonne, *Saints on the Seas*, 173.
15. "1861 England Census," Ancestry, accessed April 8, 2008, www.ancestry.com.
16. "1871 England Census," Ancestry, accessed April 9, 2008, www.ancestry.com. In the 1861 and 1871 census records, Ramsden's wife is listed as Ellen. Yet in the 1881 census record, her name is listed as Hellen. At this time, the Ramsden family was living in the town of Egremont, in the district of Wallasey, near Liverpool. As noted in the 1881 census, they were living in the "Ecclesiastical Parish or District of St. Johns Egremont."
17. "The Late Mr. George Ramsden," *Liverpool Courier*, May 27, 1896, further notes that he lived on Church Street in Egremont. In 1859 *Gore's Directory for Liverpool and Environs*, 211, has Ramsden listed as an emigration agent living at 25 Hunter Street. Nearly a decade later, in 1868, *Gore's Directory for Liverpool and Environs*, 998, has Ramsden living at 55 Church Street in Egremont.
18. British Mission History, vol. 24 (1869–1871), May 13, 1869, CHL.
19. British Mission History, June 1, 1869, CHL. However, the Guion Line did not provide food at Hull for its transmigrant European passengers as other shipping lines did. This is one way the Guion Line was able to cut the cost of the trip.
20. Joseph F. Smith to Franklin D. Richards, September 9, 1874, Joseph F. Smith Letter Book, 122, CHL.
21. Jensen, "Steaming Through," 9:7. In a letter written by Joseph F. Smith to William Burton, August 13, 1874, Joseph F. Smith Letter Book, 58–59, CHL, Smith told of Ramsden's bold efforts in breaking with the Liverpool "Shipping Conference" to offer a low bid on prices to retain the LDS immigration business. In addition, several entries in the diary of Joseph F. Smith between April and May of 1874 (Joseph F. Smith Papers, CHL) refer to business dealings with Ramsden during this period. See, for example, Smith's entries for April 9, 17, and 23 and May 1–2. Furthermore, Smith wrote to W. C. Haines of Ramsden's integrity and noted, "I believe he is as good as his word." See Joseph F. Smith to W. C. Haines, August 11, 1874, Joseph F. Smith Letter Book, 61–64, CHL. In this same year, Ramsden also showed his vigilance through a memo he sent to Joseph F. Smith, informing him

that a family of six had not been allowed to emigrate from England because one of the children had measles. See Memo of George Ramsden to Joseph F. Smith, June 26, 1874, Joseph F. Smith Papers, CHL.

22. Jensen, "Steaming Through," 9:6–7.
23. Cloward, *Steam-Ship Lines*, 17.
24. The Guion Line shortened the length of the Atlantic crossing from 32–36 days to 10–16 days. (See Evans, "Aliens En Route.") Though Morris and Co. of Hamburg was instrumental in providing good service for the European LDS emigrants from 1852 to 1869, its sailing vessels could not compete with the faster, more elaborate Guion steam vessels. Furthermore, its base was farther away from Liverpool than Guion's.
25. The topic of polygamy has been treated by scores of authors for more than a century. For example, the Studies of Mormon History website notes over 1,700 sources in discussing this controversial doctrine. See https://atom.lib.byu.edu/smh/search/?q=polygamy.
26. Anthon H. Lund, "A Good Friend Gone," MS 58, no. 23, June 4, 1896, 360–62. After the circular surfaced, Ramsden was invited to meet with Mr. Packard, U.S. consul at Liverpool, to discuss the issue of transporting Latter-day Saint immigrants. He and missionary Elder Nicholson met with Packard, and Ramsden again supported the church's position. See "The Emigration Question—Interview with United States Consul," MS 41, no. 38, September 22, 1879, 600–602.
27. Anthon H. Lund to Heber J. Grant, March 22, 1905, Lund Letter Books, CHL, as cited in Jensen, "Steaming Through," 9:7. In this same year, a letter written by William Budge to Samuel Goddard (July 15, 1879, European Mission Letter Book, CHL) sheds light on the circumstances and the LDS church's plans for dealing with the Guion Line: "Our arrangements with the [Guion] shipping company is to take only our people and they do not knowingly take others at our special rates on account of their contract with other shipping Companies[.] We however would like to send our people those who are interested in our Church and people . . . likely to become so."
28. *Liverpool, London & Paris*, 5, Maritime Archives and Library. Although the price for children under twelve is listed in the Guion travel guide as two pounds, the adult price is not mentioned. Yet an article published in the *Millennial Star* this same year notes the Saints' concern about the price of an Atlantic passage being raised to five pounds. Therefore, we can assume that the average price of an adult Atlantic passage from Liverpool to New York was about five pounds during the period the Saints worked with the Guion Line. See L. J. N., "Departure of the Fifth Company, and Prospective Change of Fares," MS 36, no. 36, September 8, 1874, 569.
29. *Liverpool, London & Paris*, 3–7.

30. For more information on the story of LDS Scandinavian transmigration through the British Isles, see Woods and Evans, "Latter-day Saint Scandinavian Migration," 75–102.
31. The 1881 England Census (Ancestry, accessed April 9, 2008, http://www.ancestry.com) describes Maples as being born in Thorne, a town thirty miles west of Hull. Since his wife and daughter were born in Australia, we can assume that Maples learned about the emigration business through his own personal experience immigrating to Australia during the late 1840s or early 1850s. Maples had returned during the early 1850s and established himself as an emigration agent working alongside Richard Cortis, Hull's leading emigration agent, who had been used by the Scandinavian Mission since the first pioneers arrived in December 1852. Later, Cortis and Maples would combine their business, with Maples taking sole control after the death of the former.
32. Latter-day Saint migrant Jesse N. Smith recalled, "Mr. Maples on behalf of the forwarding company furnished a meal for the emigrants and sent all forward the same evening to Liverpool" (Jesse N. Smith, Autobiography and Journal, 259, CHL). Another passing migrant noted, "Mr. Maples, the Guion Agent, came on board and got the list of emigrants" (Hans Jorgenson, Reminiscences and Journal, 174, CHL).
33. Apparently, this line had many staff members who also provided excellent service. Another Guion agent who is praised in several LDS immigrant accounts is a Mr. Gibson. See, for example, Letter of L. F. Monch, MS 50, December 24, 1888, 829; Letter of George Romney Jr., MS 51, December 23, 1889, 811; Letter of E. L. Sloan, MS 51, November 25, 1889, 749. However, the agency apparently did not avoid some criticism by the British government. According to government inspector W. Cowie, while other Atlantic passenger lines provided temporary lodging and meals for passing emigrants at Hull, the Guion Line transferred its passengers directly to the rails "so that those people [were] the greater portion of the day without a meal" (see *Reports Received by the Board of Trade*, 9). Yet for those traveling to Utah, such speed was often welcomed because it shortened the long journey time needed to transport converts from their homelands in mainland Europe to a new life in the Salt Lake Basin.
34. Alma Ash, Autobiography, [August 1885], 27, CHL.
35. G. O., "Detention in New York of Some of Our Emigrants," MS 48, no. 38, September 30, 1886, 601–2.
36. "The Fourth Company," MS 48, no. 38, September 30, 1886, 603. Three years later, Ramsden also reported, via telegram, a delay caused by a railway accident. None of the Latter-day Saints were killed. See "An Accident," MS 51, no. 39, September 30, 1889, 620–21. The term *Zion* in LDS theology refers to a place where God's

covenant people gather, or to the righteous themselves. In this context, *Zionward* simply implies that the converts were headed for Salt Lake City, which at this particular period of time was the main gathering place for the Latter-day Saints. For more information on this topic, see Sorensen, "Zion," 4:1624–26.

37. Daniel H. Wells to John Taylor and George Q. Cannon, September 1, 1886, European Mission Letter Book, 65–67, CHL.
38. "Statistical Emigration Report for 1874," MS 36, no. 42, October 20, 1874, 666.
39. Letter of C. C. Larsen et al. to President Joseph F. Smith, MS 37, no. 27, July 5, 1875, 428.
40. Letter of Junius F. Wells to Albert Carrington, January 6, 1876, MS 38, no. 5, January 31, 1876, 76. In another letter written by Adolph Anderson et al. to President George Teasdale, Anderson remarked, "Please extend to Mr. Ramsden my personal thanks and appreciation for his courtesies extended." See "Correspondence," MS 52, no. 22, June 2, 1890, 349.
41. "Telegram," MS 39, no. 28, July 9, 1877, 443.
42. "Departure," MS 40, no. 26, July 1, 1878, 411.
43. MS 41, no. 16, April 21, 1879, 251.
44. "Third Company of the Season," MS 41, no. 26, June 30, 1879, 412.
45. MS 41, no. 36, September 8, 1879, 571.
46. "Our Emigration," MS 48, no. 48, November 28, 1887, 763–64.
47. "Going Out of Business," *New York Times*, December 25, 1892, ProQuest Historical Newspapers, *New York Times* (1851–2004), 5.
48. Jensen, "Gathering to Zion," 189. Although this official statement was made by the First Presidency and the Quorum of the Twelve Apostles, British converts continued to trickle into America at a steady rate until the London Temple was erected in 1958. In fact, over a century after the 1894 statement, the LDS church First Presidency reissued an official policy regarding Latter-day Saint immigration to the United States: "In our day, the Lord has seen fit to provide the blessings of the gospel, including the increased number of temples, in many parts of the world. Therefore, we wish to reiterate the long-standing counsel to members of the Church to remain in their homelands rather than immigrate to the United States." See The First Presidency, "Remain in Homelands, Members Counseled," *Church News*, December 11, 1999, 7.
49. By this time the population of Salt Lake City had grown substantially, leaving fewer economic opportunities for immigrants than were available in the mid-nineteenth century.
50. "Rise and Fall of the Guion Line," 209. It is an equally impressive fact that the transatlantic LDS voyages had a perfect record of safety.

51. See British Mission History, June 30, 1894, CHL. Although the Anchor Line is mentioned herein, not only for June 30 but also for July 5–6 and September 20, 1894, the Allan Line was most likely the shipping company running from Glasgow at this time. This change rerouted LDS converts from the Scandinavian and Swiss-German Missions through the port of Leith to Glasgow, where they began the transatlantic voyage to New York. The journal of Anthon H. Lund for June 30 and July 5–7, 1894, CHL, notes that arrangements were made by Lund, the British Mission president at the time, and converts were then rerouted to travel with the Anchor Line (Allan Line), based in Glasgow. President Lund made these new arrangements known to President Sundwall of the Scandinavian Mission, President Naegle of the Swiss-German Mission, and President Wilford Woodruff.

52. "The Late Mr. George Ramsden," *Liverpool Mercury*, May 27, 1896, notes, "Mr. George Ramsden . . . died yesterday at his residence Church Street, Egremont. Mr. Ramsden, who was sixty-five years of age, had been unwell for a considerable time, his health having been seriously affected by the worry consequent on the collapse of the Guion Line. Mr. Ramsden was well known and universally respected in shipping circles, his geniality and kindly disposition having gained him hosts of friends." The Death Register lists George at age sixty-five at the time of his passing and lists his wife at age sixty-six at the time of her passing. Drawing from the 1871 census, which lists George as age forty and Ellen (Hellen) as forty-three, it is reasonable to suppose that his spouse had died about two years before he did, though the census records previously noted are not consistent in the age difference between George and Ellen (Hellen). According to *Gore's City Trade Directory for Liverpool* (1894), at the end of Ramsden's life, he was listed as the manager of the Fern House at 51 Church Street, Egremont.

53. "Late Mr. G. Ramsden."
54. "Death of Mr. George Ramsden," *Liverpool Daily Post*, May 27, 1896.
55. Anthon H. Lund, "A Good Friend Gone," MS 58, no. 23, June 4, 1896, 360–62. For more information on Anthon H. Lund, see Lund, "Out of the Swan's Nest," 77–105.
56. Anthon H. Lund, Diary, May 29, 1896, private copy in possession of Jennifer L. Lund.
57. Coman, *Economic Beginnings*, 2:184.

### 5. Crossing the Seas

1. For this chapter, I have drawn upon Woods, "Sea-going Saints," 54–60; maritime accounts I compiled in Madsen and Woods, *I Sailed to Zion*; and narrative information at Saints by Sea, http://saintsbysea.lib.byu.edu/.
2. Mary E. Fretwell Davis, Autobiography, 1, CHL.

3. Caroline Martine Anderson to Charles K. Hansen, June 17, 1864, 1, trans. Edith Melgaard Cox, in "History of Caroline Martine Anderson, First Wife of Charles Keilgaard Hansen," CHL.
4. Sutton, "[Autobiography]," 17:296.
5. J. Riley, "Poetry. On Emigration," MS 2, no. 10, February 1842, 160. For a larger treatment of LDS poetry at sea, see Brugger, "Mormon Maritime Migration."
6. "The *Metoka*," MS 4, September 1843, 80.
7. Ann Pitchforth, "To the Saints in the Isle of Man," MS 8, July 15, 1846, 12.
8. John William South, Autobiography, 5, CHL.
9. Mary Goble Pay, Autobiography, 1, CHL.
10. Joseph Beecroft, Journal, May 25, 1856, 10, CHL.
11. Ebenezer Farnes, Reminiscences, 2, CHL.
12. Simons, *Enduring Legacy*, 6:187.
13. John Daniel Thompson McAllister, Journal, vol. 4, 6, CHL.
14. Elizabeth White Steward, Autobiography, in *Barnard White Family Book*, 187, CHL.
15. B. H. Roberts, Autobiography, MS 106, bx. 1, fd. 1, bk. 1, 17, J. Willard Marriott Special Collections, University of Utah, Salt Lake City.
16. John Eden, Autobiography, MSS 1080, 3–4, LTPSC.
17. George Dunford, Reminiscences and Journal, MS 1722, 180, CHL.
18. John S. Fullmer, Diary, MS 117, fd. 1, 40, CHL.
19. James Palmer, Reminiscences, 63, CHL.
20. Ebenezer Farnes, Reminiscences, 2, CHL.
21. "History of a Polygamist Wife in Heber Valley . . ." [Contains autobiography of Jensine Marie Jensen Moulton], MS 5445, fd. 1, 8–9, CHL.
22. Simons, *Enduring Legacy*, 6:187.
23. Out of the ninety first-person LDS immigrant accounts examined during the Nauvoo years (1840–45), only 25 total deaths are mentioned. In addition, an estimated 670 Latter-day Saints died between 1847 and 1869 as they crossed the oceans. See research compiled by Woods, "I Have a Question," 41.
24. "*Monarch of the Sea*: A Compilation of General Voyage Notes," Saints by Sea, https://saintsbysea.lib.byu.edu/mii/account/932.
25. Hansen, "Mormon Family's Conversion," 717–18.
26. John Johnson, Reminiscences, MS 1779, fd. 4, 6–7, CHL.
27. Ebenezer Farnes, Reminiscences, 2, CHL.
28. Beazer, "[Autobiography]," 10:50.
29. Colonial Land and Emigration Commissioners, *Report on Necessity of Amending the Passenger's Act* (July 22, 1841), 3, cited in Davis, "Nineteenth-Century British Mormon Migration," 245.

30. Coleman, *Going to America*, 288. *Report on Necessity of Amending the Passenger's Act*, 3, informs us that the law could not be properly enforced as only one officer and an assistant were stationed at Liverpool.
31. Davis, "Nineteenth-Century British Mormon Migration," 246.
32. Piercy, *Route from Liverpool*, 19–21.
33. Letter of John Jacques, MS 18, 556.
34. Letter of James Thompson, MS 18, 623.
35. David Coombs, Journal, 3, in the author's possession.
36. For battle statistics for the *Alabama*, see Ward, Burns, and Burns, *Civil War*, 326.
37. Charles William Symons, Autobiography, in Meredith and Anderson, *Family of Charles William Symons*, 6. See also Sutton, "[Autobiography]," 17:297. Symons indicated that the ship the *Hudson* encountered was the *Georgia*, yet Sutton reported that it was the *Alabama*. However, according to Ward, Burns, and Burns, *Civil War*, 326, the *Alabama* sank in June 1864. Since the LDS immigrant accounts indicate that this particular contact with the Confederate vessel occurred on July 8, it does not seem possible that it was the *Alabama*. The *Millennial Star* reported the incident and stated that the Confederate ship was either the *Georgia* or the *Rappahannock*. "Correspondence," John M. Kay and others to President Cannon, July 19, 1864, MS 26, August 20, 1864, 540.
38. *Reminiscences of Charles W. Nibley*, 15.
39. Ann Pitchforth, "To the Saints in the Isle of Man," MS 8, July 15, 1846, 12–13.
40. Alston, "[Autobiography]," 8:36. The ship was the previously mentioned *General McClellan* in 1864.
41. Mary Ann Rawlings Aveson, [Reminiscences], in *History of the Richard Rawlings Family*, 98.
42. Isaiah M. Coombs, Diary, 40–42, CHL.
43. The one Pacific vessel that sunk was the *Julia Ann*, in 1855. Twenty-eight of the fifty-six passengers were Latter-day Saints. Of the twenty-eight Saints, only five drowned, while those who survived spent two months on an uninhabited island until they were eventually rescued. For the complete story of the *Julia Ann* shipwreck and its miraculous deliverance, see Woods, *Divine Providence*. This general study does not deal with the Pacific emigration/immigration experience due to page constraints.
44. Sonne, *Saints on the Seas*, 139.
45. Reminiscences of Wilson G. Nowers by Reinhard Maeser, *Church Emigration Book*, vol. 2, 1851, CHL. Church leaders generally tried to fill their vessels with church members, but on a number of occasions the voyages contained a mixture of people of varied faiths. In such circumstances, not only did the Saints try to do missionary work among their fellow non-LDS passengers, but LDS accounts

also provide evidence of blessings given to Saints and those of other faiths while crossing the Atlantic. For example, in 1843 Elder Lorenzo Snow blessed the steward of the *Swanton*, who was at death's door. His miraculous recovery led to the conversion of several others, including the first mate.

46. Lyon, *Diary of a Voyage*, 2, CHL.
47. See Woods, "Onboard the *International* . . . ," 23–25.
48. Letter of Christopher Arthur, MS 15, June 4, 1853, 358.
49. Letter by Thomas Fisher, MS 16, 447–48.
50. Emma Palmer Manfull, Autobiography, in "Utah Pioneer Biographies," vol. 19, 155, FHL.
51. Mary Ellison Vincent, Autobiography, 1, CHL.

## 6. Men in Motion

1. MS 5, August 1844, 46.
2. Spilsbury, *Alma Platte Spilsbury*, 40.
3. Conway, "New Orleans," 98–99.
4. Nathaniel H. Felt to Brigham Young, March 7, 1848, in Brigham Young Correspondence, CHL.
5. "Mormons in St. Louis," 5:441.
6. JH, March 12, 1849, 2–3, CHL.
7. Record of the Saint Louis Branch, 1847–50, May 3, 1849, CHL.
8. Record of the Saint Louis Branch, 1847–50, June 2, 1849, CHL.
9. Charles Dutton Miller, Reminiscences and Diary, 19, CHL.
10. David D. Bowen, Autobiography and Diary, July 18, 1849, CHL. The opposition from apostates continued for several years. William Gibson recalled a similar experience in St. Louis three years later: "We had a good number of apostates from Nauvoo to contend with who tried by every means to prevent the emigrants from going farther." William Gibson, Journals, 1:104–11, CHL.
11. Primm, *Lion of the Valley*, 155.
12. John Martin, Autobiography, 32, CHL.
13. Record of the Saint Louis Branch, 1847–50, June 16, 1849, CHL.
14. Record of the Saint Louis Branch, 1847–50, July 7, 1849, CHL.
15. Jenson, LDS *Biographical Encyclopedia*, 2:382. Felt kept a ledger while he was working as a tailor in Nauvoo, from which he extracted three pages of information regarding this deadly disease, and a detailed account of how to best treat the illness from a letter printed in the *St. Louis Republican* by a Dr. W. B. Herrek of Chicago. This ledger is in the possession of Spencer Felt, Nathaniel Henry Felt's great-grandson and heir.
16. "Mormons in St. Louis," 5:445–46.

17. Van Ravenswaay, "Years of Turmoil," 303.
18. Record of the Saint Louis Branch, 1847–50, February 16, 1850, CHL.
19. Eli B. Kelsey, "Letter to the Editor," [November 29, 1849], MS 12, January 15, 1850, 27. At this time, President Felt's office was located at no. 16 Third Street in St. Louis. See JH, January 26, 1850, CHL.
20. Record of the Saint Louis Branch, 1847–50, January 12, 1850, CHL.
21. Record of the Saint Louis Branch, 1847–50, January 19, 1850, CHL.
22. Record of the Saint Louis Branch, 1847–50, January 26, 1850, CHL.
23. Record of the Saint Louis Branch, 1847–50, February 2, 1850, CHL.
24. Bingham Bement to Sarah Bement, July 14, 1850, 2, Bement Family Letters, LTPSC.
25. Bingham Bement to Sarah Bement, August 25, 1850, 2, LTPSC.
26. Bingham Bement to Sarah Bement, October 5, 1850, 2.
27. Bingham Bement to Sarah Bement, October 20, 1850, 2.
28. Hezekiah Mitchell, Journal, April 14, 1850, CHL.
29. Record of the Saint Louis Branch, 1847–50, April 20, 1850, CHL. Nathaniel and his wife and two sons left St. Louis and joined the Edward Woolley Company at Council Bluffs on June 25, 1850, to cross the plains. Nathaniel served as a chaplain and was frequently called on to preach. Although cholera infected many emigrants as they crossed the plains, the only person who died from cholera in the entire company was Felt's teamster. Felt's company arrived in Salt Lake City on October 6, 1850.
30. "Mormons in St. Louis," *Missouri Republican*, May 8, 1851, 3.
31. Allen and Leonard, *Story of the Latter-day Saints*, 70: "The stay of the first non-Mormon officials in Utah was both brief and controversial, sowing seeds of new misunderstanding. They did not arrive until late in August 1851, and the difficulties began almost immediately.... The accusations they carried to Washington were only the beginning of a series of unfortunate and distorted reports that would again end in misunderstanding and tragedy."
32. Bingham Bement to Sarah Bement, December 7, 1850, 1.
33. Bingham Bement to Sarah Bement, December 21, 1850, 2.
34. An April 29, 1853, journal entry by William Gibson states, "The latter end of March I was appointed by Elder Orson Pratt to preach in & around St. Louis & in 1852 I was appointed by Elder Orson Hyde President of that Conference[;] in May 1853 I started with my family for the Valley." See William Gibson, Journals, April 29, 1853, 7, CHL.
35. William Gibson, Journals, May 21, 1851–52, 105–6, CHL.
36. SLR 1852–56 (May 8, 1852), 1; SLR 1852–56 (June 1, 1852), 8; SLR 1852–56 (June 12, 1852), 11. President Gibson's *local* PEF served the same purpose as the *general* church's PEF but was intended to be used solely by the Saints in St. Louis.

Although the record identifies the seven congregations as "wards," they were actually branches until the stake was officially organized.

37. William Gibson, Journals, Fall 1852, 108; Spring 1853, 112, CHL. Louis Espenschied was a German emigrant who in 1843 opened his St. Louis wagon factory at age twenty-two. His grandson, Lloyd Espenschied, in "Louis Espenschied and Family," 91–92, notes, "Strangely enough, it appears to have been a religious sect that gave Louis his first considerable business in 'prairie schooners.' When the Mormons sallied forth westward from Nauvoo in 1846, bound across the vast plains toward the Great Salt Lake, they were desperately in need of wagons. They themselves built most of them, it seems, but they were obliged to call upon others." Further, Lloyd notes that the eldest grandchild of Espenschied wrote, "Grandfather had made wagons for the Mormons when they left Illinois, and had made a special box on the back to hold fruit trees ready to plant." In addition, the author, drawing upon correspondence he received dated June 9, 1943, from LDS church assistant historian A. W. Lund, maintained that by 1855 Louis was still working with LDS emigration. Lund uncovered a letter written by John Wardle and Elder Erastus Snow to Espenschied that noted, "Paid $2,000.00 to Louis Espenschied and Co., for Wagons." Finally, later letters between President Brigham Young and Louis Espenschied reveal that Young and Espenschied were in correspondence with each other as late as 1859. See Young to Espenschied, June 1, 1857, and Espenschied to Young, August 29, 1859. See also Jeter Clinton to President Young, July 14, 1859, Brigham Young Office Files, CHL, in which Clinton discusses a $258 debt he owed to Espenschied.
38. SLR 1852–56 (October 8, 1852), 42.
39. SLR 1852–56 (October 8, 1852), 42.
40. SLR 1852–56 (October 8, 1852), 42.
41. SLR 1852–56 (October 8, 1852), 42.
42. Horace S. Eldredge, Journal, November 21, 1852, CHL.
43. SLR 1852–56 (March 18, 1853), 68.
44. SLR 1852–56 (March 18, 1853), 72. The German Branch was organized during President Eldredge's stewardship. The branch met in "the mound market room" where Elder John Gerber "preach[ed] there in the German language" to eight members (as of January 1854). Moreover, multiple entries in SLR 1852–56 mention Frederick Loba, who was called to preside over the branch, as well as the congregation's "good standing." See SLR 1852–56 (December 31, 1852), 5; (February 4, 1853), 63; (January 27, 1854), 130; (March 3, 1854), 137.
45. SLR 1852–56 (February 12, 1853), 22–23.
46. Major John Brown was the LDS emigration agent stationed at New Orleans.
47. Horace S. Eldredge, Journal, March 21–23, 25–31, 1853, CHL.

48. Horace S. Eldredge, Journal, June 1, 3, 8, 1853, CHL.
49. Horace S. Eldredge, Journal, July 24, 1853, CHL. Between November 27 and November 30, 1853, Eldredge wrote, "I attended a party at Jefferson Hall, Got up by the Saints for the benefit of the poor." Eldredge also noted on March 21, 1853, that he "attended a party at the Jefferson Hall" and on Sunday July 17, 1853, that he attended a church meeting. This record suggests that the Saints had been using Jefferson Hall for temporal, social, and spiritual purposes when Eldredge presided in St. Louis.
50. SLR 1852–56 (December 6, 1852), 83. President Gibson first suggested this idea, seeking to "make arrangements for a public party for the purpose of liquidating the church debt & also for providing fuel for the poor the coming winter" in November 1852. See SLR 1852–56 (November 12, 1852), 48.
51. SLR 1852–56 (November 11, 1853), 116, notes that the choir, led by Joseph Seel (see January 1, 1854, 125), was "provided with a room to practice in, at 2 dollars per month." SLR 1852–56 (October 28, 1853), 114.
52. SLR 1852–56 (January 30, 1854), 135.
53. Piercy, *Route from Liverpool*, 57.
54. In the fall of 1854, the St. Louis Stake comprised approximately 1,320 Saints. See SLR 1852–56 (November 4–5, 1854), 189–92.
55. SLR 1852–56 (September 1, 1854), 167. Commenting on the Saints' state in St. Louis as well as President Andrus's leadership, Elder Snow said, "A great work would be done here, many would be baptized, and he wanted the co-operation of all faithful saints, to assist him to do this work, he said he was satisfied with the moves, made by Bro M Andrus, that they were timely, judicious & wise, and had tended to establish the saints here, they were guided by the Holy Spirit, and with the Spirit he (E. S.) then felt he could bless St. Louis, and the spirit of the Lord would continue to work and [t]he saints here should be blest till they should leave for Zion." SLR 1852–56 (November 4, 1854), 190.
56. On March 1, 1857, Elder Parley P. Pratt noted that although he had several good church meetings with the St. Louis Saints, "the adversary ha[d] a great hold [t]here." See Pratt, *Autobiography*, 552.
57. For a succinct overview of the Utah War, see Poll, "Utah War." For a more detailed treatise, see Furniss, *Mormon Conflict*; and MacKinnon, *At Sword's Point*.
58. Though the St. Louis Stake was discontinued in 1857, a new stake reemerged a century later. For more information on the history of the Saints in St. Louis, see Woods and Farmer, *Saints Came Marching In*, from which some of the information for this chapter was culled. See also Farmer and Woods, "Sanctuary on the Mississippi," 42–55.
59. Hart, *Mormon in Motion*, 151–54.

60. *MS* 16, no. 43, October 28, 1854, 684.

## 7. The Knights of Castle Garden

1. See Woods, "'Pronounced Clean,'" 5–34, for information about LDS emigration through Philadelphia. *Deseret News 1997–98 Church Almanac*, 159–67, notes that only eight LDS voyages disembarked at Philadelphia during the entire nineteenth century: seven voyages during the years 1855–57 and one anomaly in 1884. Five voyages disembarked at Boston between 1855 and 1857 and only a dozen throughout the nineteenth century. Rail travel during the handcart years in the late 1850s brought some European converts through Philadelphia or Boston, as well as New York, as the First Presidency had instructed the Saints to take the railroad to the farthest rail terminus at Iowa City before beginning handcart travel. A letter from the First Presidency dated October 29, 1855, in "Thirteenth General Epistle," *MS* 18, no. 4, January 26, 1856, 54, advised emigrants, "Pursue the northern route from Boston, New York or Philadelphia, and land at Iowa city or the then terminus of the railroad; there let them be provided with hand-carts . . . thereby saving the immense expense every year for teams and outfit for crossing the plains." "Commissioners of Emigration," *The Mormon* 1, no. 13 (May 12, 1855): 3, reported that the New York commissioner had successfully passed a resolution to open Castle Garden.
2. "The Life of Charlotte Ann [Hillstead] Bates," 3, CHL.
3. Smith, "Castle Garden," 41–43. Smith's article draws heavily upon Svejda's *Castle Garden*, which is the best source for a detailed study of Castle Garden.
4. Svejda, *Castle Garden*, 44–45.
5. "The Mormon Hegira. A Fresh Importation. Mormons from England," *New York Daily Times*, January 3, 1856, 8.
6. See Woods, "Knights at Castle Garden."
7. For more information on Taylor as an LDS émigré, see Woods, "Gifted Gentleman," 161–62, which provides information about the number of LDS passengers on each voyage, as well as the port of disembarkation during the years 1855–57, when John Taylor was in New York City. For more information on Taylor as an LDS emigration agent in New York, see Woods, "Gifted Gentleman," 171–91, which is a source for this chapter.
8. *Deseret News 1997–98 Church Almanac*, 161–62, is drawn from the fact that John Taylor's first known letter written while in New York City to Brigham Young was dated April 11, 1855, and his last known letter sent to President Young from New York City was written April 18, 1857, before his return to Utah. Thus, during this two-year period, between mid-April 1855 and mid-April 1857, coupled with the fact that the Latter-day Saints did not begin to use New York as a port of disem-

barkation until late May 1855, we can hypothesize fairly accurately that Taylor supervised over 8,000 LDS immigrants (primarily British and Scandinavian) coming into these eastern seaports. Broken down by each eastern port, over 1,400 LDS passengers disembarked at Philadelphia, nearly 3,000 docked at Boston, and over 3,700 docked at New York. Moreover, a number of missionaries would have been on these voyages returning from their fields of labor in Europe.

9. John Taylor to Brigham Young, March 4, 1856, Brigham Young Correspondence, CHL.

10. McClellan, "Polemical Periodicals," 907, notes, "Soon after the Church formally announced the practice of plural marriage, Brigham Young appointed several men to go to various cities to establish periodicals to respond to antipolygamy polemic.... *The Seer* was edited by Orson Pratt and published from 1853 to 1854 in both Washington, DC, and Liverpool, England. It was followed by the *St. Louis Luminary* (November 1854–December 1855), established by Erastus Snow; *The Mormon*, founded by John Taylor in New York City in February 1855; and the *Western Standard of San Francisco*, edited by George Q. Cannon beginning in February 1856."

11. Smith, *History of the Church of Jesus Christ of Latter-day Saints*, 5:357.

12. Smith, "John Taylor," 102. Roberts, *Life of John Taylor*, 247, points out, "The Mormon office was situated on the corner of Nassau and Ann Streets, with the offices of the *New York Herald* on one side, and those of the *Tribune* on the other. Elder Taylor was thus in the very heart of Gotham's newspaper world."

13. *The Mormon* 1, no. 1 (February 17, 1855): 1.

14. Smith, "John Taylor," 102.

15. Roberts, *Life of John Taylor*, 249–50.

16. Roberts, *Life of John Taylor*, 251–52.

17. "FOREIGN CORRESPONDENCE. DESERET. Route for the Coming Emigration—General News," MS 16, no. 43, October 28, 1854, 684. See also *The Mormon*, which contains a number of lists that document the names of various vessels disembarking at New York, Philadelphia, and Boston, as well as their passengers shipped by Elder Franklin D. Richards from Liverpool. See, for example, the list of passengers on board the *Chimborazo*, 1, no. 12 (May 5, 1855): 3; the *S. Curling*, 1, no. 13 (May 12, 1855): 3; the *William Stetson*, 1, no. 15 (May 26, 1855): 3; the *John J. Boyd*, 1, no. 46 (January 5, 1856): 3; and the *Cynosure*, 1, no. 27 (August 25, 1855): 3.

18. "To the Emigration and Our Readers Generally," *The Mormon* 1, no. 1 (February 17, 1855): 3. A week later, *The Mormon* 1, no. 2 (February 24, 1855): 3, cited the *New York Evening Mirror* as stating that the main purpose of *The Mormon* was "to watch over the interests of the European Emigration, which Brigham Young ha[d] ordered."

19. *The Mormon* 1, no. 3 (March 3, 1855): 3.
20. Jenson, "Taylor, John," 1:18, points out that *The Mormon* was discontinued after Elder Taylor and other elders were called home to the Salt Lake Valley due to the threat of the Utah War.
21. See Letter of Esdras Howell, writing from "Carbondale, March 19, 1855," in *The Mormon* 1, no. 6 (March 24, 1855), 3.
22. John Taylor to Brigham Young, May 18, 1855, Brigham Young Correspondence, CHL.
23. John Taylor to Brigham Young, July 15, 1855, Brigham Young Correspondence, CHL. Two months later, Taylor again wrote Young, stating, "Since I last wrote you, part of another ship load of Emigrants have arrived, numbering 162. All poor, they have most of them obtained employment. Monetary and mercantile affairs are looking up a little, and prospects are brightening for laboring people." See John Taylor to Brigham Young, September 16, 1855, Brigham Young Correspondence, CHL.
24. John Taylor to Brigham Young, February 20, 1856, Brigham Young Correspondence, CHL.
25. The Brigham Young Correspondence located in the Church History Library in Salt Lake City contains twenty-one known letters that John Taylor wrote to Brigham Young between 1855 and 1857. There are also seventeen, possibly eighteen, known letters from Brigham Young during this time period. These letters from President Young are full of information regarding emigration. In fact, one lengthy letter dated October 30, 1856, is entirely devoted to emigration and carefully treats the challenges of a triangular correspondence between Franklin D. Richards in Liverpool, John Taylor in New York, and President Young in Salt Lake City. Perhaps more letters would have come to Taylor from the Salt Lake Valley, but getting the mail across the nation in a timely fashion posed a continual problem in the mid-nineteenth century. For example, in a letter from Young to Taylor dated July 28, 1856, President Young wrote, "In regard to the emigration, whatever we could say . . . would be long past before it reached you." In any case, the Brigham Young Correspondence provides a wealth of information, not only within the dialogue between John Taylor and Brigham Young but also among other LDS emigration agents assigned at such ports and posts as Liverpool, New Orleans, New York, Kanesville, Florence, Wyoming (Nebraska), Mormon Grove (Kansas Territory), St. Louis, Iowa City, and so on.
26. John Taylor to Brigham Young, April 11, 1855, Brigham Young Correspondence, CHL.
27. John Taylor to Brigham Young, July 15, 1855, Brigham Young Correspondence, CHL.

28. John Taylor to Brigham Young, January 18, 1856, Brigham Young Correspondence, CHL.
29. For a biographical treatise of Nathaniel H. Felt, see Woods, "Nathaniel H. Felt," 219–36.
30. John Taylor to Brigham Young, April 11, 1855, Brigham Young Correspondence, CHL.
31. Nathaniel H. Felt from New York to Brigham Young on April 28, 1855. See Brigham Young Correspondence, CHL.
32. In a letter from John Taylor to Brigham Young dated April 11, 1855, Brigham Young Correspondence, CHL, Taylor wrote of one such conference visit: "I attended Conference on the 6th of April at Philladelphia we had a very good time. The spirit of the Lord was with us introduced the subject of Tything to them, wherein they all acquiesced without a dissenting voice."
33. John Taylor to Brigham Young, May 18, 1855, Brigham Young Correspondence, CHL.
34. William Woodard, Journal, June 14, 1856, quoted in Smith, "Faithful Stewards," 95, CHL.
35. Smith, "Faithful Stewards," 95.
36. "Mormon Hegira," 8.
37. "Mormonism in New-York," *New York Daily Times*, June 1, 1857, 3; Madsen, *Presidents of the Church*, 77.
38. The best work on Castle Garden immigration in general is Svejda, *Castle Garden*. On the LDS immigration experience through Castle Garden, see Smith, "Castle Garden," 41–52.
39. Woods, Buckley, and Hallows have combined their skills to provide the full story of Wiggill's interesting life in *Life and Adventures of Mr. Eli Wiggill*.
40. Eli Wiggill, Autobiography, 454, CHL.
41. Eli Wiggill, Autobiography, 457–58, CHL. Another LDS immigrant who voyaged to New York shortly after Wiggill's group also described military music in the air: "The first thing I saw was the Military parading the streets of New York, and drumming up for volunteers to go and fight the south.... All work was stopped to make men enlist, and as I had no money, it looked rather blue for me [meaning he was tempted to join the Yankees and put on their uniform], but I had faith." William Probert Jr., Autobiography, in *Biography of William Riley and Hussler Ann*, 56.
42. Eli Wiggill, Journal, 460–61, LTPSC. See Woods, Buckley, and Hallows, *Life and Adventures of Mr. Eli Wiggill*.
43. Jacob Gates, Diary, entries for the end of 1860 and beginning of 1861, CHL, cited in Hartley, "The Great Florence Fitout," 341–42, and "'Down and Back' Wagon Trains," 29–31.

44. "Arrivals of Saints at New York," MS 23, June 22, 1861, 394. Several immigration accounts also mention that Jones aided the immigration process. That his time as an agent was limited is noted by the fact that Wilford Woodruff recorded that both Elder Nathaniel V. Jones and Elder Jacob Gates preached in the Salt Lake Tabernacle on August 18, 1861. *Wilford Woodruff's Journals*, typescript, 5:590. It seems logical that Elder Jones returned to his home in the Salt Lake Valley after the 1861 immigration season ended. He was replaced by Horace Eldredge in 1862, William Staines in 1863–64, and Thomas Taylor in 1865.

45. Nathaniel V. Jones to Rebecca Jones, April 22, 1861, 1, Special Collections and Archives, University Libraries Special Collections, Utah State University, Logan.

46. John David Thompson McAllister, Journals, 1851–1906, May 25, 1862, 4:9, CHL.

47. McAllister, Journals, 4:11, CHL. Captain Trask made three voyages with LDS immigrants across the Atlantic during the Civil War—two on the *Manchester* (1861 and 1862) and one on the *General McClellan* (1864). See Sonne, *Saints, Ships, and Mariners*, 84, 136.

48. William Jeffries, Reminiscences and Diary, 154, CHL.

49. Jeffries, Reminiscences and Diary, 156, CHL.

50. F. W. Blake, "Diary of F. W. Blake, April—December 1861," May 22, 1861, CHL.

51. Elijah Larkin, "Diaries of Elijah Larkin," typescript, 466–67, CHL.

52. [Letter] of William C. Staines, MS 31, no. 33, August 14, 1869, 536.

53. Jenson, LDS *Biographical Encyclopedia*, 2:517.

54. [Blessing of William C. Staines], MS 7071, item 1, 1–2, CHL.

55. Hart, *Mormon in Motion*, 191–92, 194. Jenson, "James Henry Hart," 2:28, notes that Hart was a prosecuting attorney from 1883 to 1884.

56. Kimball, "Saints and St. Louis," 514–15. For an account of his years in St. Louis, see Hart, *Mormon in Motion*, 124–51.

57. Hart, *Mormon in Motion*, 182, 188–89.

58. Hart, *Mormon in Motion*, 202, notes, "For the most part he was treated fairly by the New York press." See pages 201–6 for examples of his image as presented by the reporters.

59. Jno. Scofield to Elder J. H. Hart, October 24, 1883, New York Emigration Office Records, CHL.

60. James H. Johnson to Mr. James Hart, July 3, 1883, Collected material concerning James H. Hart, n.d., CHL.

61. For more information about the Interstate Railway Act, see https://www.senate .gov/artandhistory/history/minute/Interstate_Commerce_Act_Is_Passed.htm.

62. For details about LDS immigration through Norfolk, see Woods, "Norfolk & the Mormon Folk."

63. These statistics were drawn from the "Mormon Immigration Index CD," published

by The Church of Jesus Christ of Latter-day Saints (Salt Lake City, 2000), now electronically merged into https://saintsbysea.lib.byu.edu/.

## 8. LDS *Emigration through Missouri*

1. See Smith, *History of the Church of Jesus Christ of Latter-day Saints*, 3:175.
2. This prayer was given in Kirtland, Ohio, on March 27, 1836, at the dedication of the Latter-day Saint temple. This sentence, an excerpt from the dedicatory prayer, appears in D&C 109:50.
3. Smith, *History of the Church of Jesus Christ of Latter-day Saints*, 5:211.
4. "Recollections of James H. Humphreys," 2, 5, BL.
5. Albert King Thurber, Journal, 23, BL. This account also explains that shortly thereafter, Thurber "left his company and joined the church, intending to remain" (1).
6. "To California in 1850," in "Recollections of Isaac Julian Harvey," 45–46, BL.
7. Cotton, "Across the Plains to California in 1849 and After: An Autobiography," 25, BL.
8. As part of the spirit of the bicentennial commemoration of the birth of the United States, this extermination order was officially rescinded in 1976 by Missouri governor Christopher S. Bond.
9. Woods, "Gathering to Nauvoo," 50.
10. St. Louis Luminary, February 3, 1855, cited in Kimball, "Saints and St. Louis," 489.
11. Hartley and Woods, *Explosion of the Steamboat Saluda*, 53. See also Hartley and Woods, "Tragedy and Compassion," 281–305.
12. Jenson, "Fifty-Sixth Company," 414.
13. Bennett, "'We Had Everything,'" 3. Bennett maintains that while the Mormon Battalion actually brought in only $5,000, he estimates that about two hundred LDS laborers likely brought in approximately $50,000 during this period (pp. 7, 19).
14. Brooks, *On the Mormon Frontier*, 1:222.
15. In a letter dated August 2, 1854, Brigham Young instructed Elder Franklin D. Richards, a Latter-day Saint emigration agent at Liverpool, as follows: "You are aware of the sickness liable to assail our unacclimated brethren on the Mississippi river, hence I wish you to ship no more to New Orleans, but ship to Philadelphia, Boston, or New York, giving preference to the order named." Cited from "Foreign Correspondence," MS 16, October 28, 1854, 684.
16. For more detail on LDS transmigration through Missouri during the Civil War, see Woods, "East to West," 13–23.
17. Andrew Christian Neilson, Autobiography, 5, CHL.
18. Mary Charlotte Jacobs, "Story of My Life," 12, CHL.
19. Barry Wride, Journal and Autobiography 14, LTPSC.

20. Ove Christian Oveson, Journal, 23, CHL.
21. Freshwater, "Diary," 7:250.
22. "History of Mary Ann Ward Webb," 96.
23. Thomas Henry White, Autobiography, 1–2, CHL.
24. Thomas Henry White, Autobiography, 1, also adds that while at St. Joseph, White learned that the Union soldiers could collect one dollar for each man or boy on whom they could pin a ribbon; a successful ribbon pinning designated that the recipient was now in the army.

## 9. LDS *Frontier Outfitting Posts*

1. Two other temporary way stations were Garden Grove and Mt. Pisgah. For more information on these stations, see Gentry, "Mormon Way Stations," 445–61.
2. For a listing of the frontier outfitting posts and LDS pioneer companies (1847–68), see *Deseret News 1997–98 Church Almanac*, 167–76. See also https://history.churchofjesuschrist.org/chd/list?subtype=pioneer-company for a more current listing of the companies that includes links to all known first-person accounts from each company.
3. Isaac C. Haight, Journal, September 16, 1846, CHL, in Bennett, *We'll Find the Place*, 25. Bennett has also written an excellent work on the LDS history of Winter Quarters and the Kanesville region in the mid-nineteenth century titled *Mormons at the Missouri, 1846–1852*.
4. Bennett, *We'll Find the Place*, 282–83. For an excellent biography on Kane, see Grow, *"Liberty to the Downtrodden."*
5. *Frontier Guardian* 1 (April 18, 1849): 2, 6.
6. Nelson W. Whipple, Journal, Spring 1849, in Bennett, *Mormons at the Missouri*, 222.
7. Warren E. Foote, Journal, May 15, 1849, in Bennett, *Mormons at the Missouri*, 222.
8. Bennett, *Mormons at the Missouri*, 222–23.
9. *Frontier Guardian* 1, no. 7 (May 2, 1849): 2.
10. *Frontier Guardian* 1, no. 8 (May 16, 1849): 2.
11. Reuben Miller, Journals, CHL.
12. Silas Richards, Reminiscences and Journal, 6, CHL.
13. The Mormon Battalion was involved with mining at Sutter's Mill when gold was discovered. For more detail, see Bigler, *Gold Discovery Journal*.
14. *Frontier Guardian* 1, no. 7 (May 2, 1849): 2.
15. For more information on contact between the Saints in the Kanesville area and passing 49ers, see Woods, "More Precious Than Gold," 109–24, segments of which were culled and modified for inclusion in this chapter.
16. *Frontier Guardian* 1, no. 8 (May 16, 1849): 3.

17. *Autobiography of Peter Olsen Hansen*, 55–64; variant account in JH, August 7, 1849, 1–11, CHL.
18. See Nelson Wheeler Whipple, Autobiography and Journal, 88, CHL; Autobiography Sketch of Edward Phillip, CHL; and James Fisher Madison, Reminiscences, 1906, 9, CHL.
19. Jensen and Hartley, "Immigration and Emigration," 2:674.
20. See Seventh General Epistle, April 18, 1852, in Clark, *Messages of the First Presidency*, 2:99. Herein noted that one exception to this policy was when church leaders had asked foreign converts to remain in their homeland to preach the gospel before gathering to Zion.
21. For more information on this topic, see Hartley and Woods, *Explosion of the Steamboat Saluda*; and Hartley and Woods, "Tragedy and Compassion," 281–305.
22. Edward Kingsford, Autobiography, 1, CHL; Jacob Gates, Journals, vol. 5, 133, CHL. (Note: The journal pages are not numbered. This is my own pagination, and this entry is on the last page of volume 5.)
23. John Paternoster Squires, Reminiscences and Journals, May 8, 1853, CHL.
24. Christopher Jones Arthur, Autobiography, 6. CHL.
25. Christian Nielsen, Diary, May 1–2, 1853, CHL.
26. Christian Nielsen, Diary, May 8, 1853, CHL.
27. Cornaby, *Autobiography and Poems*, 31.
28. Fosdick, "On the Oregon Trail," 36. For more information on the ten-pound company, see Aird, "Bound for Zion," 300–325. On page 306, Aird notes that Brigham Young and his associates agreed that the lowest sum for which any church member could be emigrated was ten British pounds (10£).
29. Ririe, "[Autobiography]," 9:355.
30. See Ririe, "[Autobiography]," 9:355; Waters, "[Autobiography]," 11:164; Jane Ann Fowler Sparks, Reminiscences and Diary, 14, CHL. Hannah Tapfield King, Autobiography, May 1, 1853, CHL.
31. James McNaughton, Journal, May 29, 1853, CHL.
32. James McNaughton, Journal, June 5, 1853, CHL.
33. James McNaughton, Journal, June 12, 1853, CHL.
34. The Church Emigration Book 1853, CHL, notes, "Elder Isaac C. Haight, who was the Church Emigration agent at the outfitting point, selected a very healthy camping place at Keokuk, on a bluff near the river, where there was plenty of wood and grass handy. The citizens of Keokuk manifested a benevolent feeling towards the Saints, which was highly appreciated by them." For more information on Piercy, see Chatterley, "Frederick Piercy," 77–96.
35. Piercy, *Route from Liverpool*, 59–60. Lecheminant's "Entitled to Be Called an Artist," 65, details the artistic life of Piercy.

36. "Mormonism," *Keokuk Dispatch*, April 5, 1853, 2.
37. "The Mormons Are Coming," *Keokuk Dispatch*, April 12, 1853, 2.
38. *Keokuk Dispatch*, May 31, 1853. See also *Keokuk Dispatch*, June 7, 1853, 2.
39. "The Mormons at Work," *Keokuk Dispatch*, April 26, 1853, 2.
40. Cornaby, *Autobiography and Poems*, 31–32.
41. William W. Belknap to his sister, Clara, May 9, 1853, on microfilm at the Keokuk Public Library.
42. Belknap to his sister, Clara, May 9, 1853. Note that there are three microfilm reels of Belknap's correspondence. The original copies of his correspondence were given to Princeton University by the Keokuk Public Library.
43. For a full treatment of this historical event, see Woods and Atterberg, "1853 Mormon Migration," 1–23, also reprinted in *Mormon Historical Studies* 4, no. 2 (Fall 2003): 25–42, from which portions were selected for inclusion in this chapter. For a treatment of the maritime immigration narrative from Liverpool to Keokuk, see Woods, "From Liverpool to Keokuk," 3–24.
44. Unruh, *Plains Across*, 120.
45. William Y. Empey, Diary, April 9–10, 20, 1854, typescript, 115, 117, LTPSC, cited in Woods, "1854 Mormon Emigration," 233. I've culled information from this article for inclusion in my discussion of Mormon Grove in this chapter.
46. "The Cholera," MS, September 9, 1854, cited in Woods, "1854 Mormon Emigration," 233.
47. *Liberty (MO) Weekly Tribune*, July 7, 1854; "Cholera," *Weekly Missouri Statesman* (Columbia), May 12, 1854. "Cholera in Independence," *Liberty Weekly Tribune*, June 30, 1854, noted another thirty cases in the region, cited in Woods, "1854 Mormon Emigration," 233.
48. Christian Emil Neilsen, Autobiography, 1902, typescript, 10, CHL, cited in Woods, "1854 Mormon Emigration," 234.
49. Svend Larsen, "Extracts from My Autobiography," English translation, 11, CHL, cited in Woods, "1854 Mormon Emigration," 234.
50. "Foreign Intelligence-Kansas," MS, May 27, 1854, cited in Woods, "1854 Mormon Emigration," 235.
51. An account book located in HM 52587, William Y. Empey Papers, Huntington Library, San Marino, California, demonstrates that Dorr P. Curtis was assisting Empey with emigration matters during the spring and summer of 1854. Further, receipts are also included in the William Empey Account Book in HM 52614 of the William Y. Empey Papers. Three years earlier (1851), LDS British immigrant George D. Watt passed through Kansas in this same area and wrote, "The saints are all over this place some living in a large log and frame building belonging to Mr. Brewster

who is favorable to the Mormon people his house is situated on the bank of the river on the west side of the Union Hotel." See *Liverpool to Great Salt Lake*, 58.

52. Empey to Young, June 23, 1854, Brigham Young Correspondence, CHL, cited in Woods, "1854 Mormon Emigration," 236.
53. McGee to Empey, April 29, 1855, HM 52591, William Y. Empey Papers, cited in Woods, "1854 Mormon Emigration," 241.
54. Woods, "1854 Mormon Emigration," 240.
55. Woods, "1854 Mormon Emigration," 245.
56. Woods and Bashore, "Mormon Migration through Atchison," 39. Segments of this article have been culled, modified, and used in the discussion of Mormon Grove in this chapter.
57. *St. Louis Luminary*, March 3, 1855, 58, cited in Woods and Bashore, "Mormon Migration through Atchison," 41–42.
58. "The Point of Outfit for Our Spring Emigration," *St. Louis Luminary*, March 31, 1855, 74, reprinted in the *Squatter Sovereign*, April 17, 1855, 3.
59. "The Mormons," *Squatter Sovereign*, February 3, 1855, 2.
60. Woods and Bashore, "Mormon Migration through Atchison," 42.
61. Jane Charters Robinson Hindley, Reminiscences and Diary, 1855–1905, vol. 1, 17, CHL, cited in Woods and Bashore, "Mormon Migration through Atchison," 40.
62. Archibald McFarland, Reminiscences, 9, photocopy of holograph, CHL. For a descriptive history of the three homes, see "First 'Squatter' on Site of City," *Atchison Daily Globe*, December 8, 1927, sec. 6, p. 3, cited in Woods and Bashore, "Mormon Migration through Atchison," 43–44.
63. "First 'Squatter,'" 44.
64. William G. Cutler, *History of the State of Kansas*, 373, cited in Woods and Bashore, "Mormon Migration through Atchison."
65. For reference to Atchison being a "paper town" during its infancy, see Wyman, "Atchison," 298.
66. For a comprehensive historical overview of LDS policies and practices regarding African Americans, see Bush, "Mormonism's Negro Doctrine," 11–68.
67. For a discussion of the advent of the "twin relics" slogan and the double-pronged targeting of LDS polygamy and Southern slavery, see Poll, "Mormon Question," 117–31.
68. "Utah," *Squatter Sovereign*, February 3, 1855, 2.
69. "Our City," *Squatter Sovereign*, June 5, 1855, 2.
70. "Business of Atchison," *Squatter Sovereign*, June 26, 1855, 2.
71. W. J. Andrews to George J. Remsburg, February 10, 1910, in "Memoranda of Mormon Grove," *Atchison Daily Globe*, December 3, 1910, 7.

72. "First 'Squatter,'" 3. For a biographical sketch of Challis, see "Territorial Legislature of 1857–58," 10:205.

73. "Notice to Our Emigrants," *St. Louis Luminary*, April 14, 1855, 82, reprinted in the *Squatter Sovereign*, May 15, 1855, 2.

74. William G. Cutler, *History of the State of Kansas*, 371, cited in Woods and Bashore, "Mormon Migration through Atchison."

75. "More Emigrants," *Squatter Sovereign*, May 1, 1855, 2.

76. Milo Andrus to Erastus Snow, May 22, 1855, Mormon Grove, Kansas Territory, *St. Louis Luminary*, June 2, 1855, 110.

77. Article written by a newspaper reporter on January 11, 1856, appearing in the *New York Daily Tribune*, January 24, 1856, quoted in "Bypaths of Kansas History," *Kansas Historical Quarterly* 10, no. 1 (February 1941): 102.

78. Andrus to Snow, May 22, 1855, *St. Louis Luminary*, June 2, 1855, 110.

79. "More Emigrants," *Squatter Sovereign*, May 1, 1855, 2.

80. Milo Andrus to Editor, June 21, 1855, Mormon Grove, Kansas Territory, *St. Louis Luminary*, July 7, 1855, 130. In an 1855 map of Atchison County, both the LDS Camp and PEF Farm are drawn by the surveyor.

81. Andrews to Remsburg, February 10, 1910, in "Memoranda of Mormon Grove," *Atchison Daily Globe*, December 3, 1910, 7.

82. "Days of Ox Teams," *Deseret Semi-Weekly News*, June 14, 1887, 2.

83. Ballantyne to Snow, April 14, 1855, in *St. Louis Luminary*, April 28, 1855, 90.

84. "The Mormons," *Squatter Sovereign*, May 29, 1855, 2; also reprinted in the *St. Louis Luminary*, June 9, 1855, 115.

85. "Report," *St. Louis Luminary*, August 18, 1855, 155.

86. Bashore and Tolley, "Mortality on the Mormon Trail."

87. William G. Cutler, *History of the State of Kansas*, 371, cited in Woods and Bashore, "Mormon Migration through Atchison."

88. Beckman, "Atchison's First Railroad," 154.

89. Wyman, "Great Frontier Depot," 297.

90. Brigham Young was also an early advocate of the transcontinental railroad and owned stock in the Union Pacific Railroad. For more information about his involvement with the railroad, see Ambrose, *Nothing Like It*, 278–96.

91. The bulk of this segment on Iowa City as an outfitting post has been culled and modified from Woods, "Iowa City Bound," 162–89.

92. John Taylor to Brigham Young, April 16, 1856, Brigham Young Correspondence, CHL.

93. Trager, *People's Chronology*, 483, 485.

94. Letter of the First Presidency, dated October 29, 1855, in "Thirteenth General Epistle," MS 18, no. 4, January 26, 1856, 54. A later circular from the British Mission

Presidency dated February 8, 1856, MS 18, no. 8, February 23, 1856, 122, provided additional details for the westbound emigrants.
95. For a general history of nineteenth-century rail travel in America, see Schivelbusch, *Railway Journey*.
96. Andrew Smith, Diaries, May 12, 1856, CHL.
97. Autobiography of Elizabeth White Steward, in *Barnard White Family Book*, 187, CHL.
98. "Autobiography of George Harrison," 2:106–7.
99. "Journal of Peter Howard McBride," 13:360. Priscilla Merriman Evans also noted that the company of Saints she journeyed with to Iowa City by rail also traveled in cattle cars. See Priscilla Merriman Evans, Autobiography, 39, CHL.
100. See these articles denouncing the Mormon practice of polygamy: "Utah," *Davenport Daily Gazette* 20, no. 507 (June 6, 1856): 2; *Davenport Daily Gazette* 20, no. 511 (June 11, 1856): 1; *Davenport Daily Gazette* 3, no. 764 (April 15, 1857): 2.
101. "Mormon Husbands," *Daily Evening Reporter* (Iowa City) 1, no. 143 (August 16, 1856): 2.
102. *Iowa City Republican* 1, no. 15 (June 23, 1856): 3.
103. "The Republican Platform," *Davenport Daily Gazette* 2, no. 399 (February 1, 1856): 2, noted that the State Republican Convention would be held in three weeks. The article also added, "Acting in accordance with the spirit of this extract, the Convention at Iowa City will erect a pure and independent Republican Platform."
104. Daniel Spencer, Diary, March 15, 1856, typescript, 2, CHL. In an article titled "Departures," MS 18, no. 14, April 5, 1856, 217, Spencer was praised for his work in the British Isles, having left Utah for his mission there in 1852. Among other things, his appointment to supervise emigration in America was mentioned in this heartfelt statement: "We feel that a strong man has gone from us, and that in the strength of Israel's God he will be a source of great joy to the emigrating Saints."
105. Daniel Spencer, Diary, March 14, 30, 1856, typescript, 2, 4, CHL. According to the diaries of John Van Cott, March 15, 1856, vol. 2, p. 3, CHL, the two other elders were J. Goodsall and John Van Cott.
106. Daniel Spencer, Diary, March 31, 1856, typescript, 5, CHL; Diaries of John Van Cott, March 31, 1856, vol. 2, p. 12.
107. Daniel Spencer, Diary, April 1, 1856, typescript, 5, CHL.
108. See "Departures," MS 18, no. 24, June 14, 1856, 377–78. Andrew Jenson, "Ninety-Third Company," 19–20, also notes, "Owing to the competition between railway companies, the price for adult passengers from Boston to Iowa City was subsequently reduced to ten dollars, and children in proportion."
109. *Iowa City Directory and Advertiser for 1857*, 43.

110. William Woodward to Heber C. Kimball, June 11, 1856, CHL.
111. William Woodward, Journal, June 2, 1856, CHL. However, it appears that not everyone had the privilege of traveling by wagon. When the emigrants arrived, the size of their companies certainly influenced transportation to the Mormon campground. For example, Archer Walters, who arrived a few weeks before Woodward, noted, "Monday 12 of May: [1856] arrived Iowa at 3 o'clock. Dragged our luggage about 2 miles to camp ground." See Archer Walters, Journal, May 12, 1856, CHL.
112. Crandell, "Noble Woman," 318–19. Handcart construction was apparently directed by a local Iowa City wagonmaker. Charlene Hixon, "Handcart Expedition of 1856," 11, gleaned this information. Jacob E. Reizenstein, "Fact a Day about Iowa City," *Iowa City Press Citizen*, September 15, 1948, notes, "These carts were well-manufactured according to specifications, by a master craftsman, Jared Dondore." The *Iowa City Directory and Advertiser for 1857*, 11, reveals that at "S Lendry's" there was a local wagonmaker named J. Dondore. His obituary, titled "Jared Dondore Passes Away" (*Iowa Daily City Press*, December 19, 1913, 1), announces his death at age eighty-three and notes that he was "highly-esteemed" and "well-liked," adding that Dondore was a "popular member of the Odd Fellows and the Masons." In addition, an article titled "Plow Factory" (*Iowa Weekly Republican* 8, no. 20 [March 26, 1856]: 3) also mentions another business that was contracted to make handcarts for the Latter-day Saints. "This firm [Plow Factory] has a contract for supplying one hundred handcarts, for a Mormon emigrant company, that is expected to pass through our place this spring, on their way to Salt Lake." The Plow Factory is advertised in the *Iowa City Directory and Advertiser for 1857*, 32.
113. Susan Melverton R. Witbeck, Autobiography, 4, CHL.
114. "Foreign Correspondence," J. A. Little to Orson Pratt, April 26, 1857, written while Little was traveling on the Mississippi aboard the steamboat *Envoy*, *MS* 19, no. 24, June 13, 1857, 377–79. This same document demonstrates that Little was also involved in other emigration business matters. For example, he mentions a letter he wrote to a "Mr. Schuttler, the man who [was] making [their] wagons" (377). The man he is referring to is Peter Schuttler, a wagonmaker in Chicago. The autobiography of Charles Root Dana, 167, CHL, notes, "By Elder Little's request, I went to Chicago to pay a debt of one thousand dollars which he owed for wagons and also to purchase yoke, bows, etc." Apparently, the Saints had also contracted for a large number of handcarts to be made in St. Louis. For example, the previous year, an article titled "Mormon Emigration," *Davenport Daily Gazette* 2, no. 411 (February 1856): 4, drawing from the *St. Louis Republican*, publicly announced "a wheelbarrow emigration among the Saints, over the plains, to Salt Lake in the spring." The article also noted, "An establishment in this city [St. Louis] has

received an order, and are now manufacturing about five hundred of these vehicles [handcarts]." It is quite probable that the person making the handcarts was Louis Espenschied, a German immigrant who had moved to St. Louis in 1840. The Saints had been working with Espenschied as early as 1853, when St. Louis Mormon emigration agent Horace Eldredge purchased fourteen wagons at $58 apiece from Espenschied to help outfit the Saints who were gathering to Keokuk, Iowa, for their trek west. See Woods and Atterberg, "1853 Mormon Migration," 10. Furthermore, in a letter written by Erastus Snow to Brigham Young, February 14, 1857, CHL, Snow writes, "Enclosed you will find six Notes belonging to Mr. Louis Espenschied. . . . The several Notes with Int to this date amount to $9,382.06."

115. Priscilla Merriman Evans, Autobiography, 39, CHL.
116. Elizabeth Sermon, Autobiography, 2, CHL. Elizabeth crossed the Atlantic on the *Caravan*.
117. Clark, "[Autobiography]," 17:304, 306.
118. Crandell, "Noble Woman," 319.
119. For a full account of the handcart experience, see Hafen and Hafen, *Handcarts to Zion*.
120. Hartley, "Great Florence Fitout," 341.
121. Hartley, "Great Florence Fitout," 343.
122. Hartley, "Great Florence Fitout," 341–42.
123. Hartley, "Great Florence Fitout," 345. For information on church trains, see Hulmston, "Mormon Immigration in the 1860s," 32–48.
124. Hartley, "Great Florence Fitout," 367.
125. Hartley, "'Down and Back' Wagon Trains," 85.
126. Jenson, "Florence," 252. Jenson notes, "About 600 Latter-day Saint emigrants . . . were buried in the old Mormon cemetery at Florence."
127. Amos M. Musser, Diary, July 3, 1857, 20, CHL.
128. A segment of the content used on the Wyoming, Nebraska, post has been culled and modified from Woods, "East to West," 22.
129. Hansen, "Mormon Family's Conversion," 722.
130. Hartley, "Great Florence Fitout," 371; Hulmston, "Story of the Church Trains," 38.
131. Flygare, Autobiography, 54, Nils C. Flygare Collection, LTPSC.
132. Jenson, "Latter-day Saint Emigration," 116.
133. Joseph W. Young to Joseph A. Young, July 4, 1864, in Jenson, "Latter-day Saint Emigration," 116.
134. Smith, "Wyoming, Nebraska Territory," 47. Smith's treatment of the Wyoming, Nebraska, post (on pages 31–51) is the best information we have to date on the subject.

135. *Deseret News 1997–98 Church Almanac*, 175–76.
136. Hulmston, "Story of the Church Trains," 38–39.
137. Ambrose, *Nothing Like It*, 284.
138. Whitney, *History of Utah*, 2:241–42.
139. Whitney, *History of Utah*, 2:239.
140. "Autobiographical Sketch of Life and Labors of Jacob Weiler," 3–4, Church History Biographical Database, The Church of Jesus Christ of Latter-day Saints, https://history.lds.org/overlandtravels/sources/4462/weiler-jacob-autobiographical-sketch-1892-1895.
141. Ambrose, *Nothing Like It*, 279–80.
142. Ambrose, *Nothing Like It*, 282–83.
143. Ambrose, *Nothing Like It*, 284.

## 10. LDS Emigration and Military Posts

1. Zebulon Jacobs, Reminiscences and Diary, August 21, 1862, CHL.
2. Chittenden, *American Fur Trade*, 1:476; Hafen and Young, *Pageant of the West*, 13.
3. Hafen and Young, *Fort Laramie*, 20. Note that several sources list varied spellings of this trapper's name.
4. For an extensive treatment of the subject of Fort Laramie as a military post, see McChristian, *Fort Laramie and the U.S. Army*. For more information on Fort Laramie's military history, see McChristian, *Fort Laramie*.
5. Mattes, "Guardian of the Oregon Trail," 5–6. Mattes further notes, "On June 16, 1849 Major Winslow F. Sanderson arrived at Fort Laramie with four other officers and fifty-eight men who comprised Company E, Mounted Rifles."
6. Nadeau, *Fort Laramie and the Sioux*, 87–110. Although Nadeau and others have corrupted the last name of Lucien, McChristian, *Fort Laramie and the U.S. Army*, 64, points out that based on an interview with the daughter of this French interpreter, his name was Augusta Lucia. McChristian, *Fort Laramie and the U.S. Army*, 53–54, 59, further notes that a skirmish at the Platte Ferry the previous year left a smoldering feeling of ill will among the Sioux, who for the first time had seen U.S. troops react with deadly force over what they viewed as a minor incident. Apparently the Native American accused of stealing the lame LDS cow (High Forehead) viewed his act as retribution for the death of one of his relatives who had been killed during the skirmish. See McChristian, *Fort Laramie and the U.S. Army*, 55–85, for an excellent treatment of this event. For a compilation of military correspondence dealing with the Grattan Massacre, see "Engagement between United States Troops and Sioux Indians," 4–28, in the Fort Laramie National Historic Site Archive, Fort Laramie, Wyoming. A useful article dealing with the

Grattan affair is McCann, "Grattan Massacre," 1–25. For a succinct overview of the Grattan Massacre, see Metcalf, "Grattan Massacre," 446.

7. Smith, "Experience on the Plains," 756.
8. The names of the captains and members (including ages) of various LDS companies used throughout this chapter are available in the "Mormon Pioneer Overland Trail, 1847–1868 Database," https://www.familysearch.org/search/collection/2517340?cid=bl-pio-8041.
9. John Allen Sutton, Autobiography, 8, CHL.
10. Watkin Rees, Reminiscences, Watkin Rees Papers, 10, CHL.
11. Robert L. Campbell Emigrating Company Journal, in the Perpetual Emigrating Files, CHL.
12. Elizabeth Graham MacDonald, Autobiography, 1875, 18, CHL. McChristian, *Fort Laramie and the U.S. Army*, 74, notes that this slaughter ended after only ten minutes and that the Sioux immediately stripped, scalped, and mutilated the soldiers' bodies "to deprive the spirits of an afterlife." Furthermore, McChristian notes that one LDS traveler described "the sickening sight of forty dead faces upraised in the blazing sun, murdered and scalped, but still unburied beside the wreckage of a train that had been looted by the Indians" (80). At that time, it appears the emigrant did not recognize that the "mostly nude bodies" were those of Grattan's unit.
13. Poll, "Utah War," 607–8. For more information about the Utah War, see Furniss, *Mormon Conflict*. The best research to date on the Utah War is MacKinnon, *At Sword's Point*.
14. S. W. Richards and Briant Stringham to Brigham Young, August 18, 1857, Brigham Young Correspondence, CHL. The stations mentioned refer to way stations used by the Brigham Young Express and Carry Company, also known as the Y. X. Company. Arrington, *Great Basin Kingdom*, 162, notes that the Y. X. Company was "designed to provide way stations for handcart companies and other immigration, to carry the United States mail between the Missouri Valley and Salt Lake City, and to facilitate the movement of passengers and freight between Utah and the East."
15. Isaiah Moses Coombs, Diary, May 29, 1858, CHL.
16. "For the Guardian. Letter from John Taylor . . . ," *Frontier Guardian* 1, no. 25 (January 9, 1850): 1.
17. Cited from the journal of Erastus Snow in JH, October 19, 1849, 4, CHL. Three years later (1852), one emigrant remembered that some members of their company were destitute. He recalled, "Some had not money and no provisions. They laid their case before the commander of the fort and he gave them freely and

liberally, so we started, refreshed again." See David Udall, Reminiscences and Journal (1851, 1910), 9, CHL.
18. Hammer, "Story of the Life of Isaac F. Shaw (September 1, 1866)," 11, CHL.
19. More than two hundred LDS emigrants in the Willie and Martin handcart companies died during the fall of 1856 when trapped by early snows in the territory that is now Wyoming. Hafen and Hafen, *Handcarts to Zion*, 193, maintain that there were sixty-seven deaths out of a total of five hundred LDS emigrants in the Willie Company.
20. Biography of Agnes Caldwell Southworth, 4. Madsen, *I Walked to Zion*, 59, notes that Agnes and her family made it safely to Salt Lake City, arriving November 9, 1856. They settled in Brigham City, Utah, where Agnes married Chester Southworth. She later became the mother of thirteen children and died in 1924 at the age of seventy-seven in Brigham City.
21. "Rambling Reminiscences of Margaret Gay Judd Clawson," typescript, 28, CHL. Lyon, "Uncommon Aspects," explained, "The greater part of the wagon trains that traveled to California and Oregon were composed primarily of men. . . . In contrast, the Mormon pioneers . . . were families moving en masse to the Far West. . . . Women, children, and older people prevent a group from traveling as rapidly as a body of men could do."
22. For a discussion of ten unique features of the LDS emigration experience, see Lyon, "Uncommon Aspects," 33–34, 36, 38, 40.
23. Jacobs was in the Charles C. Rich Company, as noted at https://history.churchofjesuschrist.org/chd/individual/christopher-jacobs-1819?lang=eng&timelineTabs=allTabs, which lists his name and age as well as the names of other members of the Rich Company.
24. "Autobiographical Sketch of Christopher Jacobs," 1, Daughters of the Utah Pioneers Archive, Salt Lake City.
25. Nathan Hale Gardner, "Biographical Sketch of Ann Rogers Snow," 10, CHL.
26. Mosiah Hancock, Journal, 25–26, CHL.
27. Thomas Ambrose Poulter, Journal, in "Utah Biographies," 44:140, FHL.
28. The Giles family traveled in the Philemon C. Merrill Company. Kezia's age and the company members' names are noted at https://history.churchofjesuschrist.org/chd/individual/keziah-giles-1840?lang=eng&timelineTabs=allTabs.
29. Seegmiller, "Biographical Sketch of Kazia [Kezia] Giles Carroll, in Family Histories," [n.d.], CHL.
30. McChristian, *Fort Laramie and the U.S. Army*, 355–56, indicates that this attack took place nine miles below Fort Laramie, on the exact day the Sixth West Virginia unit had arrived at the fort to begin their military duties. He further notes

that two men were killed and seven wounded and that two women were carried off by the Native Americans in the assault.

31. Francis and Jensine Grundvig (also spelled Grundtvig) were members of the Minor G. Atwood Company. See https://history.churchofjesuschrist.org/chd/individual/francis-christian-grundtvig-1836?lang=eng&timelineTabs=all-events for a list of emigrants' names and ages and a surviving documentary describing Francis and Jensine Grundvig's overland travel to Utah in 1865.

32. Francis Christian Grundvig, Autobiographical Sketch, 1909, 12–15, CHL. Company member James P. Anderson, Autobiographical Sketch, 1, CHL, provided additional details about the attack: "One woman was captured and carried away by the Indians; her name being Mrs. Grundvig. We never heard from her any more. They also threw a rope one [on] a girl 18 years of age by the name of Stena Kemfy Jenson, but she managed to free herself from the ropes and in doing so she escaped from the Indians." Maria Lofdahl Andellin, "Life Sketch of Grandma Maria Lofdahl Andelin," noted, "One of our women by the name of Gruntvig, was kidnapped by the Indians, and we never heard a word of her after. From then on we traveled at night and camped in the day, so the Indians wouldn't know where we were camped." Peter Nielsen, Reminiscences, August 22, 1865, CHL, recalled, "Two of the Indians met brother and sister Gruntvig on the road, the[y] shot Gruntvig, and he run for the camp. One of the men jumped of[f] his hors[e], lifted sister Gruntvig up to the other man and both road into the trees, taking her with them. Sister Gruntvig hase never been heard of since." See also Romney, "Exciting Trip," 34–35, for a brief published account of this story.

33. Joel Judkins Terry, Diary, June 15, 1847, CHL.

34. Ann Gregory Wilkey, Autobiography, 1–2, CHL.

35. Henry Pugh, Journal, in JH, October 10, 1853, 18, CHL.

36. The standard, though dated, study on handcarts is Hafen and Hafen, *Handcarts to Zion*. A more recent article is Carter, "Mormon Handcart Companies," 2–13. An excellent updated treatment of various aspects of the handcart experience, especially as it pertains to Iowa, appears in the *Annals of Iowa* 65, nos. 2–3 (Spring/Summer 2006), a special commemorative issue devoted to this topic.

37. Mary Powell Sabin, Autobiography, 12, CHL.

38. Jesse Morgan, Journal, in Morgan, *Trip Across the Plains*, 13, LTPSC.

39. Levi Hammon Emigrating Company, August 20, 1851, 16, CHL.

40. Ossian F. Taylor, Journal, August 15, 1851, CHL.

41. Hannah Cornaby, Autobiography and Poems, [1881], typescript, 35, LTPSC.

42. Jens C. A. Weibye, September 23, 1862, 10–11, CHL.

43. Unruh, *Plains Across*, 244–301. In addition, beginning in 1861, the Saints began to transport provisions and oxen from the Salt Lake Valley in what were referred to as Church Trains.

44. Piercy, *Route from Liverpool*, 92. Referring to an attempt to begin drawing Fort Laramie the previous day, Piercy wrote, "Sketched what little I could see of it, but not having time to cross the river, I was unable to obtain a complete view of it until my return, when I made that which is used in this work" (91–92; see his sketch on page 94).

45. Sloan was a member of the LDS-operated Levi Stewart Freight Train. See "Autobiography of William K. Sloan," 245.

46. "Life of Perrigrine Sessions," 1839–1886, vol. 1, 43, CHL.

47. Sylvester Henry Earl, Diary, August 2, 1855, CHL.

48. Jesse Wentworth Crosby, Reminisces, 43–44, CHL.

49. Andrew Jackson Shupe, Journal, June 14, 1847, CHL.

50. [Autobiography] of Henry Frederick McCune, in McCune, "Henry Frederick McCune," 4, CHL. Henry traveled overland in 1857 with the Jacob Hofheins/Matthew McCune Company.

51. Thomas McIntyre, Journal, July 27, 1859, CHL.

52. *Life Incidents and Travels of Elder William Holmes Walker and His Association with Joseph Smith the Prophet* [1943], 15, CHL.

53. "Autobiography of William K. Sloan," 245.

54. For an overview of the Willie Company's harrowing experience, see Fleek, "Ordeal by Handcart," 20–26.

55. Autobiography of Amasa Christian Linford, in *Autobiography of James Henry Linford Sr.*, 54, LTPSC. However, in this autobiographical account, Linford may have forgotten or not been aware of flour that was apparently purchased. In George Cunningham, Reminisces, 1876, 2–5, CHL, Cunningham, also a member of the Willie Company, remembered, "As our provisions were very exhausted our captain went to Fort Laramie and bought a ton or two of flour for which he had to pay $20.00 per hundred pounds." That provisions were purchased at Fort Laramie is also demonstrated in the journal of Levi Savage, October 1, 1856, CHL. Savage was also a member of this company and wrote, "Went to the Fort and perchased provisions. They are exstreamly costly."

56. Luke William Gallup, Reminiscences and Diary, May 1842–March 1891, 131, CHL.

57. Alfred Cordon Emigrating Company Journal, August 20, 1851, CHL.

58. Charles R. Savage, Diaries, 1855–1909, July 21, 1860, vol. 3, 70, CHL. Apparently the price was lowered if emigrants were headed east instead of west. For example, Robert, who noted that his company paid twenty dollars per one hundred pounds of flour, added, "They said if we were traveling East instead of West they

would let us have it for government price to wit $4.00 per 100 lbs." See Journals of Robert McQuarrie (1854–1917), August 4, 1857, vol. 1, 11–12, CHL.

59. McChristian, *Fort Laramie and the U.S. Army*, 24.
60. Hartley and Woods, *Explosion of the Steamboat Saluda*, 37–38.
61. Charles Ramsden Bailey, Autobiography, 11, in Joel Edward Ricks, Cache Valley Historical Material, CHL. The diaries and reminiscences of Richard Ballantyne (1852–1896), August 14, 1855, CHL, further note that on this same day Captain Ballantyne also took Isabella Race in a wagon to the fort for surgical aid, but she died on the way. Isabella appears to be the same woman spoken of in the autobiographical sketch of Mary Ann Ford Simmons, 3, CHL, also a member of the Ballantyne Company, who wrote, "When we were about two days journey from Laramie, a sister was making her bed in the wagon, a gun was there and it went off and shot her arm, breaking the bone halfway betwen the sholder and elbow. She ran out in camp with her arm swinging by a piece of flesh. they took her to Laramie, but she died on the way."
62. "Autobiography of Elizabeth Isabelle Jacobson Pulsipher," 499–500. See also Pulsipher, "[Reminiscences]," 7:50–51.
63. Samuel Amos Woolley, Diaries (1846–1899), 7:239, July 15, 1856, CHL.
64. William I. Appleby, Autobiography and Journal, September 5, 1849, typescript, 268, CHL.
65. Miles Romney, Journal, Summer 1855, 2, CHL.
66. Albert Jones, Autobiography, 2–3, in the LDS biographical sketches collection, CHL. Jones later wrote about helping dig the graves of fourteen people in his company. Hafen and Hafen, *Handcarts to Zion*, 193, estimate that between 135 and 150 of the 576 members in the Martin Company died.
67. Isabella S. Armstrong, Autobiography, in Emma Louise Armstrong, Notebook, 1917–1950, 170–71, CHL. See also Fleek, "Ordeal by Handcart," 20–26, for an overview of the Martin Company's hardships.
68. That the Platte River could be dangerous at times is attested by Andrew Jackson Allen, Reminiscences and Journal, 1857–July 1884, 2, CHL, who wrote, "It war verry difficult to cro[ss] all got over safe[,] then crossed the south fork of the laremy."
69. Hafen, *Overland Mail*, 56–58.
70. Hafen, *Overland Mail*, 59. See JH, February 28, 1852, CHL, for Brigham Young's letter. At the close of the following year, Brigham again wrote of his dissatisfaction with the government's mail service: "It might also be well to suggest to the department that it would be proper that is, if they wish to accommodate us with the mails to let their contracts to such persons as make bids with the expectation of fulfilling them, and who will provide suitably to do it with some prospects of

success. The contract heretofore would never justify extra expense; consequently, the contractors feeble attempts of course proved fruitless, and we have been left without a solitary mail, for over half a year at a time." See *JH*, December 13, 1853, CHL.

71. John Brown, Reminiscences and Journals, 1843–1896, vol. 1, 193, CHL.
72. The same sense of delight and relief is conveyed in an 1866 letter from a member of the Daniel Thompson Company, which simply states, "At Fort Larima we received letters from home." See "Reminiscences of James Gale," in McGrath, *Ancestors and Descendants of James Gale*, 33, LTPSC.
73. Samuel Amos Woolley, Diaries (1846–1899), 7:239–40, July 15, 1856, 10, CHL.
74. John Parson Camp Journal, in *JH*, September 3, 1855, 10, CHL.
75. Charles Ramsden Bailey, Autobiography, 11, CHL, reveals that the Richard Ballantyne Company was in contact with Fort Laramie on August 14, 1855. Erastus Snow was active in overseeing emigration matters at this time.
76. Homer Duncan to Brigham Young, August 5, 1861, CHL.
77. Samuel Amos Woolley, Diaries, 1846–1899, reel 1, box 1, fd. 3, vol. 9, 74, CHL.
78. Henry Stokes, History and Diary, September 12, 1862, typescript, 13, Pioneer Memorial Museum, Daughters of Utah Pioneers, Salt Lake City.
79. This chapter has been culled and revised from Woods, "Fort Bridger Connection," 2–14.
80. Chittenden, *American Fur Trade*, 1:476. For a biography on the life of Jim Bridger, see Alter, *Jim Bridger*.
81. *Wilford Woodruff's Journals*, vol. 3, typescript. Vanguard member Jacob Weiler remembered the meeting with Bridger as follows: "We were met by an old mountaineer who told us we never could raise a crop in the valley of the Great Salt Lake. He said he would give one thousand dollars for the first ear of corn we raised in this valley, for it could not be done, but we came here to try and we did, and all the world knows the result." See "Autobiographical Sketch of Life and Labors of Jacob Weiler," 4, CHL. Regarding Bridger's reputed statement that he paid $1,000 for an ear of corn, see Gowans and Campbell, *Island in the Wilderness*, 28, who suggest that "there is some question as to what the old mountain man really said on that occasion." Drawing on a July 8, 1859, entry in the *Journal History of the Church of Jesus Christ of Latter-day Saints (JH)*, these authors suggest two possibilities. They note that the *JH* for this date states, "The mountaineers never thought we could raise corn here, Mr. Bridger says he would give a thousand dollars per bushel of all the corn we could raise in the family." The authors also point out, "It is interesting that part of this statement has been rubbed out and someone has written in pencil, 'This is edited wrong.' The right version is on the opposite page which reads, 'Mr. Bridger says he would give $1,000.00 if he only knew if we

could raise an ear of corn.' This is signed by Andrew Jenson and William Lund as being correct."
82. *Wilford Woodruff's Journals*, vol. 3, July 8, 1847.
83. Erastus Snow, Journal, in "Journey to Zion," 272; Benjamin Ashby, [Autobiography], 21–22, CHL.
84. Ashby, [Autobiography], 21–22, CHL.
85. Lorenzo Brown, Journal, September 11, 1848, CHL. The following year, James Terry told of his brother's employment at the post: "When we got to Fort Bridger My brother Joshua Terry was working there and he let us have a yoke of oxen to help us on to the valley." See James Parshall Terry, Reminiscences and Journal, 106, 112–15, CHL. Louis Vasquez and Jim Bridger co-owned the fort. For more information on Vasquez, see Bray, "Louis Vasquez, Mountain Man," 1–25.
86. Journal of John Pulsipher ([n.p.], 1970), 27, CHL.
87. Isaac Russell, Autobiography, CHL.
88. *Howard Egan*, 140–45, CHL.
89. See http://www.lds.org/churchhistory/library/source/0,18016,4976-4631,00.html under the heading "De La Mare, Philip, Deseret Manufacturing Company," 1908, 6–7. Note also that Philip De La Mare was in the 1852 Philip De La Mare Independent Company.
90. Piercy, *Route from Liverpool*, 97–98.
91. Gowans, "History of Fort Bridger," 86.
92. Gowans, "History of Fort Bridger," 86.
93. Isaac B. Haight to F. W. Richards, August 31, 1853, cited in Gowans, "History of Fort Bridger," 101.
94. Gowans and Campbell, *Island in the Wilderness*, 66, note that Bridger sold the fort to a Latter-day Saint named Lewis Robison. Bridger received two payments of $4,000 each for the fort. See pages 66–78 for the complete story.
95. William Knox, Diary, [August] 25, [1855], typescript, CHL.
96. Thomas Evans Jeremy, Journal, in Marjorie Monro Renick, "Andrew Robertson, the Mormon Immigrant, 1802–1864," [October 18, 1855], Appendix, 22, CHL. "History of Fort Bridger and Supply," JH, 35–36, CHL, notes that at this time Elder George W. Boyd was the caretaker at Fort Bridger.
97. Ahmanson, *Secret History*, 35, CHL.
98. Amasa Christian Linford, [Autobiography], in Linford, Autobiography of James Henry Linford, 63–67, CHL. Another member of the James G. Willie Company wrote, "We came to Fort Bridger and teams came from Salt Lake City to meet us, and here we left our carts. We came to Salt Lake City on the 9th day of November 1856." See Jense Nielsen, [Reminiscences], in Albert R. Lyman, "Bishop Jense Nielsen (1936)," 4, 6–8, CHL.

99. Jesse Haven, Journal, December 4, 6, 1856, CHL.
100. Lewis Robison to Brigham Young, April 17, 1856, CHL.
101. Lewis Robison to Daniel H. Wells, July 12, 1857, Lewis Robison Collection, CHL; Gowans and Campbell, *Island in the Wilderness*, 93.
102. Gowans and Campbell, *Island in the Wilderness*, 99–101; Jenson, "Fort Bridger and Fort Supply," 39. For more information on the Utah War, see Furniss, *Mormon Conflict*.
103. James Palmer, Reminiscences, 185, CHL. Palmer was in the 1858 emigration company led by Horace S. Eldredge.
104. Thomas McIntyre, Diary, 64–65, CHL.
105. "Diary of John Young Smith," in *Joseph McKay—Martha Blair: Their Progenitors, Posterity and Lineal Lines—A Documented History, 1135–1967*, by Ila May Fisher Maughan (privately printed, 1967), 47, CHL.
106. Annie Taylor Dee, "Memories of a Pioneer," 18, CHL.
107. Lt. Col. Alex Lambers to H. H. Bancroft (regarding the early history of Ft. Bridger), Miner MSS, 8, BL.
108. [Reminiscences] of Sally M. Porter, in "Utah Pioneer Biographies," vol. 10, 10, FHL.
109. Lorenzo Hadley [Interview], in "Utah Pioneer Biographies," vol. 12, 16, FHL.
110. Elijah Larkin, Diary, typescript, vol. 2, 499, CHL.
111. Paxton, Passing Thoughts [1939], [3], https://www.lds.org/churchhistory/library. See also James Mills Paxton, Autobiography, 5–7, LTPSC.
112. William McLachlan, Reminiscences and Journals, 1863–1886, vol. 1, 115–39, CHL.

## 11. Arrival at the Final Post

1. For additional sources treating Salt Lake City in the nineteenth century, see Tullidge, *History of Salt Lake City*; and Alexander, *Mormons and Gentiles*. For an outsider's view, see Burton, *City of the Saints*.
2. The Old Fort was located about three blocks west and three blocks south of modern Temple Square in what is now known as Pioneer Park.
3. William Clayton, Diary, August 1, 1847, CHL. See also "Letter of Thomas Bullock," in "Camp of Israel, Winter Quarters, Council Bluffs, January 4, 1848," MS 10, no. 8, April 15, 1848, 118.
4. Cited in Morgan, *Old Fort*, 14.
5. J. C. Ensign, Reminiscences, in *Utah Semi-Centennial Commission Book of the Pioneers* [ca. 1897], Utah State Archives Series 14107, Utah Division of Archives and Records Service.
6. "Brief Biography of Rachel Emma Woolley Simmons," 11–14 (trail excerpt tran-

scribed from "Pioneer History Collection," available at the Pioneer Memorial Museum, Daughters of Utah Pioneers, Salt Lake City).
7. "Autobiography of Ann Woodbury Cannon," 167–69.
8. Daniel Davis, Diary, September 24, 1848, 101, CHL.
9. Aroet Lucious Hale, Diary, typescript, 17–18, CHL. Emeritus CHL archivist and Salt Lake City historian W. Randall Dixon noted that the Old Utah Fort was the primary gathering place for the pioneers in the late 1840s and that some Saints continued to settle there until the fort was torn down in 1851. Dixon also explained that during the 1850s, Union Square, also known as the Public Square and referred to as the Sixteenth Ward, served as the arrival place for the incoming emigrants. Phone conversation with W. Randall Dixon, March 12, 2010.
10. Dixon also noted that the Old Fort in Salt Lake City once stood at what is now known as Pioneer Park. He further explained that Union Square was located near downtown Salt Lake City where West High School now stands, between Third and Fourth West and between Third and Fourth North.
11. "Reminiscences of William Goforth Nelson," in JH, September 9, 1850, 7, CHL.
12. Peter McIntyre, Autobiography, [ca. 1850–1854], typescript, 40, CHL.
13. "Autobiography of Isaac Brockbank," 9–15. Arrington, *Great Basin Kingdom*, 64, explains that the Perpetual Emigrating Company, also known as the Perpetual Emigrating Fund or PEF, was launched in Salt Lake City in 1849, following the California gold rush, which brought tens of thousands of overlanders through the Latter-day Saint mecca. Unruh, *Plains Across*, 253, maintains that "at least 10,000 forty-niners detoured via the Mormon oasis."
14. Woodward, "In Early Days," 415.
15. Ann Gregory Wilkey, Autobiography, n.d., 2, CHL.
16. Joseph W. Young Emigrating Company, Journal, October 10–11, 1853, CHL.
17. Autobiographical Sketch of Ann Lewis Clegg, [ca. 1911], 2–3, CHL.
18. Watkin Rees, Reminisces, 8–12, CHL.
19. "[Autobiography] of John Crook," in "Utah Pioneer Biographies," vol. 7, 252–56, FHL.
20. Wilford Woodruff, "Correspondence from Utah," *The Mormon*, November 15, 1856, 3.
21. Crandell, "Noble Woman," 427.
22. Robert McQuarrie, Journals, September 12, 1857, CHL.
23. The Eighth Ward Square is located in downtown Salt Lake City. "It is bounded by 4th and 5th South and State [1st East] and 2nd East Streets." Email from W. Randall Dixon to the author, January 14, 2011.
24. [Autobiography] of Ellen Wasden, in "Two Pioneer Stories," 2–5, CHL.

25. Robert Bodily, Journal, typescript, 11, CHL.
26. Eli Wiggill, Autobiography, 484–85, CHL.
27. "[Autobiographical Sketch] of Hannah Harrison Snow," 316.
28. Charles Henry John West, Reminiscences, 7, CHL.
29. At this time Edward Hunter was serving as a general authority in the capacity of the presiding bishop of the church. In addition to supervising the temporal needs of the church under the direction of Brigham Young, Hunter was also responsible for helping LDS emigrants adapt to their new Utah home. Bishop Hunter served in this capacity for over three decades (1851–83). For a succinct overview of Hunter's life, see Hartley, "Edward Hunter Pioneer Presiding Bishop." For a complete treatment of Hunter's life, see Hunter, *Edward Hunter*.
30. Burton, *City of the Saints*, 249–50.
31. "Home Items," *Deseret Weekly News*, November 9, 1864, 44.
32. Editorial, "Hints for the Emigrating Saints, and Which May Profit Those Who Remain," MS 23, no. 15, April 13, 1861, 233.
33. "Commendable," *Deseret News* 15, no. 39 (August 30, 1866): 309.
34. Hans J. Zobell, Reminiscences, 73, translated from Danish by Albert L. Zobell, copy in private possession. It is not known why Zobell experienced this lack of hospitality. However, it is possible that the number of incoming emigrants affected the normal care given in such transitional circumstances. Evidence also shows that during the trail years of the mid-nineteenth century, members of a few LDS companies reported that no one greeted them upon their arrival in Salt Lake City, or they simply did not mention any reception upon entrance into the valley.
35. William George Davis, Diary, June 3–4, 1882, 48–49, CHL. Strack, "Railroads in Utah," 451, notes, "The growth of a network of railroads in Utah began with the completion of the Utah Central between Ogden and Salt Lake City in January 1870." Thus, Davis and those traveling with him would have taken the Utah Central to Salt Lake City in 1882.
36. Samuel R. Bennion, Diary, November 9, 1885, CHL.
37. Anthon H. Lund, Diary, November 10, 1885, CHL. Although Lund recorded the date as November 10 and Bennion noted it as November 9, both recorded that they arrived on Tuesday.
38. The high cost of rail travel in 1887 led to route changes. Instead of departing from New York City, incoming immigrants now began their rail travel at Norfolk. See Woods, "Norfolk & Mormon Folk," 72–92.
39. "For Emigrants," MS 14, no. 35, April 8, 1873, 221.
40. Jens C. A. Weibye, Reminiscences and Journals, September 29, 1873, CHL.
41. *Diary and Missionary Journal of William Kilshaw Barton, Pioneer of 1852*, November 1873, 33, privately printed, CHL.

42. James Samuel Bowler, Autobiography, 41, CHL.
43. P. [Peter] C. Carstensen, "Correspondence," written to Joseph F. Smith, July 23, 1874, MS 36, no. 34, August 25, 1874, 538–39. Elder Erastus Snow opened up LDS missionary work in Scandinavia in 1850 and therefore was beloved by the Danish Saints.
44. James H. Hansen, Daybook, July 10, 1882, 29–30, CHL.
45. Nielson, "[Autobiography]," 11:300–301.
46. "Immigrants Arrived," *Deseret News* 44, no. 32 (November 12, 1883).
47. Letter of C. J. Arthur, dated November 12, 1885, "The Last Company," MS 47, no. 49, December 7, 1885, 778.
48. Letter of E. [Edwin] T. Woolley, dated May 22, 1886, "Home in Zion—Incidents of Travel—Labors and Experience," MS 48, no. 25, June 21, 1886, 398–99.
49. Letter of C. F. Olsen, dated July 20, 1886, "Correspondence," MS 48, no. 33, August 16, 1886, 524.
50. John William Craven, "Correspondence," MS 51, no. 20, May 20, 1889, 310.
51. "Life of Charlotte Ann Bates," 3, CHL.
52. Alma Ash, Autobiography, 30–31, CHL.
53. Thomas Meikle Forrest, Diary, 6, submitted to the author by Keith Forrest.
54. John MacNeil to David and Ann MacNeil, September 27, 1870, in Buchannan, *Good Time Coming*, 100.
55. Jesse N. Smith, Autobiography and Journal, August 10, 1870, 262, CHL.
56. Letter of Elder George Goddard, "Incidents of Travel," MS 46, no. 50, December 15, 1884, 798.
57. See Arrington, *Great Basin Kingdom*, 108–12, on public works in Salt Lake City.
58. Silas Richards to Brigham Young, August 11, 1860, Correspondence of Brigham Young, CHL.
59. Arrington, *Great Basin Kingdom*, is the most reputable source in treating the Utah colonies directed by Brigham Young.
60. Joseph Smith, Sidney Rigdon, and Hyrum Smith, "A Proclamation to the Saints Scattered Abroad," MS 1, no. 2, March 1841, 274.
61. Park Valley is located about seventy-five miles west of Brigham City, near Promontory Point, where the transcontinental railroad was joined together.
62. Zaugg, "[Autobiography] of Frederick Zaugg," 33, in the author's possession.

# Bibliography

## Archives and Manuscript Materials

Andellin, Maria Lofdahl. "A Life Sketch of Grandma Maria Lofdahl Andelin, as Written by Her Own Hand..." Pioneer Memorial Museum, Daughters of Utah Pioneers, Salt Lake City.

"Autobiographical Sketch of Christopher Jacobs." Daughters of Utah Pioneers Archive, Salt Lake City.

"Autobiographical Sketch of Life and Labors of Jacob Weiler." Church History Biographical Database, The Church of Jesus Christ of Latter-day Saints. https://history.churchofjesuschrist.org/chd/transcript?lang=eng&name=transcript-for-jacob-weiler-autobiographical-sketch-1892-1895-3-4.

Bancroft Library, University of California, Berkeley.

"Biography of Agnes Caldwell Southworth." Pioneer Memorial Museum, Daughters of Utah Pioneers, Salt Lake City.

"Brief Biography of Rachel Emma Woolley Simmons." Pioneer Memorial Museum, Daughters of Utah Pioneers, Salt Lake City.

Church History Library, Salt Lake City.

Coombs, David. Journal. In the author's possession.

"Engagement between United States Troops and Sioux Indians," 4–28. Fort Laramie National Historic Site Archive, Fort Laramie WY.

Ensign, J. C. Reminiscences. In *Utah Semi-Centennial Commission Book of the Pioneers* [ca. 1897]. Utah State Archives Series 14107. Utah Division of Archives and Records Service.

Family History Library, Salt Lake City.

Forrest, Thomas Meikle. Diary. Submitted to the author by Keith Forrest.

"History of John Irwin Forsyth." Unpublished manuscript compiled by Grace Meldrum Smith. Copy in the author's possession.

Hixon, Charlene. "The Handcart Expedition of 1856 in Johnson County." Unpublished manuscript, 1975.

Hunter, J. Michael. "Mormonism in Europe: A Bibliographic Essay." Unpublished manuscript, Brigham Young University, Provo UT. https://scholarsarchive.byu.edu/facpub/1389/.

Jacobs, Christopher. Autobiographical Sketch. Daughters of Utah Pioneers Archive, Salt Lake City.

"John Irwin Forsyth." Unpublished manuscript compiled by Grace Meldrum Smith. Copy in the author's possession.

Joseph Smith Papers. Discourse, 11 June 1843–A, as Reported by Wilford Woodruff. https://www.josephsmithpapers.org/paper-summary/discourse-11-june-1843-a-as-reported-by-wilford-woodruff/1.

Joseph Smith Papers. History, 1838–1856.

J. Willard Marriott Special Collections, University of Utah, Salt Lake City.

*Liverpool, London & Paris Guide and Continental Indicator for Gratuitous Distribution to the Passengers Sailing by the Steamships of the Guion Line Proprietors*. Maritime Archives and Library, National Museums Liverpool, Liverpool, England.

"Liverpool to New York 28 Apr 1864–3 Jun 1864: A Compilation of General Voyage Notes." Saints by Sea. https://saintsbysea.lib.byu.edu/mii/voyage/249.

L. Tom Perry Special Collections. Harold B. Lee Library, Brigham Young University, Provo UT.

Lund, Anthon H. Diary, May 29, 1896. Private copy in possession of Jennifer L. Lund.

"Mormon Immigration Index CD." The Church of Jesus Christ of Latter-day Saints, Salt Lake City. Now electronically merged into Saints by Sea, https://saintsbysea.lib.byu.edu/.

"The Mormon Pioneer Overland Trail, 1847–1868 Database." https://www.familysearch.org/search/collection/2517340?cid=bl-pio-8041.

Special Collections and Archives, University Libraries Special Collections, Utah State University, Logan.

Stokes, Henry. History and Diary, September 12, 1862, typescript, 13. Pioneer Memorial Museum, Daughters of Utah Pioneers, Salt Lake City.

*Utah Semi-Centennial Commission Book of the Pioneers* [ca. 1897]. Utah State Archives Series 14107. Utah Division of Archives and Records Service.

William Y. Empey Papers. Huntington Library, San Marino CA.

Zaugg, Frederick. "[Autobiography] of Frederick Zaugg." In the author's possession.

Zobell, Hans J. Reminiscences. Translated by Albert L. Zobell. In private possession.

## Published Works

Aird, Polly. "Bound for Zion: The Ten-and-Thirteen-Pound Emigrating Companies, 1853–54." *Utah Historical Quarterly* 70 (Fall 2002): 300–325.

Alder, Douglas D. "From Beautiful Switzerland." *Pioneer* 55, no. 2 (2008).

———. "The German-Speaking Immigration to Utah: 1850–1890." Master's thesis, University of Utah, 1959.

Alexander, Thomas G. *Mormons and Gentiles: A History of Salt Lake City*. Western Urban History Series, vol. 5. Boulder CO: Pruett, 1984.

Allen, James B., and Glen Leonard. *The Story of the Latter-day Saints*. 2nd ed. Rev. and enl. Salt Lake City: Deseret Book, 1992.

Allen, James B., and Malcolm R. Thorp. "The Mission of the Twelve to England 1840–41: Mormon Apostles and the Working Class." BYU *Studies* 15 (Summer 1975): 499–526.

Allen, James B., Ronald K. Esplin, and David J. Whittaker. *Men with a Mission 1837–1841: The Quorum of the Twelve Apostles in the British Isles*. Salt Lake City: Deseret Book, 1992.

Alston, Christopher. "[Autobiography]." In *Our Pioneer Heritage*, compiled by Kate B. Carter, vol. 8. Salt Lake City: Daughters of Utah Pioneers, 1952–57.

Alter, J. Cecil. *Jim Bridger*. Rev. ed. Norman: Oklahoma University Press, 1966.

Ambrose, Stephen E. *Nothing Like It in the World: The Men Who Built the Transcontinental Railroad 1863–1869*. New York: Simon and Schuster, 2000.

Anderson, Shauna C., Ruth Ellen Maness, and Susan Easton Black. *Passport to Paradise: The Copenhagen Mormon Lists*. Vols. 1–2, covering the years 1872–94. West Jordan UT: Genealogical Services, 2000.

Armytage, W. H. G. "Liverpool, Gateway to Zion." *Pacific Northwest Quarterly* 48, no. 2 (April 1957).

Arrington, Leonard J. *Great Basin Kingdom: An Economic History of the Latter-day Saints 1830–1890*. Lincoln: University of Nebraska Press, 1966.

———, ed. *Presidents of the Church*. Salt Lake City: Deseret Book, 1986.

Aughton, Peter. *Liverpool: A People's History*. Preston: Carnegie Press, 1990.

"[Autobiographical Sketch] of Hannah Harrison Snow." In *Valiant in the Faith: Gardner and Sarah Snow and Their Family*, by Archibald Bennett, F. Ella M. Bennett, and Barbara Bennett Roach. N.p., 1990.

"Autobiography of Ann Woodbury Cannon." In *Cannon Family Historical Treasury*, edited by Beatrice Cannon Evans and Janath Russell Cannon. N.p.: George Cannon Family Association, 1967.

"Autobiography of Elizabeth Isabelle Jacobson Pulsipher." In *Pioneer Women of Arizona*, compiled by Roberta Flake Clayton, edited by Catherine H. Ellis and David F. Boone. Provo UT: Religious Studies Center, Brigham Young University; Salt Lake City: Deseret Book, 2017.

"Autobiography of George Harrison." In *Treasures of Pioneer History*, compiled by Kate B. Carter, vol. 2. Salt Lake City: Daughters of Utah Pioneers, 1953.

"Autobiography of Isaac Brockbank." In *Isaac Brockbank, Jr. 1837–1927: Autobiography*, compiled by Stephen W. Brockbank. N.p., 1997.

*Autobiography of James Henry Linford Sr.* Logan UT: J. P. Smith, 1947.

*An Autobiography of Peter Olsen Hansen, 1818–1895.* Compiled by Leland Hansen Ashby. N.p.: L. H. Ashby, 1988.

"Autobiography of William K. Sloan." *Annals of Wyoming* 4, no. 1 (July 1926).

Backman, Milt, Jr. "A Warning from Kirtland." *Ensign* (April 1989).

Bashore, Melvin L., and H. Dennis Tolley. "Mortality on the Mormon Trail, 1847–1868." *BYU Studies Quarterly* 53, no. 4 (2014): 109–23.

Beazer, Ellen Burton. "[Autobiography]." In *Our Pioneer Heritage*, compiled by Kate B. Carter, vol. 10. Salt Lake City: Daughters of Utah Pioneers, 1952–57.

Beckman, Peter. "Atchison's First Railroad." *Kansas Historical Quarterly* 21 (Autumn 1954).

Bennett, Archibald, F. Ella M. Bennett, and Barbara Bennett Roach. *Valiant in the Faith: Gardner and Sarah Snow and Their Family.* N.p., 1990.

Bennett, Richard E. *Mormons at the Missouri, 1846–1852: "And Should We Die..."* Norman: University of Oklahoma Press, 1987.

———. "'We Are a Kingdom to Ourselves': The Council of Fifty Minutes and the Mormon Exodus West." In *The Council of Fifty: What the Records Reveal about Mormon History*, edited by Matthew J. Grow and R. Eric Smith, 153–66. Provo UT: Religious Studies Center, Brigham Young University, 2017.

———. "'We Had Everything to Procure from Missouri': The Missouri Lifeline to the Mormon Exodus, 1846–1850." Paper presented at the Heritage Conference, Independence MO, September 15–16, 2000.

———. *We'll Find the Place: The Mormon Exodus 1846–1848.* Salt Lake City: Deseret Book, 1997.

Berrett, LaMar C. "History of the Southern States Mission 1831–1861." Master's thesis, Brigham Young University, 1960.

Bigler, David L., ed. *The Gold Discovery Journal of Azariah Smith.* Salt Lake City: University of Utah Press, 1990.

*Biography of William Riley and Hussler Ann, Probert Stevens.* Compiled and edited by Orvilla Allred Stevens. Privately printed, 1981.

Black, Susan Easton. "New Insights Replace Old Traditions: Membership of the Church in Nauvoo, 1839–1846." Paper presented at "Nauvoo, the City of Joseph," Brigham Young University, Provo UT, September 21, 1989.

Bray, Lauren C. "Louis Vasquez, Mountain Man." *Trail Guide* 3 (December 1954): 1–25.

Brooks, Juanita, ed. *On the Mormon Frontier: The Diary of Hosea Stout, 1844–1861.* 2 vols. Salt Lake City: University of Utah Press, 1964.

Brugger, William H. "Mormon Maritime Migration in Meter." PhD diss., Drew University, 2007.

Buchannan, Fredrick S., ed. *A Good Time Coming: Mormon Letters to Scotland.* Salt Lake City: University of Utah Press, 1988.

Buice, David. "The Saints Came Marching In: The Mormon Experience in Antebellum New Orleans, 1840–1855." *Louisiana History* 23, no. 3 (1982): 221–37.

Burton, Richard F. *The City of the Saints and Across the Rocky Mountains to California.* Edited by Fawn M. Brodie. New York: Alfred A. Knopf, 1963.

Bush, Lester. "Mormonism's Negro Doctrine: An Historical Overview." *Dialogue: A Journal of Mormon Thought* 8, no. 1 (1973): 11–68.

Cannon, George Q. *George Cannon, the Immigrant.* N.p., 1927.

Cannon, M. Hamblin. "Migration of English Mormons to America." *American Historical Review* 52, no. 3 (April 1947): 436–55.

*Cannon Family Historical Treasury.* Edited by Beatrice Cannon Evans and Janath Russell Cannon. N.p.: George Cannon Family Association, 1967.

Carter, Kate B. *Our Pioneer Heritage.* 20 vols. Salt Lake City: Daughters of Utah Pioneers, 1952–57.

Carter, Lyndia McDowell. "The Mormon Handcart Companies." *Overland Journal* 13 (1995): 2–13, 55.

Chandler, George. *Liverpool Shipping: A Short History.* London: Phoenix House, 1960.

Chatterley, Matthew L. "Frederick Piercy: English Artist on the American Plains." *Mormon Historical Studies* 4, no. 2 (Fall 2003).

Chittenden, Hiram Martin. *The American Fur Trade of the Far West.* 2 vols. Palo Alto CA: Academic Reprints, 1954.

*Church History in the Fullness of Times.* Salt Lake City: The Church of Jesus Christ of Latter-day Saints, 1989.

Clark, James R., comp. *Messages of the First Presidency of the Church of Jesus Christ of Latter-day Saints.* 6 vols. Salt Lake City: Bookcraft, 1965–75.

Clark, Louisa Mellor. "[Autobiography]." In *Our Pioneer Heritage*, compiled by Kate B. Carter, vol. 17. Salt Lake City: Daughters of Utah Pioneers, 1952–57.

Clayton, Roberta Flake, comp. *Pioneer Women of Arizona.* Edited by Catherine H. Ellis and David F. Boone. Provo UT: Religious Studies Center, Brigham Young University; Salt Lake City: Deseret Book, 2017.

Cloward, Edward. *The Steam-Ship Lines of the Mersey and Export Trade Register.* Liverpool: Nautical, May 1880.

Coleman, Terry. *Going to America.* New York: Pantheon Books, 1972.

Colonial Land and Emigration Commissioners. *Report on Necessity of Amending the Passenger's Act* (July 22, 1841). In Ray Jay Davis, "Law and the Nineteenth-Century British Mormon Migration." In *Mormons in Early Victorian Britain*, edited by Richard L. Jensen and Malcolm R. Thorp. Salt Lake City: University of Utah Press, 1989.

Coman, Katherine. *Economic Beginnings of the Far West.* 2 vols. New York: Macmillan, 1912.

Conway, A. A. "New Orleans as a Port of Immigration, 1820–1860." Master's thesis, University of London, 1949.

Crandell, Mary B. "Autobiography of a Noble Woman." *Young Woman's Journal* 6, no. 7 (April 1895).

Davis, Ray Jay. "Law and the Nineteenth-Century British Mormon Migration." In *Mormons in Early Victorian Britain,* edited by Richard L. Jensen and Malcolm R. Thorp. Salt Lake City: University of Utah Press, 1989.

*Deseret News 1997–98 Church Almanac.* Salt Lake City: The Church of Jesus Christ of Latter-day Saints, 1998.

*The Doctrine and Covenants of the Church of Jesus Christ of Latter-day Saints.* Salt Lake City: The Church of Jesus Christ of Latter-day Saints, 1981.

Ellsworth, George. "A History of Mormon Missions in the United States and Canada, 1830–1860." PhD diss., University of California, Berkeley, 1951.

Enders, Donald L. "The Steamboat *Maid of Iowa*: Mormon Mistress of the Mississippi." *BYU Studies* 19 (Spring 1979): 321–35.

Espenschied, Lloyd. "Louis Espenschied and Family." *Missouri Historical Bulletin* 18, no. 2 (January 1962).

Evans, Nicholas J. "Aliens En Route: European Transmigration through Britain, 1836–1914." PhD diss., University of Hull, 2006.

Farmer, Tom L., and Fred E. Woods. "Sanctuary on the Mississippi: St. Louis as a Way Station for Mormon Emigration." *Confluence* 9, no. 2 (Spring/Summer 2018): 42–55.

Fleek, Sherman L. "Ordeal by Handcart: The Handcart Pioneers' Winter of Discontent." *Mormon Heritage Magazine* 1 (December 1994): 20–26.

Fosdick, Stephen, Jr., ed. "On the Oregon Trail to Zion in 1853: Memoirs of Stephen Fosdick." In *The Denver Brand Book,* vol. 9. Boulder CO: Johnson, 1953.

Freshwater, William H. "Diary." In *Our Pioneer Heritage,* compiled by Kate B. Carter, vol. 7. Salt Lake City: Daughters of Utah Pioneers, 1952–57.

Furniss, Norman F. *The Mormon Conflict, 1850–1859.* New Haven CT: Yale University Press, 1960.

Garner, Hugh, ed. *A Mormon Rebel: The Life and Travels of Frederick Gardiner.* Salt Lake City: University of Utah Library, 1993.

Gentry, Leland H. "The Mormon Way Stations: Garden Grove and Mt. Pisgah." *BYU Studies* 21, no. 4 (Fall 1981): 445–61.

Gillett, Edward, and Kenneth A. MacMahon. *A History of Hull.* Hull: University of Hull Press, 1989.

*Gore's City Trade Directory for Liverpool.* Liverpool, 1894.

*Gore's Directory for Liverpool and Environs.* Liverpool, 1859 and 1868.

Gowans, Fred R. "History of Fort Bridger." PhD diss., Brigham Young University, 1972.

———. "Journey to Zion." *Utah Humanities Review* 2–3 (July 1948).

Gowans, Fred R., and Eugene E. Campbell. *Fort Bridger: Island in the Wilderness.* Provo UT: Brigham Young University Press, 1975.

Grant, Jedidiah. "Instructions to Newcomers." In *Journal of Discourses*, vol. 3. London: Latter-day Saints Book Depot, 1855–86.

Grow, Matthew J. *"Liberty to the Downtrodden": Thomas L. Kane, Romantic Reformer.* New Haven CT: Yale University Press, 2009.

Hafen, LeRoy R. *The Overland Mail.* Lawrence MS: Quarterman, 1976.

Hafen, LeRoy R., and Ann W. Hafen. *Handcarts to Zion: The Story of a Unique Western Migration, 1856–1860.* Lincoln: University of Nebraska Press, in association with Arthur H. Clark, Spokane WA, 1960.

Hafen, LeRoy R., and Francis Marion Young. *Fort Laramie and the Pageant of the West, 1834–1890.* 1938. Reprint, Lincoln: University of Nebraska Press, 1984.

Hansen, H. N. "An Account of a Mormon Family's Conversion to the Religion of the Latter-day Saints and Their Trip from Denmark to Utah." *Annals of Iowa* 41, no. 1 (Summer 1971): 717–22.

Hansen, Lorin K. "Voyage of the *Brooklyn*." *Dialogue: A Journal of Mormon Thought* 21, no. 3 (1988): 46–72.

Hansen, Marcus Lee. *The Atlantic Migration, 1607–1860: A History of the Continuing Settlement of the United States.* New York: Harper, 1961.

Hart, Edward L. *Mormon in Motion: The Life and Journals of James H. Hart 1825–1906 in England, France and America.* Salt Lake City: Windsor Books, 1978.

Hartley, William G. "'Down and Back' Wagon Trains." *Ensign* (September 1985).

———. "Edward Hunter Pioneer Presiding Bishop." In *Supporting Saints: Life Stories of Nineteenth-Century Mormons*, edited by Donald Q. Cannon and David J. Whittaker, 275–304. Salt Lake City: Bookcraft, 1985.

———. "The Great Florence Fitout of 1861." *BYU Studies Quarterly* 24, no. 3.

Hartley, William G., and Fred E Woods. "Compassion at Lexington, Missouri, 1852." *Missouri Historical Review* 99, no. 4 (July 2005): 281–305.

———. *Explosion of the Steamboat Saluda.* Salt Lake City: Millennial Press, 2002.

Hawthorne, Nathaniel. *The English Notebooks.* New York: Modern Language Association of America, 1941.

"The History of Mary Ann Ward Webb and Her Diary to Utah (1864)." In *Mary Ann Ward Webb: Her Life and Ancestry*, by Robert R. King and Kay Atkinson King. McLean VA: American Society for Genealogy and Family History, 1966.

*A History of the Richard Rawlings Family.* Compiled by Gladys Rawlings Lemmon. Privately printed, 1986.

Hulmston, John K. "Mormon Immigration in the 1860s: The Story of the Church Trains." *Utah Historical Quarterly* 58, no. 1 (Winter 1990): 32–48.

Hunter, William Edward. *Edward Hunter: Faithful Steward*. Salt Lake City: Publisher's Press, the Hunter Family, 1970.

*Iowa City Directory and Advertiser for 1857*. Compiled by John Kennedy. Iowa City: A. G. Tucker, 1857.

*Isaac Brockbank, Jr. 1837–1927: Autobiography*. Compiled by Stephen W. Brockbank. N.p., 1997.

Jackson, Gordon. "The Ports." In *Transport in Victorian Britain*, edited by Michael J. Freeman and Derek H. Aldcroft, 218–52. Manchester: Manchester University Press, 1988.

———. *Transport in Victorian Britain*. Edited by Michael J. Freeman and Derek H. Aldcroft. Manchester: Manchester University Press, 1988.

Jensen, Richard L. "The Gathering to Zion." In *Truth Will Prevail: The Rise of The Church of Jesus Christ of Latter-day Saints in the British Isles 1837–1987*, edited by V. Ben Bloxham, James R. Moss, and Larry C. Porter. Solihull: The Church of Jesus Christ of Latter-day Saints, 1987.

———. "Steaming Through: Arrangements for Mormon Emigration through Europe, 1869–1887." *Journal of Mormon History* 9 (1982): 3–23.

———. "Transplanted to Zion: The Impact of British Latter-day Saint Immigration on Nauvoo." *BYU Studies* 31 (Winter 1991).

Jenson, Andrew. "Church Emigration." *The Contributor* 13, no. 4 (February 1892).

———. "Fifty-Sixth Company—Kennebec." *The Contributor* 13, no. 9 (July 1892).

———. "Florence." In *Encyclopedic History of the Church of Jesus Christ of Latter-day Saints*. Salt Lake City: Deseret News, 1941.

———. "History of Fort Bridger and Fort Supply." *Utah Genealogical and Historical Magazine* 4 (January 1913).

———. "James Henry Hart." In *Latter-day Saint Biographical Encyclopedia*, vol. 2. Salt Lake City: Andrew Jenson Company, 1901.

———. *Latter-day Saint Biographical Encyclopedia: A Compilation of Biographical Sketches of Prominent Men and Women in the Church of Jesus Christ of Latter-day Saints*. 4 vols. Salt Lake City: Andrew Jenson Company, 1901.

———. "Latter-day Saint Emigration from Wyoming, Nebraska." *Nebraska History Magazine* 17 (April–June 1936).

———. "Ninety-Third Company." *The Contributor* 14, no. 1 (November 1892).

———. "Sixtieth Company." *The Contributor* 13, no. 10 (August 1892).

———. "Taylor, John." In *Latter-day Saint Biographical Encyclopedia*, vol. 1. Salt Lake City: Andrew Jenson Company, 1901.

"Journal of Peter Howard McBride." In *Our Pioneer Heritage,* compiled by Kate B. Carter, vol. 13. Salt Lake City: Daughters of Utah Pioneers, 1952–57.

"Journey to Zion." *Utah Humanities Review* 2–3 (July 1948).

Kimball, Stanley B. "The Saints and St. Louis, 1831–1857: An Oasis of Tolerance and Security." BYU *Studies* 13 (Summer 1973): 489–519.

King, Robert R., and Kay Atkinson King. *Mary Ann Ward Webb: Her Life and Ancestry.* McLean VA: American Society for Genealogy and Family History, 1966.

Lecheminant, Wilford Hill. "Entitled to Be Called an Artist: Landscape and Portrait Painter Frederick Piercy." *Utah Historical Quarterly* 48 (1980): 49–65.

*Liverpool to Great Salt Lake: The 1851 Journal of Missionary George D. Watt.* Edited by LaJean Purcell Carruth and Ronald G. Watt. Transcription by LaJean Purcell Carruth. Introduction by Fred E. Woods. Lincoln: University of Nebraska Press, 2022.

Lund, Jennifer L. "Out of the Swan's Nest: The Ministry of Anthon H. Lund, Scandinavian Apostle." *Journal of Mormon History* 29, no. 2 (Fall 2003): 77–105.

Lyon, T. Edgar. "Uncommon Aspects of the Mormon Migration." *Improvement Era* 72, no. 9 (September 1969).

Mackay, Charles. *The Mormons or Latter-day Saints.* London, 1852.

MacKinnon, William P., ed. *At Sword's Point.* Part 1, *A Documentary History of the Utah War to 1858.* Kingdom in the West: The Mormons and the American Frontier, vol. 10. Norman OK: Arthur H. Clark, 2008.

Madsen, Susan Arrington. *I Walked to Zion.* Salt Lake City: Deseret Book, 1994.

Madsen, Susan Arrington, and Fred E. Woods. *I Sailed to Zion: True Stories of Young Pioneers Who Crossed the Oceans.* Salt Lake City: Deseret Book, 2000.

Madsen, Truman G. *Presidents of the Church: Insights into Their Lives and Teachings.* Salt Lake City: Deseret Book, 2004.

Mattes, Merrill J. "Fort Laramie, Guardian of the Oregon Trail." *Annals of Wyoming* 17, no. 1 (January 1945).

McCann, Lloyd E. "The Grattan Massacre." *Nebraska Monitor* 37, no. 1 (1956): 1–25.

McChristian, Douglas C. *Fort Laramie and the U.S. Army on the High Plains 1849–1890.* National Park Service, Historic Resource Study, Fort Laramie National Historic Site. February 2003. http://www.nps.gov/history/history/online_books/fola/high_plains.pdf.

———. *Fort Laramie: Military Bastion of the High Plains.* Norman OK: Arthur H. Clark Co., 2008.

McClellan, Richard D. "Polemical Periodicals." In *Encyclopedia of Latter-day Saint History,* edited by Arnold K. Garr, Donald Q. Cannon, and Richard O. Cowan. Salt Lake City: Deseret Book, 2000.

Meredith, Carley Budd, and Dean Symons Anderson. *The Family of Charles William Symons and Arzella Whitaker Symons.* Privately printed, 1986.

Metcalf, P. Richard. "The Grattan Massacre." In *The New Encyclopedia of the American West*, edited by Howard R. Lamar. New Haven CT: Yale University Press, 1998.

Morgan, Nicholas Groesbeck, Sr. *The Old Fort: Great Salt Lake City, Great Basin, North America [cartographic material]: As Constructed by the Pioneers upon Their Arrival in the Salt Lake Valley in 1847*. Salt Lake City: N.p., 1950.

*Mormons in Early Victorian Britain*. Edited by Richard L. Jensen and Malcolm R. Thorp. Salt Lake City: University of Utah Press, 1989.

"Mormons in St. Louis." In *Our Pioneer Heritage*, compiled by Kate B. Carter, vol. 5. Salt Lake City: Daughters of Utah Pioneers, 1952–57.

Mulder, William. *Homeward to Zion: The Mormon Migration from Scandinavia*. Minneapolis: University of Minnesota Press, 1957; reprinted in 2000.

———. "Mormons from Scandinavia, 1850–1900: A Shepherded Migration." *Pacific Historical Review* 23 (1954).

Nadeau, Remi. *Fort Laramie and the Sioux*. Santa Barbara CA: Crest, 1997.

Nelson, Russell M. "The Gathering of Scattered Israel." The Church of Jesus Christ of Latter-day Saints. https://www.churchofjesuschrist.org/study/general-conference/2006/10/the-gathering-of-scattered-israel?lang=eng.

———. "Let God Prevail." The Church of Jesus Christ of Latter-day Saints. https://www.churchofjesuschrist.org/study/general-conference/2006/10/the-gathering-of-scattered-israel?lang=eng.

———. "The Temple and Your Spiritual Foundation." The Church of Jesus Christ of Latter-day Saints. https://www.churchofjesuschrist.org/study/general-conference/2021/10/47nelson?lang=eng.

*The New Encyclopedia of the American West*. Edited by Howard R. Lamar. New Haven CT: Yale University Press, 1998.

Nielson, Andrew Christian. "[Autobiography]." In *Our Pioneer Heritage*, compiled by Kate B. Carter, vol. 11. Salt Lake City: Daughters of Utah Pioneers, 1952–57.

Parrish, Alan K. "Beginnings of the *Millennial Star*: Journal of the Mission to Great Britain." In *Regional Studies in LDS Church History: British Isles*, edited by Donald Q. Cannon. Provo UT: Department of Church History and Doctrine, Brigham Young University, 1990.

Piercy, Frederick Hawkins. *Route from Liverpool to Great Salt Lake Valley, Illustrated with Steel Engravings and Woodcuts from Sketches Made by Frederick Piercy*. Edited by James Linforth. Liverpool: Franklin D. Richards, 1855.

Poll, Richard D. "The Mormon Question Enters National Politics, 1850–1856." *Utah Historical Quarterly* 25 (April 1957): 117–31.

———. "The Utah War." In *Utah History Encyclopedia*, edited by Allan Kent Powell, 607–8. Salt Lake City: University of Utah Press, 1994.

Porter, Larry C. "Ye Shall Go to the Ohio: Exodus of the New York Saints to Ohio, 1831." In *Regional Studies in Latter-day Saint Church History: Ohio*, edited by Milton V. Backman Jr., 1–25. Provo UT: Department of Church History and Doctrine, Brigham Young University, 1990.

Pratt, Parley P., Jr. *Autobiography of Parley P. Pratt.* Salt Lake City: Deseret Book, 1985.

Primm, James Neal. *Lion of the Valley: St. Louis, Missouri, 1764–1980.* 3rd ed. St. Louis: Missouri Historical Society Press, 1998.

Pritchard, Lily. "Across the Waves: Mormon Emigration of British Saints, 1840–1870." PhD diss., University of Bradford, England, 1989.

Pulsipher, Elizabeth J. "[Reminiscences]." In *Our Pioneer Heritage*, compiled by Kate B. Carter, vol. 7. Salt Lake City: Daughters of Utah Pioneers, 1952–57.

Ravenswaay, Charles van. "Years of Turmoil, Years of Growth: St. Louis in the 1850s." *Missouri Bulletin* 23, no. 4, part 1 (July 1967).

*Reminiscences of Charles W. Nibley, 1849–1931.* Privately printed, 1934.

*Reports Received by the Board of Trade and the Local Government Board Relating to the Transit of Scandinavian Emigrants through the Port of Hull*, July 11, 1882. https://www.norwayheritage.com/articles/templates/voyages.asp?articleid=39&zoneid=6.

Richards, Samuel W. "Missionary Experience." *The Contributor* 11 (February 1890): 155–59.

———. "Missionary Experience Recalled by the Death of Queen Victoria." *Improvement Era* 4 (1901).

Ririe, James. "[Autobiography]." In *Our Pioneer Heritage*, compiled by Kate B. Carter, vol. 9. Salt Lake City: Daughters of Utah Pioneers, 1952–57.

Roberts, B. H. *Life of John Taylor: Third President of The Church of Jesus Christ of Latter-day Saints.* Salt Lake City: George Q. Cannon and Sons, 1892.

Romney, Junius. "An Exciting Trip across the Plains." *Juvenile Instructor* 30, no. 1 (January 1, 1895).

Schivelbusch, Wolfgang. *The Railway Journey: The Industrialization of Time and Space in the Nineteenth Century.* Oakland: University of California Press, 2014.

*Scraps of Biography—Tenth Book of the Faith Promoting Series.* Salt Lake City: Juvenile Instructor Office, 1883.

Simons, Fanny Fry. *An Enduring Legacy.* Vol. 6. Salt Lake City: Daughters of Utah Pioneers, 1983.

Slaughter, Sheri Eardley. "'Meet Me in St. Louie': An Index of Early Latter-day Saints Associated with St. Louis, Missouri." *Nauvoo Journal* 10, no. 2 (Fall 1998): 49–108.

Smith, Craig S. "Wyoming, Nebraska Territory: Joseph W. Young and the Mormon Emigration of 1864." *BYU Studies* 39, no. 1 (2000).

Smith, Don H. "Castle Garden, the Emigrant Receiving Station in New York Harbor." *Nauvoo Journal* 10 (Spring 1998): 41–52.

Smith, Job. "An Experience on the Plains." *Improvement Era* (August 1908).

Smith, Joseph. *History of the Church of Jesus Christ of Latter-day Saints*. Edited by B. H. Roberts. 7 vols. Salt Lake City: Deseret News, 1952.

Smith, Joseph, Jr. *History of the Church of Jesus Christ of Latter-day Saints*. Edited by B. H. Roberts. 2nd ed. Salt Lake City: Deseret Book, 1980.

Smith, Lucy Mack. *History of Joseph Smith by His Mother, Lucy Mack Smith*. With notes and comments by Preston Nibley. Salt Lake City: Bookcraft, 1958.

Smith, Paul Thomas. "John Taylor." In *The Presidents of the Church*, edited by Leonard J. Arrington. Salt Lake City: Deseret Book, 1986.

Sonne, Conway B. "Liverpool and the Mormon Emigration." Paper presented at the Mormon History Association Conference, Liverpool, England, July 10, 1987.

———. *Saints, Ships, and Mariners: A Maritime Encyclopedia of Mormon Migration 1830–1890*. Salt Lake City: University of Utah Press, 1987.

———. *Saints on the Seas: A Maritime History of Mormon Migration 1830–1890*. Salt Lake City: University of Utah Press, 1983.

Sorensen, A. D. "Zion." In *Encyclopedia of Mormonism*, edited by Daniel B. Ludlow, vol. 4. New York: Macmillan, 1992.

Spilsbury, George, ed. *The Life and Posterity of Alma Platte Spilsbury*. Compiled by Viva Skousen Brown. Privately printed, 1983.

Stegner, Wallace. *The Gathering of Zion: The Story of the Mormon Trail*. New York: McGraw, 1964.

Strack, Don. "Railroads in Utah." In *Utah History Encyclopedia*, edited by Allan Kent Powell, 451. Salt Lake City: University of Utah Press, 1994.

*Supporting Saints: Life Stories of Nineteenth-Century Mormons*. Edited by Donald Q. Cannon and David J. Whittaker. Salt Lake City: Bookcraft, 1985.

Sutton, James T. "[Autobiography]." In *Our Pioneer Heritage*, compiled by Kate B. Carter, vol. 17. Salt Lake City: Daughters of Utah Pioneers, 1952–57.

Sveyda, George J. *Castle Garden as an Immigration Depot, 1855–1890*. National Parks Service, U.S. Department of the Interior, 1968.

Taylor, P. A. M. *Expectations Westward: The Mormons and the Emigration of Their British Converts in the Nineteenth Century*. Ithaca NY: Cornell University Press, 1966.

———. "Mormons and Gentiles on the Atlantic." *Utah Historical Quarterly* 24, no. 3 (July 1956).

———. "Why Did British Mormons Emigrate?" *Utah Historical Quarterly* 22, no. 3 (July 1954): 249–70.

"Territorial Legislature of 1857–58." In *Transactions of the Kansas State Historical Society, 1907–1908*, edited by Geo. W. Martin, 10:205. Topeka: State Printing Office, 1908.

Trager, James. *The People's Chronology: A Year-by-Year Record of Human Events from Prehistory to the Present.* New York: Holt, Rinehart and Winston, 1979.

*Treasures of Pioneer History.* Compiled by Kate B. Carter. 6 vols. Salt Lake City: Daughters of Utah Pioneers, 1952–57.

Tullidge, Edward W. *The History of Salt Lake City and Its Founders.* Salt Lake City: Edward W. Tullidge, 1886.

———. *The Women of Mormondom.* New York: N.p., 1877.

Underwood, Grant. "Millenarianism and the Early Mormon Mind." *Journal of Mormon History* 9 (1982).

———. *The Millenarian World of Early Mormonism.* Urbana: University of Illinois Press, 1993.

Unruh, John, Jr. *The Plains Across: The Overland Immigrants and the Trans-Mississippi West, 1840–1860.* Chicago: University of Illinois Press, 1979.

*Utah History Encyclopedia.* Edited by Allan Kent Powell. Salt Lake City: University of Utah Press, 1994.

Van Orden, Bruce. *Building Zion: The Latter-day Saints in Europe.* Salt Lake City: Deseret Book, 1996.

Ward, Geoffrey C., Ken Burns, and Ric Burns. *The Civil War: An Illustrated History.* New York: Alfred A. Knopf, 1990.

Ward, Maurine Carr, ed. *Winter Quarters: The 1846–1848 Life Writings of Mary Haskin Parker Richards.* Logan: Utah State University Press, 1996.

Waters, Sarah Birch. "[Autobiography]." In *Our Pioneer Heritage,* compiled by Kate B. Carter, vol. 11. Salt Lake City: Daughters of Utah Pioneers, 1952–57.

Whitney, Orson, F. *History of Utah.* 4 vols. Salt Lake City: George Q. Cannon and Sons, 1904.

———. *Life of Heber C. Kimball.* Salt Lake City: Bookcraft, 1978.

*Wilford Woodruff's Journals, 1833–1898.* Edited by Scott G. Kenney. 9 vols. Midvale UT: Signature Books.

Woods, Fred E. "The Arrival of Nineteenth Century Mormon Emigrants in Salt Lake City." Edited by Scott Esplin and Ken Alford. Provo UT: Religious Studies Center, Brigham Young University, 2011.

———. "Between the Borders: Mormon Transmigration through Missouri 1838–1868." In *The Missouri Mormon Experience,* edited by Thomas M. Spencer, 151–77. Columbia: University of Missouri Press, 2010.

———. *Divine Providence: The Wreck and Rescue of the Julia Ann.* Springville UT: Cedar Fort, 2014.

———. "East to West through North and South." *BYU Studies* 30 (2000).

———. "The 1854 Mormon Emigration at the Missouri-Kansas Border." *Kansas History: A Journal of the Central Plains* 32, no. 4 (Winter 2009–10).

———. "Fort Laramie . . . Halfway to Our Mountain Home (1847–68)." *Annals of Wyoming* 80, no. 3 (Summer 2008): 17–32.

———. "From Liverpool to Keokuk: The Mormon Maritime Migration Experience of 1853." *Mormon Historical Studies* 4, no. 2 (Fall 2003): 3–24.

———. *Gathering to Nauvoo*. American Fork UT: Covenant Communications, 2002.

———. "Gathering to Nauvoo: Mormon Immigration 1840–46." *Nauvoo Journal* 11, no. 2 (Fall 1999).

———. "George Ramsden, the Guion Line, and the Mormon Immigration Connection." *International Journal of Mormon Studies* 2, no. 1 (Spring 2009): 83–97.

———. "A Gifted Gentleman in Perpetual Motion: John Taylor as an Emigration Agent." In *Champion of Liberty: John Taylor*, edited by Mary Jane Woodger. Provo UT: Religious Studies Center, Brigham Young University, 2009.

———. "I Have a Question." *Ensign* (July 1998).

———. "Iowa City Bound: Mormon Migration through Sail and Rail, 1856–1857." *Annals of Iowa* 65, nos. 2 and 3 (Spring/Summer 2006): 162–89.

———. "The Knights at Castle Garden: Latter-day Saint Immigration Agents at New York." In *Regional Studies in Church History: New York*, edited by Alexander L. Baugh and Andrew H. Hedge, 3:103–24. Provo UT: Religious Studies Center, Brigham Young University, 2002.

———. "The Latter-day Saint Gathering." In *Liverpool to Great Salt Lake: The 1851 Journal of Missionary George D. Watt*, edited by LaJean Purcell Carruth and Ronald G. Watt, transcribed by LaJean Purcell Carruth. Lincoln: University of Nebraska Press, 2022.

———. "Men in Motion: Administering and Organizing the Gathering." In *A Firm Foundation: Church Organization and Administration*, edited by David Whittaker and Arnold K. Garr, 197–22. Provo UT: Religious Studies Center, Brigham Young University, 2011.

———. "More Precious Than Gold: The Journey to and through Zion in 1849–1850." *Nauvoo Journal* 11, no. 1 (Spring 1999): 109–24.

———. "Mormon Migration and the Fort Bridger Connection (1847–1868)." *Annals of Wyoming* 80, no. 1 (Winter 2008): 2–14.

———. "Mormon Migration on Lake Erie and through Fairport Harbor." *Inland Seas: Quarterly Journal for the Great Lakes Historical Society* 60, no. 4 (Winter 2004): 291–305.

———. "Nathaniel H. Felt: An Essex County Man." In *Regional Studies in Latter-day Saint Church History: The New England States*, edited by Donald Q. Cannon, Arnold K. Garr, and Bruce A. Van Orden, 219–36. Provo UT: Religious Studies Center, Brigham Young University, 2004.

———. "Norfolk & the Mormon Folk: Latter-day Saint Immigration through Old Dominion (1887–1890)." *Mormon Historical Studies* 1, no. 1 (Spring 2000): 72–92.

———. "Onboard the *International* . . ." *Log of Mystic Seaport* 51, no. 1 (Summer 1999).

———. "'Pronounced Clean, Comfortable, and Good Looking': The Passage of Mormon Immigrants through the Port of Philadelphia." *Mormon Historical Studies* 6, no. 1 (Spring 2005): 5–34.

———. "Sea-going Saints." *Ensign* (September 2001).

———. "The Tide of Mormon Migration: Flowing through the Port of Liverpool, England." *International Journal of Mormon Studies* 1 (2008): 60–86. https://vdocuments.mx/the-tide-of-mormon-migration-flowing-through-the-port-of-ijms-1-2008-fred-woods.html?page=1.

Woods, Fred E., and Doug Atterberg. "The 1853 Mormon Migration through Keokuk." *Annals of Iowa* 61, no. 1 (Winter 2002): 1–23. Reprinted in *Mormon Historical Studies* 4, no. 2 (Fall 2003): 25–42.

Woods, Fred E., and Melvin L. Bashore. "Mormon Migration through Atchison in 1855." *Kansas Journal* 25, no. 1 (Spring 2002).

Woods, Fred E., and Nicholas Evans. "Latter-day Saint Scandinavian Migration." *BYU Studies* 41, no. 4 (2002): 75–102.

———. "LDS Migration through Hull, England." *BYU Studies* 41, no. 4 (2002): 75–102.

Woods, Fred E., and Thomas L. Farmer. *When the Saints Came Marching In: A History of the Latter-day Saints in St. Louis.* Salt Lake City: Millennial Press, 2009.

Woods, Fred E., Jay H. Buckley, and Hunter T. Hallows, eds. *The Life and Adventures of Mr. Eli Wiggill: South African 1820 Settler, Wesleyan Missionary, and Latter-day Saint.* 5 vols. Salt Lake City: Greg Kofford Books, 2024.

Woodward, William. "In Early Days." *Juvenile Instructor* 31, no. 14 (July 15, 1896).

Wrigley, Thomas. "[Autobiography]." In *Our Pioneer Heritage*, compiled by Kate B. Carter, vol. 5. Salt Lake City: Daughters of Utah Pioneers, 1952–57.

Wyman, Walker D. "Atchison, a Great Frontier Depot." *Kansas Historical Quarterly* 11 (August 1942).

# Index

*Page numbers in italics refer to illustrations.*

abduction, 116–17, 159–60
Adams, William, 26–27, 30
advice to emigrants, 53, 96, 104, 122, 188, 220n48
agents, emigration: in Boston, 143–44; in Florence, 147; in Iowa City, 143–44; in Kanesville, 120; in Keokuk, 124; list of, 199–201; in Liverpool, 16–17, 36; in New Orleans, 77–78; in New York and Castle Garden, 95–101, 102, 103, 104, 115; in St. Louis, 84–89; in Wales, 40; in Wyoming NE, 149
Allan Line (shipping company), 221n51
Alston, Christopher, 69
Anderson, Caroline Martine, 57
Anderson, James P., 245n32
Andrus, Milo, 134–36, *135*, 139, 200
apostates, 28, 78–79, 147–49, 174, 175, 224n10
Appleby, William I., 166, 199
argonauts. *See* gold rush and argonauts
Armstead, James, 86
Arthur, Christopher Jones, 73, 124, 191–92
Ash, Alma, 50–51, 192–93
Ashby, Benjamin, 11, 170
Atchison KS, 134–41

Atkin, Thomas, 39
Aveson, Mary Ann Rawlings, 69

the Balize, 21–22
Ballantyne, Richard, 168
baptisms, 72, 73
Barton, William Kilshaw, 190
Bates, Charlotte Ann, 192
Bates, Ormus E., 199
Baxter, Robert, 184
Beatie, N. S., 200
Beazer, Ellen Burton, 63
Beecroft, Joseph, 59
Belknap, William K., 129–30, *129*
Bement, Bingham, 82, 84
Bennett, Richard E., 113
Bennion, Samuel R., 190
Bigler, J. G., 200
Blake, F. W., 103
Bodily, Robert, 185
Boggs, Lilburn W., *110*
boiler explosion, 113
Book of Mormon, 2
Boston, 101–2
Bowen, David D., 79
Bowler, James Samuel Page, 190
Boyle, Henry, 10
branches and wards. *See* church units

Brannan, Samuel, 212n98
Bridger, Jim, 169–70, *169*, 172–73, 248n81
Bristol, England, 208n24, 209n37
Brockbank, Isaac, 181
Brown, Benjamin, 10–11
Brown, David, 72
Brown, Ira, 165
Brown, John, 167, 199
Brown, Lorenzo, 170
Burgess, James, 30
Burton, Richard F., 185–86

Callister, John, 15
Callister, Thomas, 15
Campbell, Robert L., 155
Cannon, Angus M., 200
Cannon, George Q., 16, 20–21, 199
captains, relations with, 19–21, 60
Carstensen, Peter C., 190–91
Carter, Jared, 4
Castle Garden, 91–92, *92*, 103, 108
cattle, 61, 163
Charity Branch, 11
children, 20–21, 60
cholera, 79–80, 131, 139, 224n15
Church of Jesus Christ of Latter-day Saints: counseling of, on route changes, 18, 90, 108, 233n15; leaders of, meeting arriving emigrants, 180–86, 193–94; purchase of Fort Bridger by, 173; teachings of, 1–3. *See also* Quorum of the Twelve Apostles
church units, 207n11; in St. Louis, 82–84, 89; temporary, during voyages, 65–66; traveling together to Kirtland, 3–5; traveling together to Nauvoo, 9–10
Civil War, U.S., 66–68, 101–4, 115–17

Clark, Hiram, 29
Clawson, Hiram B., 200
Clawson, Margaret Gay Judd, 157
Clayton, William, 19, 31–32, 77
Clegg, Ann Lewis, 183
Colesville Branch, 3–4
Colonial Land and Emigration Commission, 63
colonization, 195–96
conduct of Saints during voyages, 20, 65
Confederate warships, 66–68
consecration, xv
Coombs, David, 67
Coombs, Isaiah M., 69–70, 71, 156
Cordon, Alfred, 19–20, 24, 164
Cornaby, Hannah Last, 125, *126*, 161
costs, 13; estimated, of Liverpool to Nauvoo, 35–36; of packet ship from St. Louis to Keokuck, 88; of railroad travel from New York, 98; of railroad travel to Iowa City, 144, 239n108; reducing, 17, 50; of steamship to eastern ports, 48, 218nn27–28; of supplies at Fort Bridger, 172; of supplies at Fort Laramie, 164, 166, 246n55, 246n58
Cowley, James, 211n80
Crandell, Mary Brannigan, 144, 146, 184
Craven, John William, 192
Crook, John, 183
Crookston, Robert, 16, 30
Crosby, Jesse, 10–11
Crosby, Jesse Wentworth, 163
Cunningham, George, 246n55
Curtis, Dorr P., 131–32, 236n51
Cutler, William G., 140

dancing, 60
Davidson, William, 39

Davis, Daniel, 180
Davis, Mary E. Fretwell, 57
Davis, Ray Jay, 64
Davis, William George, 189–90
deaths: from cholera, 79–80, 131, 139, 140; during Nauvoo years compared to pioneer-era years, 222n23; at sea, 62–63; from steamboat explosion, 113; in Willie and Martin handcart companies, 244n19, 247n66
Dee, Annie Taylor, 175–76
De La Mare, Philip, 172
*Deseret Weekly News*, 186–88
Dondore, Jared, 240n112
"down and back" wagons, 147
Duncan, Homer, 168
Dunford, George, 40, 60

Earl, Henry Sylvester, 163
economic difficulties, 13, 23, 75–78. *See also* employment
Eden, John, 60
Egan, Howard, 171, *171*
1842 Passenger Act, 63–64
Eighth Ward Square. *See* Emigration Square
Eldredge, Horace S., 84, 85, 86–89, 199, 200, 201
Ellsworth, Edmund, 183–84
Emigrant House, 190–91
"emigration revelation," xv
Emigration Square, 184–86
Empey, William, 131, 200, 236n51
employment: in Iowa City, 145–46; in Keokuk, 127, 128–29; in New Orleans, 23, 82; in New York City, 97, 230n23; in northwestern Missouri, 113; recommended as means to extend funds, 13, 76–77; in Utah, 195–96
Ensign, J. C., 180
entertainment. *See* recreation and entertainment
Epistle of First Presidency, Thirteenth General, 141–42, 228n1
Epistle of the Twelve: announcing building of stockade and fort, 180; announcing mission districts, 12; encouraging group travel, 16–17, 36; on time to gather, 123; on when and through where to immigrate, 18, 210n58
Espenschied, Louis, 86, *87*, 226n37, 241n114
European Mission Headquarters, 34
Evans, Priscilla Merriman, 145
explosion, boiler, 113
extermination order, 109

Fairport Harbor, 206n17
family, difficulty of leaving, 15–16, 57–58
Fango, Gobo, 101–2
Farmer, James, 40
Farnes, Ebenezer, 59, *59*, 62–63
Fayette Branch, 4–5
Felt, Nathaniel H., 77, 79–80, *81*, 83, 99–100, 200, 224n15, 225n29
Fielding, Amos, 17, 199
Fielding, Joseph, 28
fire, 26
Fisher, Thomas F., 73
Florence NE, 146–47
Folsom, William H., 200
Foote, Warren E., 122
Forrest, Thomas Meikle, 194
Forsgren, John, 81
Forsyth, William, 73

Index | 273

Fort Bridger: burning of, 174; emigrants banned from, 172; occupation of, by U.S military, 174–77; selling of, to the church, 173; supplies at, 170–71
Fort Laramie, 154; medical care at, 164–66; missionaries at, 156–57; Native Americans and, 154–55; supplies at, 164, 166, 243n17; wagon repair and fresh animals at, 163
Fosdick, Stephen, 125
French traders, 163
*Frontier Guardian*, 120–23
Fuller, Mr., 95
Fullmer, John S., 60
funds for assisting immigrants, 84, 97, 123, 194–95, 225n36, 227n50, 251n13

Gallup, Luke, 164
games, 60
Gardiner, Frederic, 40
Gates, Jacob, 102, 147, 200
*General McClellan* (ship), 67
*Georgia* (ship), 68, 223n37
Gerber, John T., 149, 226n44
German Branch, 226n44
Gibson, William, 84–85, 225n34
Giles, Kezia, 159
Giles, William, 159
Glasgow, Scotland, 221n51
gold rush and argonauts, 121–23, 153–54, 157–58, 251n13
Gowan, Andrew, 39–40
Gowans, Fred, 172
Grattan, John L., 154–55
Grattan Massacre, 154–55, 243n12
Griggs, Thomas, 39
Grundvig, Francis Christian, 159–60
Grundvig, Jensine, 159, 245n32
Guion, Stephen Barker, 46, 216n12

Guion Line (Liverpool and Great Western Steamship Company), 46–53, 217n19, 218n24, 218nn27–28, 219n33

Hadley, Lorenzo, 176
Haight, Isaac C., 120, 172–73, 235n34
Hale, Aroet Lucius, 180–81
Hammer, Mary, 157
Hancock, Mosiah, 158
handcarts, 98, 146, 173–74, 240n112, 240n114, 244n19
Hannibal and St. Joe Railroad, 115–17
Hansen, H. N., 62, 148–49
Hansen, James, 191
Hansen, Joseph, 42
Harrison, George, 142
Harrison, Hannah, 185
Hart, James H., 51, 106–8, *107*, 200
Hawthorne, Nathaniel, 38–39
Hedlock, Reuben, 199
Hill, Lewis, 200
Hilstead, Charlotte Ann, 91
Hindley, Jane Charters Robinson, xv, xvi, 136, *137*
Hoth, Hans, 39
Howe, Eber D., 5
Howells, William, 71
*Hudson* (ship), 67–68, 223n37
Hull, England, 41–42
Humphreys, James H., 110
Hunter, Edward, 186, *187*, 252n29
Hyde, Orson, 120, *121*, 200
hymns, 58–59

ice, 4–5, 27
iceberg, 69
Iowa City IA, 141–42, 240n111
*Iowa City Republican*, 143

Jacobs, Christopher, 158
Jacobs, Zebulon, 153
Jacobson, Elizabeth Isabelle, 166
Jacobson, Lorena, 166
Jaques, John, 65, 66
Jeremy, Thomas Evans, 40, 173
Jews, gathering of, xiv–xv
Johnson, John, 62
Jones, Albert, 166
Jones, Dan, 26–27
Jones, Nathaniel V., 102, 103, 181, 199, 232n44
*Julia Ann* (ship), 223n43

Kanesville IA, 120–23
Kay, William, 20
Kelsey, Eli B., 80
Keokuk IA, 124–30
Kimball, Heber C., 6–7, 7, 30, 180
Kirtland OH, 3–5
Knight, Newel, 3–4
"knights near Castle Garden," 92
Knox, William, 173

land sharks, 23. *See also* thieves
Lapish, Hannah, 166–67
Laramie WY, 150
Larkin, Elijah, 103–4, 176
Larsen, C. C., 52
Larsen, Svend, 131
*Latter-day Saints' Emigrants' Guide* (Clayton), 77
letters encouraging immigration, 14, 31–32, 36
Linford, Amasa Christian, 164
Linforth, James, 13
Little, Feramorz, 200
Little, James A., 145, 240n114
Little, Jesse C., 199

Liverpool, England, 13, 16–17, 37, 38–40
London, 213n9
lottery ticket, 78
Lund, Anthon H., 47, 48, 54, 190
Lund, Hans Peter, 39

MacDonald, Elizabeth Graham, 155
MacNeil, John, 194
Maiben, Henry, 72
*Maid of Iowa* (steamboat), 26–27
mail, 167–68
*Manchester* (ship), 102–3
Manfull, Emma Palmer, 73
Maples, Charles, 50, 219nn31–32
Martin, John, 79
Maughan, Mary Ann Weston, 18, *19*
McAllister, John, 60, 102
McBride, Peter Howard, 142
McCune, Henry, 163
McGaw, James, 199, 200
McGee, Elijah Milton, 132–33, *133*
McIntyre, Peter, 181
McIntyre, Thomas, 163, *165*
McKenzie, Thomas, 199
McLachlan, William, 177
McNaughton, James, 125–26
McNeil, Christina, 157
McQuarrie, Robert, 184
measles, 131
medical care, 164–66, 247n61
Mellor, Louisa, 146
*Millennial Star*, 33–36, 37, 188, 190, 212n2
Miller, Charles Dutton, 78–79
Miller, Daniel A., 162
Miller, Henry W., 168
missionaries, 9–11, 12, 80–82, 156–57
Mississippi River, 21–22, 27
Missouri, 6

Missourians, Mormon attitudes toward, 110–11
Mitchell, Hezekiah, 83
Moon, Francis, 13–14
Moon, Hugh, 13
Morgan, J., 73–74
Morgan, Jesse, 161
*The Mormon*, 94–95, 96–97, 229n12, 229nn17–18
Mormon Grove ks, 134–40
Morris, David H., 39
motives for gathering, xiv–xv, 9, 204n7, 213n2
Moulton, Jensine Marie Jensen, 61
Musser, Amos Milton, 39, 147, *148*

nationalities of emigrants, 8, 13, 15, 40–41, 68, 101, 130, 149, 213n9
Native Americans, 120, 154–55, 158–61, 170–71, 244n30
Nauvoo il, 29–32
Nauvoo Temple, 14, *31*
Neibaur, Alexander, 19, 25–26, *25*, 29–30
Neilsen, Rasmus, 215n40
Nelson, Russell M., 2
Nelson, William Goforth, 181
New Orleans, 17–18, 21–23, 75–77
newspapers: anti-Mormon, 5; in Atcheson, 138, 140; in Iowa, 143; in Kanesville, 120–23; in Keokuk, 127–28; in Liverpool, 215n2; in London, 45–46; in New York, 94–95, 100–101, 106, 229n12; reporting of, about cholera, 131; reporting of, about polygamy, 138, 142–43, 229n10; in St. Louis, 83–84, 138
New York City: during Civil War, 102, 104; as economic center, 13; as port of disembarkation, 17, 108, 209n38; as railhead, 98–99, 108. *See also* Castle Garden
New York Commissioners of Emigration, 91
*New York Daily Times*, 92, 100
*New York Daily Tribune*, 139
*New York Mirror*, 95
*New York Sun*, 95
Nibley, Charles W., 68
Nielsen, Christian, 124
Nielsen, Christian Emil, 131
Nielson, Andrew Christian, 191
Norfolk va, 108
North Eastern Railway (ner), 41

oath of allegiance, 176–77
O'Connell, John, 43, 44, 45
Old Fort, 179–80, 250n2, 251nn9–10
Olsen, C. F., 192
orderliness, 18, 65
outfitting posts, 119–20, 124, 130, 131–39, 141–42, 146–47, 149–50

Palmer, Ann, 165–66
Palmer, James, 22, 61
Parson, John, 167–68
passengers: conditions for, at sea, 47, 63–64; conditions for, prior to embarking, 38–40, 44; relations among, 18–19, 223n45
Paxton, James Mills, 176–77
Pay, Mary Goble, 59
Peers (Pierce), Captain, 19–20
Pennsylvania Railroad Company, 99
Perpetual Emigrating Fund (pef), 123, 194–95, 251n13
persecution, 19–20, 26–28
Philadelphia, 99, 228n1

Piercy, Frederick, 126–27, 162, 172, 246n44
Piper, Agent, 201
Pitchforth, Ann, 58, 68–69
Pixton, Robert, 16
*The Plains Across* (Unruh), 162
poetry, 58
polygamy, 84, 138, 142–43, 229n10
Pomfret Branch, 10
Porter, Sally M., 176
ports of disembarkation: on East Coast, 17–18, 75, 90, 91–92, 96, 101, 108, 209nn38–39, 210n59, 229n8; in England, 41–42; at New Orleans, 17–18, 21, 75
ports of embarkation, 13, 16–17, 37–38, 209n37, 213n9
postal service, 167–68
Poulter, Thomas Ambrose, 158–59
Pratt, Orson, 199
Pratt, Parley P., 27, 33, 35, 199
Probert, William, Jr., 231n41
Public Square (Salt Lake City), 181–84
Pugh, Henry, 160, 182–83
Pulsipher, John, 170

Quorum of the Twelve Apostles, 8; epistle of, announcing building of stockade and fort, 180; epistle of, announcing mission districts, 12; epistle of, encouraging group travel, 16–17, 36; epistle of, on time to gather, 123; epistle of, on when and through where to immigrate, 18, 210n58

Race, Isabella, 247n61
railroads: from Boston, 141; across England, 41–42, 208n17; from New York, 97–99, 141; transcontinental, 151–52; unpleasantness of travel by, 115–16, 142
Ramsden, George, 47–55, 49, 217n21, 218n26, 221n52
recreation and entertainment, 39, 57–60, 84, 88, 125
Rees, Watkin, 155, 183
Reeves, John, Jr., 201
regulations, 63–65
Reid, Robert, 18
*Reunion of the Saints* (painting), 195
Richards, Franklin D., 199, 201
Richards, Mary Haskin Parker, 15, 20
Richards, Samuel W., 43–46, 44, 199
Riley, J., 57
Roberts, B. H., 60
Robinson, Lewis, 174
Romney, Miles, 166
*Route from Liverpool to the Great Salt Lake Valley* (Piercy), 64–65
Rowley, William, 29

Sabin, Mary Powell, 160–61
sailors, 19, 59, 60
Salt Lake City: Emigration Square in, 184–86; Old Fort in, 179–80, 250n2; Public Square in, 181–84; temporary lodgings for new arrivals in, 180–93; Tithing Yard in, 188–92
*Saluda* (steamboat), 113
sandbars, 21, 27
Sanderson, Winslow F., 156
Savage, Charles R., 164
Schmid, Robert, 39
Schofield, Brother, 107
Scofield, Jno., 107
Scott, Andrew H., 157
Scovil, Lucius N., 23, 77–78, 199

seasickness, 61–62
Sermon, Elizabeth, 145–46
Sessions, Perrigrine, 163
Sheets, Elijah Funk, 9
Shupe, Andrew Jackson, 163
Simmons, Rachel Emma Woolley, 180
Simons, Fanny Fry, 60
singing, 58–60, 160
Sioux, 154–55, 158, 160, 161, 242n6
slavery, 24, 137–38
Sloan, William K., 163, 164
Smith, Andrew, 142
Smith, George A., 151
Smith, Jesse N., 194
Smith, Job, 155
Smith, Joseph: beginnings of Church of Jesus Christ and, 1; and gathering places, 11–12; on Missouri mobs, 109–10; on not expecting perfection, 196; on reason for gathering, xiv–xv; revelations of, to gather, 3, 4; on thrift in choosing immigration route, 17–18; welcoming immigrants to Nauvoo, 30
Smith, Joseph F., 47, 217n21
Smith, Lucy Mack, 4–5
Smoot, Abraham O., 113, *114*
Snow, Ann Rogers, 158
Snow, Erastus: as agent in St. Louis, 200; preaching of, in St. Louis, 81–82, 227n55; and St. Louis Stake, 89; and trade at Fort Bridger, 170; treatment of, at Fort Laramie, 156–57
Snow, Lorenzo, 82
soldiers: emigrants and, during U.S. Civil War, 103–4, 115–17; kindness of, to emigrants, 156–57, 175–76, 243n17; Native Americans and, 154–55; during Utah War, 156; and women, 116–17, 157, 175
songs, 58–59, 72–73
South, John William, 58
Southworth, Agnes Caldwell, 157
Spencer, Daniel, 143–44, 200, 239n104
Spilsbury, George, 75–76, *76*
Staines, Priscilla, 15–16, 26, 30–31
Staines, William C., 24, 104–6, *105*, 200
stakes and wards. *See* church units
Stenhouse, Thomas B. H., 199
Steward, Elizabeth White, 60, 142
St. Joseph MO, 113
St. Louis, 27–28, 78–80, 83–85, 112, 131, 211n81
St. Louis Stake, 89, 227n55, 227n58
Stokes, Henry, 168
storms, 18, 26, 68–74, 125
Stout, Hosea, 114
Stratton, Joseph A., 9
Sutton, James T., 57
Sutton, John Allen, 155
Symons, Charles William, 67–68

Taylor, George, 99
Taylor, John, *94*; as Eastern Mission president, 93–94; as editor of *The Mormon*, 94–95, 96–97; as emigration agent, 95–101, 141, 199, 228nn7–8; and improvements at Fort Laramie, 156; preaching of, in St. Louis, 82
Taylor, Ossian F., 161
Taylor, Thomas, 200
temple: in Nauvoo, 14; as reason for gathering, xiv–xv
Terry, Joel Judkins, 160
Terry, Joshua, 249n85
thieves, 17, 23, 91, 163

Thompson, James, 65
Thurber, Albert King, 110–11, *111*
Tithing Office and Deseret Store, *191*
Tithing Yard, 188–92
Toronto, Joseph, 81
trading, 158–59, 161, 166, 170–71
trailheads. *See* outfitting posts
trains. *See* railroads
Trask, Captain, 102–3
tugboats, 21–22
Turnbull, George, 199

Union Pacific Railroad, 150–52
Union Square. *See* Public Square (Salt Lake City)
Utah Central Rail, 194, 252n35
Utah War, 89, 155–56, 174, 225n31

Van Cott, John, 143
Vincent, Mary Ellison, 73–74
Volker, John W. F., 67

wagons, 85, 86, 125, 138, 147, 162–63
Walker, William Holmes, 164
Wasden, Ellen, 184–85
Washington Square. *See* Emigration Square
Webb, Mary Ann Ward, 116
Weibye, Jens C. A., 161, *162*, 190
Weiler, Jacob, 151, *152*
Wells, Daniel H., 51
Wells, Junius F., 52
West, Charles Henry John, 185
Westport MO, 130
Wheelock, Silas, 58
Whipple, Nelson, 122
Whitaker, George, 22–23

White, Thomas Henry, 116–17
Wiggill, Eli, 101–2, 185
Wilkey, Ann Gregory, 160, 181–82
Williams, Thomas, 199
Wilson Line, 50
Winter Quarters NE, 119, 120
women: Native Americans and, 158–59; soldiers and, 116–17, 157, 175
Woodbury, Ann Cannon, 180
Woodruff, Wilford, 21, 170, 183–84
Woodson, Samuel H., 167
Woodward, William, 144, 181
Woolley, Edwin T., 192
Woolley, Samuel, 166, 167, 168
Wrigley, Thomas, 28, 84
*Wyoming* (ship), 47, 52
Wyoming NE, 147–49

Young, Brigham, *xvii*, *182*; appointment of district leaders by, 12; changing of port of entry by, 90; correspondence of, about emigration, 97–98, 230n25; Jim Bridger and, 170, 172; and mail service, 167, 247n70; revelation of, to emigrate west, xv; revelation of, to not fear enemies, 117; on singing and dancing, 60; Union Pacific Railroad and, 151–52, 238n90; welcoming of emigrants by, 183, 194
Young, John W., 200
Young, Joseph A., 200
Young, Joseph W., 149, *150*, 200
Y. X. Company, 243n14

Zaugg, Frederick, 196–97
Zion, finding, 189, 193, 196–97
Zobell, Hans J., 188–89